Copyright © 2020 by Institute of Competition Law
106 West 32nd Street, Suite 144, New York, NY 10001, USA
www.concurrences.com
books@concurrences.com

First Printing, March 2020
978-1-939007-89-6 (paperback)
LCCN: 2020933462

Cover: Yves Buliard, www.yvesbuliard.fr
Book design and layout implementation: NordCompo

Women & Antitrust
Voices from the Field

Curation & Foreword
Evelina Kurgonaite

Editors
Nicolas Charbit
Sonia Ahmad

Concurrences Books

Liber Amicorum

Eleanor Fox - Liber Amicorum
Nicolas Charbit, Sonia Ahmad (eds.), 2021

Laurence Idot - Liber Amicorum
Christophe Lemaire, Francesco Martucci (eds.), 2021

Richard Whish QC (Hon) - Taking Competition Law Outside the Box
Nicolas Charbit, Sonia Ahmad (eds.), 2020

Herbert Hovenkamp - Liber Amicorum
Nicolas Charbit, Sonia Ahmad (eds.), 2020

Albert Foer - Liber Amicorum
Nicolas Charbit, Sonia Ahmad (eds.), 2020

Frédéric Jenny - Standing Up for Convergence and Relevance in Antitrust, Vol. I & II
Nicolas Charbit, Sonia Ahmad (eds.), 2019 & 2020

Douglas H. Ginsburg – An Antitrust Professor on the Bench, Vol. I & II
Nicolas Charbit, et al. (eds.), 2018 & 2020

Wang Xiaoye - The Pioneer of Competition Law in China
Adrian Emch, Wendy Ng (eds.), 2019

Ian S. Forrester - A Scot Without Borders, Vol. I & II
Assimakis Komninos et al. (eds.), 2015

William E. Kovacic: An Antitrust Tribute, Vol. I & II
Nicolas Charbit et al. (eds.), 2013 & 2014

Practical Books

Mergers in South America
Paulo Burnier da Silveira & Pamela Sittenfeld (eds.), 2020

**Competition Law Inquiries in the EU -
A Practitioner's Guide**
Nathalie Jalabert-Doury, 2020

Gun-Jumping in Merger Control - A Jurisdictional Guide
Catriona Hatton, Andrea Hamilton & Yves Comtois (eds.), 2019

Choice - A New Standard for Competition Analysis?
Paul Nihoul et al.(eds.), 2016

EU Law and Life Science
Peter Bogaert, Damien Geradin (eds.), 2014

PhD Theses

The Role of Media Pluralism in the Enforcement of EU Competition Law
Konstantina Bania, 2019

Buyer Power in EU Competition Law
Ignacio Herrera Anchustegui, 2017

General Interest

Antitrust Conversations with Nobel Laureates
Thibault Schrepel (ed.), (2020)

Women & Antitrust: Voices from the Field, Vol. I & II
Evelina Kurgonaite & Kristina Nordlander, 2020

Conference Proceedings

Antitrust in Emerging and Developing Countries, Vol. I & II
Eleanor Fox, Harry First (eds.), 2015 & 2016

Global Antitrust Law - Current Issues in Antitrust Law and Economics
Douglas Ginsburg, Joshua Wright (eds.), 2015

Competition Law on the Global Stage: David Gerber's Global Competition Law in Perspective
David Gerber (ed.), 2014

e-Book versions are available to **Concurrences+** subscribers.

Foreword

EVELINA KURGONAITE

Competition rules, in some form or other, can be traced back over two millennia. The more formal study of competition is at least two centuries old, while modern antitrust law began with the Sherman Act in 1890.

Today, more than a hundred countries have competition laws, and the international antitrust community is vast. While no data on the number of competition professionals is readily available, one of the largest annual antitrust events in Washington DC brings together over 3,800 attendees. And even that is just a fraction of competition professionals across jurisdictions.

Not only is it an old area of law that keeps a lot of people busy – competition is also about economics, dynamic market realities, numerous policy considerations, and, indeed, also about national and international politics. By its very nature, competition is interdisciplinary – it is all intertwined, quite literally.

Arguably, this interdisciplinary nature of competition is one of the key reasons why it susceptible to pressures stemming from developments in various related areas. And competition law has adapted, continuously. But never has it been challenged quite as much as in the recent years, amidst expanding digitalisation, calls for antitrust overhaul, enforcement toolbox review, integration of policies such as consumer protection and data privacy, and quests for levelling the playing field in the global context.

At this unprecedented juncture for the competition field, this book offers more than two dozen interviews with leading figures in the field from around the world and from different parts of the competition profession.

In the book, competition professionals – including senior enforcement authority representatives, experienced in-house counsel, economists, prominent academics and leading private practitioners – have shared with their peers their perspectives, based, in most cases, on decades of experience and the ever-changing antitrust world, as well as reflections on key challenges they have observed in the past and anticipated in the future and they have, on occasion, also offered thoughts on possible solutions.

Last but not least, the reader will also find in this book insights into the professional paths and personal anecdotes of competition women in different parts of world – from Brussels to Washington DC, Paris, London, Stockholm, Copenhagen, Lisbon, Madrid, Hong Kong, Singapore, Beijing, Sydney, Johannesburg, Sao Paolo, Mexico City, and others.

W@Competition is delighted to have partnered with Concurrences to bring this project to fruition. Together, we have sought to amplify the voices of women in the competition profession and hope this book will facilitate connections among professionals in this field in different parts of the world.

Contributors

Paula Azevedo
Administrative Council for
Economic Defense
Brasília

Louise Åberg
McDermott Will & Emery
Paris / Washington, DC

Stefania Bariatti
Chiomenti
Milan / Brussels

Jeannine Bartmann
Allianz
Munich

Sabrina Borocci
Hogan Lovells
Milan

Patricia Brink
US Department of Justice
Washington, DC

Sarah Cardell
Competition and Markets
Authority
London

Fiona Carlin
Baker McKenzie
Brussels

Winnie Ching
Competition & Consumer
Commission of Singapore
Singapore

Silvia D'Alberti
Gattai, Minoli, Agostinelli
& Partners
Rome

Beatriz de Guindos
Spanish National Markets and
Competition Commission
Madrid

Pia de la Cuesta
thyssenkrupp
Madrid

Cani Fernández
Cuatrecasas
Madrid / Brussels

Amelia Fletcher
University of East Anglia
London

Karina Flores
Mexican Federal Economic
Competition Commission
Mexico City

Ethel Fonseca
RBB Economics
London

Katrin Gaßner
Freshfields Bruckhaus Deringer
Düsseldorf

Adriana Giannini
Tauil & Chequer, associated
with Mayer Brown
São Paulo

Renata Hesse
Sullivan & Cromwell
Washington, DC

Samantha Hynes
Sullivan & Cromwell
Washington, DC

Nicola Ilgner
Nortons Inc
Johannesburg

Heather Irvine
Bowmans
Johannesburg

Maria Jaspers
DG COMP, European
Commission
Brussels

Claudia Koken
C-Law
Amsterdam

Evelina Kurgonaite
W@
Brussels

Carina Lange
AILI Consulting
Amsterdam

Felicity Lee
Ashurst
Melbourne

Karin Lunning
Swedish Competition Authority
Stockholm

Martina Maier
Siemens
Brussels / Munich

Iona McCall
AlixPartners
London

Amelia McKellar
Gilbert + Tobin
Sydney

Laura Méndez Rodriguez
Infonavit
Mexico City

Teresa Moreira
United Nations Conference on
Trade and Development
Geneva

Irene Moreno-Tapia
Cuatrecasas
Barcelona

Kirstie Nicholson
BHP Billiton
Singapore

Susan Ning
King & Wood Mallesons
Beijing

Siún O'Keeffe
Academy of the Netherlands
Authority for Consumers &
Markets
The Hague

Alejandra Palacios
Mexican Federal Economic
Competition Commission
Mexico City

María Pilar Canedo
Spanish National Markets and
Competition Commission
Madrid

Sandra Potlog
O2 Telefónica UK
Slough

Sophia Real
Google
Brussels

**Margarida Rosado da
Fonseca**
CS Associados
Lisbon

Emily Smith-Reid
HSBC
London

Anneleen Straetemans
ZX Ventures
London

Marie-Claire Strawbridge
Freshfields Bruckhaus Deringer
London

Wendy Thian
Baker McKenzie
Hong Kong

Bitten Thorgaard Sørensen
Danish Competition and
Consumer Authority
Copenhagen

Barbara Veronese
Oxera
Milan

Auraellia Wang
Google
Hong Kong

Maria Wasastjerna
Hannes Snellman
Helsinki

Rose Webb
New South Wales Department
of Customer Services
Sydney

Meng Yanbei
Renmin University
Beijing

Rasa Zaščiurinskaitė
Cobalt Legal
Vilnius

Table of Contents

Part I – Enforcers & Academics

Part II – In-house Counsels

Part I
Enforcers & Academics

Paula Azevedo
CADE

Adriana Giannini

Paula Azevedo is a Commissioner in Brazil's Administrative Council for Economic Defense. Before taking office, she worked in private practice as a competition and trade law expert at two of the largest firms in Brazil. From 2007 to 2008, she worked as a Coordinator at the former Secretariat of Economic Law on cartel and unilateral conduct investigations and as the Mercosur negotiator for competition, services, and intellectual property issues. She is currently a Professor of Law and Economics and International Trade at the Brasília Institute for Public Law and a volunteer Professor of Competition Law at the University of Brasília. She holds a Masters in International Economic Law from Georgetown University Law Center, where she was an IIEL fellow, and a law degree from the University Centre of Brasília.

Adriana Giannini is a partner of the competition law group of Tauil & Chequer, in association with Mayer Brown, in Brazil. For over 20 years, she has focused her work in cross-border complex merger cases and cartel investigations, as well as on abuse of dominance investigations and procurement. Adriana holds a post-graduate degree from Fundação Getulio Vargas in law and economics and a master of laws degree (LLM) in EU Competition Law from King's College London.

Paula, you are a very young and accomplished practitioner, with one of the most important jobs in relation to competition law enforcement and policy in a key jurisdiction. I am sure many young lawyers are curious about your career and how it led to your current position as a Commissioner in CADE. Could you please tell me a bit about that?

My career in competition started by accident. My intention was to work in international trade law, but I resided in Brasília and there were almost no firms working with international trade at the time. The closest field that also dealt with economics and the day-to-day business of large corporations and markets was antitrust law. I began as an intern at a global firm, that allowed me to work directly with the competition team and remotely with their trade team in São Paulo. I later interned in other law firms and in the public sector, but ultimately decided that I wanted to practice economic law. The direct and palpable impact of the work on the client, the market and the consumer truly intrigued me.

In order to transition into trade law (which was my goal at the time), I attended the LLM programme at Georgetown immediately after I graduated, and I divided my time between competition and trade. I was the second-youngest person in my class that year, which was a challenge since I lacked some of the real-world experience of my peers. However, it later allowed me to grow quite quickly in my career.

When I was about to leave Georgetown, Professor Steve Salop suggested that I go work at the Brazilian Ministry of Justice. A former student of his, Mariana Tavares, was the head of the competition investigation unit and was building her team. It was a very interesting moment in Brazilian antitrust: leniency agreements and dawn raids were just beginning and there was a lot of innovation in cartel enforcement. I worked at the Ministry for two years; I participated in dawn raids and was the head negotiator for Mercosur. We wrote the first guidelines for trade associations and best practices for companies. Competition policy was changing and it was great to be there at a time where I was able to understand how policy was being shaped from the enforcers' point of view.

I spent the next decade in private practice and worked at two of the most prestigious firms in competition and trade. I was very fortunate to work for extremely talented and hard-working people. My career was pretty much the same as everyone else's: I worked very hard, focused on my clients and my cases, and read constantly to ensure that I was up to date on global trends in my fields.

In 2016, I was forced to step away from the office because my husband fell ill and I was pregnant with my third daughter. Fortunately, everything worked out and in late 2017 I returned to my position as a senior associate. I was thinking about how to make partner when I received a phone call from a friend asking if I would like to have my name presented to the President as a candidate for CADE Commissioner. I said yes, but only after very long conversations with trusted friends.

I was fortunate that I was the kind of candidate the President and Congress wanted at the time. I would love to say that I am one of a kind and that is why I received the nomination, but the truth is that I was at the right place at the right time, and had built up a solid technical CV and the respect of my peers. I later learned that my reputation among government stakeholders for being fair, transparent and technical also greatly helped in my appointment. Since I was a lawyer in Brasília, I had very close contact with players from several ministries and agencies, who followed my career over the years.

Thank you. As we have known each other for quite a while, I know that family and friends are very important to you as well. At the risk of asking a very clichéd question, how do you manage the pressure and time requirements from your job with your family and friends? Do you have any tips that you would like to share? I am personally interested in this last bit of advice…

Yes, family and friends are very important to me. So much so, that at certain moments in my career, I prioritised my family and not my career. In fact, when I was a young lawyer, I was concerned that I would never make partner or be a good lawyer because I was not willing to abdicate having a family and being a mom. The response I received from a partner at the time was: if the firm wants you, they will have to accommodate your needs.

Throughout my career I saw practical examples of this attitude. One of the partners I worked for arrived at the office about two hours before everyone else, after dropping her kids off at school, and left every day, no matter what, at 5.15 pm in order to be home for dinner. I saw that if you scheduled in your priorities, it was possible to rearrange your work schedule.

As my family grew, I found that if I had an honest conversation with the partners and my team about my home life, we were able to work something out. When I was pregnant, I did a lot of home office work. When my husband was ill, I stepped back and worked only on the most essential projects and later stepped away completely for several months. Whenever one of my kids was sick, I would work from home. I can honestly say that I was never demoted, reprimanded or thought less of for prioritising my family

I guess my tip would be: prioritise and be honest.

Coming back to CADE, the CADE Tribunal has four new commissioners, which now form a new majority in terms of decision-making going forward. That is quite a big change for the authority as a whole. What do you see as the main challenges for the new commissioners in the coming years?

A change of four commissioners at once is not ideal. Therefore, the main challenge now is to ensure a smooth transition. The new commissioners are all experienced in different areas of the law or economics, and have different backgrounds. This allows for rich debates and renewed discussions, but all seven of us are committed to ensuring that there is respect for the rule of law and precedent.

Brazil's economy seems to be finally picking up the pace after a long period of economic recession. This, coupled with a favourable exchange rate, is likely to result in a significant increase of merger control notifications being filed, thus an increase of CADE's work, and we all know that CADE's resources are already overstretched. Is there any plan to hire more staff soon?

That is true. We are currently expanding our staff through rounds of recruitment from other agencies and the federal government. Coupled with this, we are focusing on training staff through in-house executive education and establishing internal guidelines, best practices and common procedures in order to reduce the time it takes for a new recruit to fully understand competition law and how to analyse cases. The plan is to continue recruiting over the next couple of years and to reduce turnover. This is a problem at CADE because we are one of the few Brazilian agencies that does not have a dedicated staff. Therefore, we are working on creating long-term incentives and career goals in order to retain staff.

In terms of mergers that have been filed recently, I noticed that there has been a good number of conglomerate mergers recently. However, CADE never blocked any merger based on conglomerate effects only – do you think that CADE might start to look into these effects more deeply?

Conglomerate mergers are definitely a trend that will continue as the economy picks up and post-recession consolidation occurs. As conglomerate mergers increase, CADE will definitely look into these effects more deeply. Conglomerate effects were central in the analysis of several mergers recently in the healthcare, software and banking industries, for example. The Tribunal has provided guidance on how to look at conglomerate effects, such as in the recent *IBM/Red Hat* merger. If needed, CADE could block a merger based on conglomerate effects, but this would have to be done on a case-by-case basis.

In relation to cartel enforcement, there is a consensus among practitioners that there is lower number of investigations being opened by CADE, compared with previous years. What do you believe are the reasons for that? Do you think it is a direct result of the end of the many investigations related to the larger Car Wash investigation or do you feel that this is part of a global trend? If yes, why is that?

It is hard to say whether this is a temporary lull or a trend. Until 2018, the number of leniency investigations signed with CADE was at an all-time high. This translates into new investigations, but the timing may not be automatic. In some cases, for example, the investigation may be opened only after dawn raids or other confidential procedures are carried out.

With respect to the Car Wash cases, there are still many ongoing investigations and, due to our internal firewall, I do not know if there are new investigations that will be made public this year. However, I believe the Car Wash investigations thoroughly tested CADE's leniency system and showed that CADE is able to handle a large volume of extremely complex leniency requests and investigations. It is important for future applicants to know that the system is mature and trustworthy.

You recently spoke at the celebrated NYU conference about antitrust and development, where you talked about the issues surrounding cartel and corruption enforcement in developing countries. This is a topic close to my heart, as I believe both cartels and corruption are among the main obstacles to development. However, in many instances, it is difficult to enforce against both cartels and corruption consistently for several reasons, such as the lack of resources from public administration, unhelpful legal framework etc. What were the big takeaways from this conference and what do you think that we in Brazil should be doing to increase enforcement?

CADE believes that cartel and corruption enforcement has to be carried out in a concerted manner in order to effectively deter these practices. The NYU conference was extremely important to show that we are on the right track. The biggest takeaway from the conference was the consensus that cartels and corruption can be complementary and part of the same cycle. As such, inter-agency cooperation is key because everyone knows what corruption looks like, but many agencies and public officials are not well versed in competition and cannot readily identify a cartel. We need to increase our advocacy measures to assist in identifying cartels. We also need to work even more closely with agencies that prosecute corruption. This close engagement is essential for a concerted and, most importantly, cohesive enforcement policy.

As you know, there is an increased scrutiny by antitrust authorities worldwide to launch investigations into super-dominant companies such as Google, Amazon, Apple, Facebook etc. We see, for instance, the US Department of Justice and Federal Trade Commission dividing their oversight over the potential antitrust implications arising from these companies and the recent fines imposed by the Germany's Federal Cartel Office against Facebook. Is that something you see CADE doing as well? Do you think CADE might launch a sector enquiry into these companies, e.g., with a study by the economic study department at CADE?

CADE has been looking into super-dominant tech companies for some time and we are aware of the effects they may have on the market. Recently, CADE headed the initiative by the BRICS countries to issue a report on digital markets. Last year, CADE concluded three investigations into different Google practices and initiated two new investigations. The three investigations that were concluded did not result in fines because the Tribunal understood that the practices either did not exist (in the Scraping and API cases) or did not produce effects in Brazil (in the Shopping case). Despite these cases, CADE is still looking into the effects of tech companies on the market and will continue to monitor the Brazilian market closely.

We have talked a bit about merger control, cartels and antitrust investigations. But what do you see as overall trends for CADE in terms of policy in the next couple of years? What do you think CADE should be focused on and what topics will come up?

I believe that there are a couple of topics that CADE will focus on. The first is cooperation between CADE and other agencies. These cooperation efforts among agencies are highly important for a coherent approach aiming at economic development. The dialogue between the competition authority and the regulatory agency is a productive way to combine and ponder the different interests in a certain sector.

CADE and the Brazilian Central Bank have increased dialogue in response to the recent changes in the financial sector, and as a response to some recurrent cases investigated by CADE in the context of that sector. The recurrence may indicate that some rules, dynamics and structures of the market could be better designed.

Further, cooperation and increased dialogue is a way for the competition authority to increase its knowledge of the market and better understand the regulatory framework surrounding certain practices.

The second is the use of behavioural and structural remedies in conduct cases. The main challenge we face today is to keep up with the rapid pace of economic change in a globalised and digitalised world, so we have been trying to develop new methods and ways to continue to effectively promote and defend competition.

Under Article 38 of the Brazilian Antitrust Law (Law 12.529/2011), the competition authority is allowed to determine other measures, such as the divestment of assets or a corporate split, as well as behavioural commitments, in order to protect general public interest and to hinder serious consequences arising from the conduct. Therefore, CADE has the authority to use other non-financial sanctions in order to attain an effective decision.

While there are critics that state that such measures are extreme, it is important to note that these types of remedies are exceptional and are used by CADE only when fines are insufficient to prevent or cease the practice. This could be the case when the anticompetitive conduct is directly related to the market structure or dynamic.

Thank you so much for all of that, which was all very enlightening for me. My last question is about being the main challenges you have faced as a female practitioner and how you overcame those. Did you have any mentor or sponsor, and how did she or he help you? What is your advice for the next generation of female antitrust lawyers in Brazil?

I believe the main issue women face is in overcoming certain preconceived notions of women's roles in society. At work, a woman is usually expected to have a demure personality, not ask for money and be accommodating. At home, she is expected to be the primary caregiver and be responsible for the majority of household tasks. Deviating from these standards at work or at home can be difficult and is not always second nature to some women.

In some respects, I was fortunate because my parents have always held equal roles at home, and my mother has a very distinguished career as a diplomat. Growing up, there was no doubt in my mind that I would also have a career and that my husband would be my partner and equal. Looking back, this naturally shaped my early career because I never felt that my place was anywhere other than sitting at the table as an equal. The legal profession is still a very masculine world, but I never felt out of place for being the only woman at a meeting or at a dinner – or anywhere for that matter. However, I did feel pressure to behave and react as a man would, which sometimes made me feel embarrassed for reacting as myself and not as I thought a male colleague would react.

Throughout my professional career, I had two mentors, one male and one female. Surprisingly, the fact that I am a woman was hardly ever an issue we discussed. They helped me hone my skills, fight for recognition and balance my professional and personal life. They also helped me develop the confidence I needed to be feminine in a masculine world, and to know that I would not be less of a professional for being so.

Therefore, my advice for the next generation of female antitrust lawyers in Brazil is: realise that you deserve "a seat at the table" as much as anyone else. Do not let yourself believe that the legal profession is too masculine. If you are good, the world will accommodate your needs and not the other way around.

Patty Brink
US Department of Justice

Samantha Hynes

Patty Brink is currently the Director of Professional Development and Counsel to the Assistant Attorney General at the Department of Justice's Antitrust Division. She joined the Antitrust Division in 1989 after graduating from University of California, Davis King Hall. Patty was the Director of Civil Enforcement from 2010 to 2019 and the Deputy Director of Operations from 2006 to 2010. Prior to joining the Office of Operations, Patty was in the Networks and Technology Enforcement Section of the Antitrust Division and was the Special Counsel for Microsoft Decree Enforcement.

Samantha Hynes is an associate in the Litigation Group at Sullivan & Cromwell. Her practice focuses on antitrust matters, including civil litigation and merger reviews at the US Department of Justice and the Federal Trade Commission. The clients she has represented span a variety of industries, such as airlines, automobiles, financial services, food and grocery, industrial gases, oil and gas exploration and production, paper and print services, and pharmaceuticals.

Civil Enforcement

In September 2018, Assistant Attorney General Makan Delrahim announced a series of changes to modernise the Antitrust Division's merger review process, with the goal of increasing transparency and resolving most investigations within six months. What steps has the Division taken to meet its goals of increased transparency and expedited reviews? Is the Division on track to resolve most investigations that it has opened since the announcement within six months?

As Director of Civil Enforcement and Deputy Director in Operations, I was in the Antitrust Division's Front Office for 13 years. I had the privilege of working with new senior leadership to implement their priorities. So when AAG Delrahim told us that he wanted to improve the efficiency and transparency of our merger investigations, my team first studied what factors have the most impact on the duration of our merger reviews. Obvious to all merger practitioners: the increase in the amount of documents and data produced to us (roughly a 250% increase in the last five years), and the agencies' need to prepare for complex merger trials, if necessary. Other factors are not so obvious: the agencies' increasing use of upfront buyers and internal recognition that for the increasing percentage of our investigations in which we coordinate with international competition agencies, those jurisdictions' timelines mean that parties are not able to close as quickly as they would be if we were the only reviewer.

To implement the suggestions Makan made in his September 2018 speech, we undertook a revision (and subsequent publication) of our model timing agreement, which largely structures the timing of meetings, depositions, productions, etc. We also held extensive conversations with our attorneys and economists about how we could better structure our reviews, particularly focusing on Makan's view that merging parties can facilitate our review by providing information earlier in the process. The new timing agreement requires rolling productions, limits the number of documents that can be "de-privileged", and anticipates earlier data productions. It also includes presumptive limits on the number of custodians to be searched and a shorter (60 day) post-compliance waiting period. As Makan reported at a speech on 5 February 2020, the Division has been meeting his goal of a six-month review of merger transactions from the time of the last HSR filing to the investigating team providing their view of their competitive concerns to the parties.

As Director of Civil Enforcement, you reviewed and advised on all consent decree packages to ensure that the remedies proposed will adequately preserve competition in the relevant markets. What do you look for when assessing the adequacy of a remedy package? How has the Division's approach to merger remedies evolved during your time at the Division?

I considered the review of consent decrees, a responsibility I shared with Dorothy Fountain, the Division's Chief Legal Adviser, to be one of the most important aspects of my job. Unlike the FTC (Federal Trade Commission), we do not have a "compliance shop"; instead we use a "model" final judgment and in-depth staff and Front Office review of the draft final judgments (FJs) to ensure that divestiture agreements will be effective and enforceable. Of course, we look closely at the precise language in the FJ: are the assets to be divested all assets "used in" or only those "primarily used in" the making of the product at issue? How are shared IP rights allocated? While certain aspects of merger remedies have remained consistent over my time at the Division, such as preferences for structural remedies and divestiture of standalone businesses, other mechanisms are used less frequently than in the past, such as crown jewels and fix-it-firsts.

In addition to the day-to-day review of remedy proposals, both Dorothy and I remain current on remedy studies and issues. Together with my counsel, Amy Fitzpatrick, we had regular meetings with a group from the FTC's compliance shop to discuss current cases as well as the lessons learned through the FTC's thoughtful and comprehensive remedies studies. Nor do we limit our exploration to the US. A few years ago, I participated in a thoughtful and eye-opening series of calls and meetings with the FTC and the EU on merger remedies. The calls culminated with an article authored by me, Dan Ducore, Johannes Luebking and Anne McFadden comparing US/ EU merger remedies, which I think practitioners would find very helpful.[1]

Even though the Division, unlike the FTC, does not have funding to do retrospectives or market studies, we do think through our own decrees and consider what worked well and what didn't. Dorothy, Amy and I regularly revisited many of the questions that are always key to constructing a good remedy: how do we best ensure that the buyer of the divested assets is getting the correct assets and personnel? How can we best ascertain the plans of a purchaser of the divestiture assets? What if the upfront buyer falls through? Failing to preserve the competition that existed prior to an anticompetitive merger puts at risk all of the Division's efforts to investigate and prosecute that merger.

Both the Division and the Federal Trade Commission have identified the healthcare industry and, in particular, rising healthcare costs, as an area of focus. How is the Division acting to ensure competition in healthcare markets?

Antitrust enforcement is an essential tool for protecting healthcare consumers. When I first started in the Division, I was in the now-disbanded Professions and Intellectual Property Section and worked on several healthcare cases, primarily involving agreements between healthcare providers. I learned from those investigations the important role that competition plays at the many different levels of the health care industry to contain costs and improve quality. Fast forward to 2017, when the Division successfully challenged two multi-billion dollar health insurance mergers that would have consolidated the number of national insurance

---

1   Patricia Brink, Daniel Ducore, Johannes Luebking and Anne Newton McFadden, "A Visitor's Guide to Navigating US/EU Merger Remedies" (2016) 12 Competition Law International 1, 85.

companies from five to three. Those trials, which ran simultaneously in two DC District Court courtrooms, were a herculean effort by our teams, and are among the Division accomplishments of which I am most proud. Virtually every civil section, as well as many criminal and policy sections, "volunteered" lawyers and paralegals to work on those trials. So now, whenever one of my doctors asks what I do, I say, "I work for DOJ and we stopped Aetna from buying Humana and Anthem from buying Cigna." They always reply, "Thank you!"

I also would like to draw attention to a case we filed in 2016 against Atrium Health, formerly known as Carolinas HealthCare System. Our suit challenged Atrium's use of steering restrictions in its contracts with commercial health insurers in the Charlotte, North Carolina area. Those restrictions prevented health insurers from developing health plans that encouraged patients to use cost-effective providers. We found that increased consumer access to these types of health benefit plans invigorates competition between providers to offer lower premiums and better overall healthcare services. Ultimately, we were able to agree to a resolution of this case, which was filed in April 2019.

International Cooperation

Since you have been at the Division for many years, you must have seen tremendous changes in the international aspects of the Division's work. What has been your involvement in international work and what have you found most enlightening or fulfilling?

When I started at the Division in 1989, there were approximately 30 competition agencies around the world; that number is now over 130. This international prioritisation of competition law and policy has been accompanied by a global economy that is much more interconnected and interdependent than it was when I first started at the Division. Certainly, international cooperation is playing a far more central role in our work now than it was even 10–20 years ago, as is our work in providing technical assistance to agencies around the world. I've been very involved in both of these efforts.

Over the years, I worked closely with the civil sections and our International Section to oversee our civil case cooperation with sister agencies. Lynda Marshall, Chief of the International Section, and I get reports on all of our case teams' interactions with international enforcers. One of the most personally fulfilling aspects of seeing global competition agencies work together is how we can enhance each other's understanding of competition, how global markets are working, where there are sticking points, and how we can best protect both businesses and consumers in a world that is constantly changing and shifting.

As international connections become more important, the competition agency community has developed methods to learn from each other, build relationships, and support each other. In 2018 alone, the International Section of the Antitrust Division participated in over 60 meetings with its fellow enforcement agencies at home and abroad, led technical assistance programmes in 15 countries, and participated in 22 different technical cooperation programmes. Over the years, I've been very fortunate to travel to meet with many competition agencies, including those in India, China, Vietnam, and agencies participating in the OECD's Budapest and Korea Regional Competition Centres, as well as to meet with the countless others who come to Washington. We've discussed topics ranging from analysis of merger and anticompetitive conduct, remedies, investigative techniques and best practices to agency resources and organisation. Relationships with international agencies are long-term commitments that the Antitrust Division takes very seriously and that can ultimately yield great benefits. Building these relationships has been one of the greatest joys of my career in international competition work.

In May 2019, the International Competition Network (ICN) held its annual conference in Cartagena, Colombia, which was attended by 500 delegates from more than 80 jurisdictions. At the conference, the ICN enacted two documents to promote and strengthen procedural fairness in competition agency proceedings: the Framework on Competition Agency Procedures (CAP) and Recommended Practices for Investigative Process. How is the Division leading on promoting procedural fairness across the globe? How does the Division strive to provide parties procedural fairness here in the United States?

The Division has long been a leader in the international dialogue on procedural fairness, so our engagement here isn't new, but the 2019 ICN conference was important due to the enactment of both the CAP and the Recommended Practices for Investigative Process. The CAP was adopted by the ICN Steering Group in early April. It officially opened for all national, supranational, and customs territory-specific competition agencies to join on 1 May, and the ICN Annual Conference was a time to celebrate its entry into effect. I'm happy to report that the DOJ's Antitrust Division signed on as a founding member, as did, to date, 66 other competition agencies around the world. The success of the CAP and the Recommended Practices are historic achievements for transparency and procedural fairness in antitrust enforcement.

The origins of the CAP can be found in the Antitrust Division's work on the Multilateral Framework on Procedures in Competition Law, Investigation, and Enforcement (MFP), which the Division developed under the leadership of AAG Delrahim. When AAG Delrahim took up his post, international cooperation, and specifically international procedural fairness and due process, were among his top priorities. He immediately charged the International Section to think creatively about how we could take the lead on fundamental due process in the antitrust and competition sphere with the goal of garnering greater confidence in and respect for antitrust enforcement globally. The MFP was not developed in a vacuum, and we borrowed liberally from initiatives already in place, ideas derived in other contexts, and international models, to create an agreement that has truly been an international creation. Our goal was to identify norms that are truly universal and then take advantage of the groundswell of international support for fundamental due process. The MFP, which ultimately became the CAP, are great advancements towards those goals.

Domestically, I think we and the FTC do a good job in providing parties and third parties with the types of transparency and due process outlined in the CAP and Recommended Practices: non-discrimination, transparency, notice and meaningful engagement, timely resolution, confidentiality protections, impartiality, access to information and opportunity to defend, representation by counsel, written decisions, and independent review. Further, in my experience, one thing the US agencies do well is to recognise that we do not have all the answers – and that we need to listen, too. Engagement with the parties to a proposed merger, or whose conduct is under investigation, is critical to reaching fully informed decisions. Our standard procedures include: 1) transparency about who makes decisions and the timetable of likely milestones; 2) regular meetings between investigating staff and parties/ counsel; 3) opportunity to meet with the decision-makers before a decision is made; and 4) regular updates to parties on theories of competitive harm the nature of the evidence/economic analysis and 5) encouraging parties to provide written submissions, including legal and economic analyses.

During the ICN's annual conference, the ICN's Merger Working Group, of which you are an active member, presented a report comparing different National Competition Authorities' (NCAs) approaches to assessing vertical mergers, using three mergers as case studies: *Broadcom/Brocade*,

Essilor/Luxottica, and *Ticketmaster/Live Nation*. How does the Division's approach to vertical mergers differ from the approaches taken by other NCAs? How is it similar?

As a Division, we have made substantial progress towards international convergence in our approaches to assessing non-horizontal mergers. For example, in the vertical context, there is broad consensus that input and customer foreclosure are the most likely theories of harm, and we generally agree on using an "ability, incentive and effect" analytical framework. The differences are really in the details. As in all mergers, but particularly in the vertical context, the analysis is highly fact-intensive, and different jurisdictions will inevitably face different market conditions.

For example, in *AT&T/Time Warner*, the European Commission was able to clear the transaction in Phase 1, while the Division had to grapple with significant US-based effects, ultimately bringing a challenge in federal court. These differences were the result of very different activities and market positions of the parties in Europe and the US, not different substantive approaches to vertical mergers by our agencies.

Another example is the *Bayer/Monsanto* merger, which raised a variety of horizontal concerns relevant to a number of jurisdictions, but also some vertical issues that were specific to the United States. Without a remedy, the merger would have resulted in vertical foreclosure effects from the combination of Monsanto's strong position in corn and soybean seeds with Bayer's strong position in certain critical seed treatments. We required the divestiture of Bayer's seed treatment businesses to eliminate the incentive and ability to increase prices to Monsanto's rivals post merger. Although this was a US-specific concern, we worked very cooperatively with other jurisdictions reviewing the merger, particularly the EU, to ensure that there was no conflict among the remedies imposed by the different jurisdictions.

One area where there appears to be some variation among jurisdictions is with respect to the use of more detailed economic modelling to analyse foreclosure incentives. As reported in the ICN 2018 survey on vertical mergers, a number of agencies indicated that they sometimes or always use detailed economic modelling techniques, but a substantial proportion of jurisdictions said that they never use them.[2] So this is an area where we could work towards a common approach.

Another area where discussion may be warranted is with respect to remedies. As you may know, AAG Delrahim has repeatedly stated a strong preference for structural remedies in both horizontal and vertical contexts. That is in part why the Antitrust Division withdrew the 2011 Policy Guide to Merger Remedies. An important benefit of structural settlements is that they solve, for good, the competitive problem resulting from the merger. Other competition agencies appear be more open to behavioural remedies, particularly in the vertical context.

Another area of potential variation among jurisdictions is how agencies are approaching other non-horizontal merger theories of harm, such as conglomerate theories. Particularly as more mergers involve global companies that trigger concurrent reviews across jurisdictions, it is critical to work towards consistent outcomes. For example, we would want to avoid a situation where one jurisdiction blocks a merger on the basis of a theory that other jurisdictions believe risks sacrificing important efficiencies to prevent speculative future harm to competition. By so doing, that jurisdiction denies consumers around the world the benefits the merger might have delivered.

Today, many jurisdictions either don't have any guidelines for assessing vertical and conglomerate mergers or have outdated guidelines. The US agencies are now in the process of drafting and issuing new guidelines for assessing vertical mergers. We are hopeful that in updating those

---

2   <http://icn2018delhi.in/images/ICN-survey-report-on-vertical-mergers-17-03-18.pdf>.

guidelines we will improve transparency and effectiveness of merger review not only in the United States but to contribute to the dialogue across jurisdictions as others are reviewing their own frameworks.

Reflections and Advice to Antitrust Practitioners

Over the course of your career at the Division you have served in many different roles, including the Deputy Director of Operations, the Special Counsel for Microsoft Decree Enforcement, and a staff attorney in numerous Division sections. How did your experience across the Division informed the way you approached your role as Director of Civil Enforcement?

My years at the Division have given me a broad and deep knowledge of the Antitrust Division's excellent staff and our work. As an interface between our senior leaders and the career managers and staff, I learned the importance of representing the various interests fairly and openly.

Because I started at the staff level, I also understand the nuts and bolts of how a case is put together (or put to bed). My experiences as a staff attorney enable me to appreciate and understand how our attorneys do their work, what their concerns are and how to address them. I drew on this experience in terms of substance, mechanics and logistics, and to make sure our attorneys have the tools, such as models, policies and guidance, to do their job well. On a personal level, my years in the Division have enabled me to develop a network of alliances across the Division that I can fall back on for guidance and perspective. And this is true internationally as well. I think the world has grown a great deal smaller than when I first started.

Finally, I take great pride in representing American consumers and advocating on their behalf.

You have said on a number of occasions that your work between 2004 and 2005 as the Special Counsel for Microsoft Decree Enforcement was among the "most interesting, significant, and rewarding" work of your career. What was it about that work that you found so interesting, significant, and rewarding?

Working on the Microsoft case was pretty formative for my career. I've come to realise that Microsoft was the dawn of modern case cooperation. Our team, which included Renata Hesse and Paula Blizzard, met with the EU case team, including the EU's Cecilio Madero and Nick Banasevic, every four to six months for several years. Add to that the job of coordinating with the two groups of state plaintiffs and the Technical Committee that was set up to help enforce the compliance of the decree, and on any given day I had quite a number of balls in the air. Substantively, this role gave me insight into the value of cooperation with other agencies, procedural skills on how to engage in cooperation effectively, and first-hand experience with the challenges of developing workable, impactful remedies that are meaningful to competition and consumers and enforceable in the long-term.

What advice can you give to women starting their careers as antitrust practitioners?

First, kudos for choosing a fascinating area of law. A day doesn't go by that I haven't been intellectually challenged. Second, and here I think I'm stealing a line from Renata Hesse, a law career should be viewed as a marathon, not a sprint. Your willingness and ability to take on new roles and challenges may change dramatically over time; the difficulty is how to cut yourself some slack in the hard times and challenge yourself when you can. Also, consider government service for some or all of your career. FTC and DOJ attorneys and economists work on the most significant US competition cases and have the luxury of seeking to do the right thing for American consumers, whether that is to bring a lawsuit against anticompetitive conduct or transactions, or to close investigations. When people ask about my working at the Division for 30 years, I just think, "You should be so lucky."

Sarah Cardell
Competition and Markets Authority
Marie-Claire Strawbridge

Sarah Cardell was appointed as General Counsel at the Competition and Markets Authority (CMA) in September 2013. She heads the CMA's Legal Service which provides legal advice across the CMA's functions. She is also a member of the CMA's senior executive team and is the legal adviser to the CMA's Board. Previously, she was partner in the Competition Group at Slaughter and May, where she advised across wide range of EU and UK merger and antitrust cases and Legal Partner of the Markets Division at Ofgem, where her responsibilities included leading on competition law matters.

Marie-Claire Strawbridge is a counsel with Freshfields Bruckhaus Derringer. She acts across a broad range of sectors on all aspects of EU and UK competition law for clients including Tesco, CVC and RWE. She has a strong focus on retail and consumer markets clients as well as running the firm's antitrust associate-led sector group focused on financial investors. She has extensive experience in advising corporate clients, private equity houses and financial investors in relation to merger control aspects of global and UK transactions. She also advises on antitrust investigations, abuse of dominance and complex vertical agreements.

Competition reforms: Obviously there is a lot going on in terms of potential reforms to the UK competition regime, not least in order to make the UK regime fit for purpose in a post-Brexit world. I read with interest Lord Tyrie's letter to the Secretary of State for Business, Energy and Industrial Strategy in February 2019. This all makes for interesting times for competition lawyers – but should businesses brace themselves for a long period of uncertainty and ongoing regulatory change? Or is this an opportunity to be seized in order to improve and refine the UK regime?

I certainly see this as an opportunity to improve the regime and make sure that it delivers real benefits for consumers, which is its ultimate objective. But we are not proposing to tear up the substantive framework of competition analysis – the legal framework for antitrust and merger control investigations will look broadly the same to businesses (although we are proposing to look at whether more bespoke rules are needed for digital mergers). The reform proposals in Lord Tyrie's letter are principally intended to ensure that the Competition and Markets Authority (CMA) can act to address new and emerging forms of consumer detriment quickly and effectively, particularly in digital markets and in markets where vulnerable consumers are disadvantaged.

If the proposals are implemented, aspects of the way we investigate and enforce would feel different for businesses, and inevitably any change creates a degree of uncertainty. But this needs to be set against the possible consequences for businesses if we did nothing. We don't want to be passive bystanders while confidence in the regime – and the underlying belief that the model of market competition under a framework of independently enforced rules is key to delivering good consumer outcomes – is further undermined.

Post-Brexit: What will be the CMA's priorities post-Brexit, in terms of sectors and market issues to focus on, and how will it make sure the UK remains a leading international competition authority? Do you think we are likely to see divergence of approach between the CMA and the European Commission in any particular areas, whether procedurally or substantively?

In terms of priorities, we continue to see robust enforcement as central to our purpose and will maintain a high volume of enforcement investigations. Post-Brexit, it will be critical for us to work effectively in parallel with the major jurisdictions both in antitrust and merger cases to deliver good outcomes for consumers.

But we also believe that we should seek to eliminate unfair practices through wider reviews in markets that are at the heart of people's everyday lives and at the centre of UK economic life. So alongside our competition enforcement cases, you can expect to see an equal focus on market studies and consumer enforcement cases. Our priorities include protecting vulnerable consumers, improving trust in markets, promoting better competition in online markets, and supporting economic growth and productivity. Digital markets are a key priority for us, as discussed further below.

The scope for UK and EU competition regimes to diverge will depend in part on the nature of the UK's future relationship with the EU. While ongoing alignment with the EU competition regime could provide beneficial consistency for businesses in similar markets, greater flexibility would give the CMA more freedom to reach decisions that reflect the particularities of UK markets and to set its own agenda. Of course, both regimes will start from a similar place and, regardless of the precise terms of a future relationship, we are clear that it will be critical for us to continue to cooperate very closely with our EU partners.

Internal documents: A lot of private practitioners would probably agree that antitrust regulators are increasingly focusing their investigations on internal documents as compelling contemporaneous evidence of how businesses really operate and competition really works. This raises practical challenges, which I will come on to. Do you think this remains the right focus?

In our mergers cases it would be a fair observation that the CMA is increasingly assessing the internal documents of the merging parties at both Phase 1 and Phase 2. They can be especially useful in fast-changing and dynamic markets, where they can provide some insight into not only how the merging parties view each other and their competitors, but also how they see upcoming changes in their industry and how the merger might help them address any challenges they expect to face.

Taking a couple of recent merger cases by way of example, in *Experian/ Clearscore*, we needed to understand how the parties and their rivals were positioning themselves in competition with each other, how rivals were investing in future growth strategies and how broader developments in the market were likely to affect competition in the industry. Similarly, in *PayPal/ iZettle*, we needed to understand the parties' rationale and valuation model for the transaction, as well as the parties' plans for their businesses, absent the merger. More generally, in both antitrust and merger investigations, internal documents are clearly an important (but not the only) source of contemporaneous evidence to inform our assessment of the market content and underlying purpose of the transaction or conduct in question.

So – to answer your question – I do think this remains the right focus and (subject to continuing to refine our approach) I don't expect the CMA to move away from focusing on internal documents as a key source of evidence for its investigations going forward.

Formal information-gathering powers: We have seen an increasing trend on the part of the CMA to use its formal information-gathering powers under section 109 of the Enterprise Act during merger control proceedings to request documents from the parties. I think this creates real challenges in the modern era, given the vast volumes of documents produced by most businesses. Not only does it put a lot of burden on businesses given the severe penalties at stake, but it also requires a great deal of resources to process, at the CMA end, material which might not even be relevant to an investigation. Of course, we have all seen the document guidance and indications that the use of section 109 document requests is to become standard. Particularly the increased workload the CMA is expected to have post-Brexit, do you think this remains the right approach and use of resources or will there be a place again for informal requests allowing for a more pragmatic, iterative (and more proportionate) approach?

We recognise the burden that requests for internal documents can impose on businesses, and that ultimately it is for the business in question to ensure their chosen search tools and methodology are adequate for their intended purpose (noting that we can and have taken enforcement action where this has proved inadequate). Within the constraints of the statutory merger control timeframe, we generally seek to reduce this burden by (a) sending requests for internal documents in draft, (b) commenting on a party's proposed search methodology, and (c) in some cases, attending at a business' external advisers' offices to conduct an initial screening to further reduce the number of documents submitted. This can help the parties focus on producing the documents that are most likely to advance the CMA's substantive case.

More generally, across both merger control and antitrust enforcement, we think it is essential for parties and their advisers to treat our requests for documents and information with appropriate diligence and priority. The majority do, but where that is not the case we will take robust enforcement action to follow up on this. Ultimately it is in all our interests to ensure that our investigations and decisions are timely, robust and based on complete and accurate information.

Judicial review: The CMA will of course always be open to appeal risk but there have been some quite significant examples in the past year or so – *Pfizer/Flynn* is an obvious one as well as *Sainsbury's/Asda's* procedural appeal on the CMA timetable during Phase 2 at the end of 2018. Given the Competition Appeal Tribunal (CAT) has shown it can handle these cases expeditiously, do you think the CMA will see more procedural appeals of this kind coming from merging parties and, if so, what is the CMA doing to prepare for these kinds of actions?

Within the constraints of the statutory time limits in merger cases, we ensure that our process is as fair and transparent as possible and consider very carefully any procedural concerns that are raised with us by parties. There will be occasions – such as in the *Sainsbury's/Asda* merger – where, for good reason, we are unable to agree to what the parties are asking for and this may lead to our decision being challenged before the CAT.

We welcome the fact that the CAT is able to deal with judicial review challenges in merger cases expeditiously, as this minimises the disruption caused to the CMA's investigation (where the challenge is brought during an investigation) or to any remedy being implemented (where the merging parties challenge the CMA's final decision).

It is difficult to say whether the number of procedural appeals is likely to increase in the future. However, we are anticipating that the increase in both our merger and antitrust caseload following Brexit will lead to an increase in the number of challenges in the CAT. That is one of the reasons why we are already taking steps to bolster our litigation team, so that we have the resources to deal with any litigation that arises.

Policy: What do you see as the biggest challenges facing antitrust regulators around the world in preventing consumer harm in the modern era?

It seems trite and obvious to say it, but digital is the biggest challenge. It's no surprise that the European Commission, the FTC, and the UK

Treasury's Furman Review have all shone their light on competition in digital markets. Those and other reviews, including our own reform thinking, have sought to address challenges posed by the growth in the digital economy, which – while bringing great benefits to consumers and in many ways intensifying competition – raises new questions of competition law and policy, gives rise to new forms of consumer detriment, and exposes deficiencies in the speed and effectiveness of the current regime. This becomes all the more salient given the changing nature of cases the CMA is expected to take on post-Brexit.

There's also a populist and political challenge to the regime and the model of market competition, reflecting genuine and widespread public concern that the system doesn't appear to be working for many people, with ordinary consumers being ripped off or left behind. This is something that our chairman, Lord Tyrie, has been speaking on. I think he is right to do so. It is an issue that, to varying degrees, all competition authorities are having to face up to.

Your role at the CMA: What does being General Counsel to the CMA involve and what takes up most of your time, day to day?

It's an incredibly wide-ranging, challenging and satisfying role. I head up the CMA's Legal Service, comprising around 100 lawyers at present, and have ultimate oversight of the legal advice provided across all of our investigations as well as overall responsibility for the CMA's litigation. Of course, I'm very ably supported by an excellent team of Senior and Legal Directors who lead the legal work on individual cases, but I'm in regular touch with them to act as a sounding-board on tricky issues and to assist with decision-making on strategic litigation calls. Alongside that, I'm an active member of the CMA's senior executive team reviewing both management and policy issues arising across the CMA, and I'm the Legal Adviser to the Board. Additionally, I'm the Senior Executive responsible for managing our Policy, Advocacy and

International Directorate. Perhaps not surprisingly therefore my days are incredibly varied but almost always involve a mix of both management and legal issues, which is a combination I very much enjoy.

Your career: what has been your most challenging experience in your career? And the most rewarding?

There have been many challenges along the way but one I would highlight would be my move to head up the legal team at Ofgem after I left Slaughter and May. I'd been there from a trainee through to Partner in the Competition Group so it was a big change moving in-house to a regulator in an area in which I'd had only limited experience prior to the move. It was a major challenge to take on leadership of a new team at the same time as building my credibility and experience in a new area of law, but one which I relished and where, in fact, I gained a huge amount of experience which proved invaluable when subsequently moving to the CMA as General Counsel.

The most rewarding experience has undoubtedly been building the CMA Legal Service effectively from scratch. The original legal structure planned for the CMA was very dispersed and lacked any central cohesion. Early on, I and the senior legal team concluded that it was not fit for purpose and worked with colleagues across the organisation to consolidate the CMA's litigators and advisory lawyers into a single Legal Service. We then embarked on a major recruitment initiative which has continued, more recently supported by initiatives such as the launch of a CMA legal trainee programme, a campaign to recruit and train non-(competition) specialist lawyers and a "legal returners" programme. I'm proud and honoured to lead such a committed and exceptionally talented and hard-working team of lawyers.

Winnie Ching
Competition and Consumer Commission of Singapore

Kirstie Nicholson

Winnie Ching is Director (Legal) at the Competition and Consumer Commission of Singapore. She is responsible for reviewing decisions, supervising investigations, assessing mergers and providing advice on legal and policy matters. Winnie was instrumental in developing CCCS' Fast Track Procedure and enhancing CCCS' Leniency Guidelines. Prior to joining CCCS, she was an Assistant Director of Litigation in the UK Office of Fair Trading, litigating competition and consumer cases in the UK Courts and Competition Appeal Tribunal. Winnie has also worked in private practice and at the Australian Competition and Consumer Commission as a Principal Investigator. Winnie was recently appointed as a Member of the Data Protection Panel in Singapore.

Kirstie Nicholson is the global competition counsel at BHP. Based in Singapore, Kirstie is responsible for the group's competition law compliance framework and advises clients located across the entire BHP group globally on the full range of competition law matters, including merger control, investigations and day-to-day counselling. Before joining BHP, Kirstie spent over a decade in private practice as a competition law specialist with international law firms in London, Brussels, Shanghai and Singapore and was among the first European competition lawyers to relocate to China to assist clients with aspects of the developing competition laws in Asia. Kirstie was also a founding partner of Landmark Asia in Singapore, a boutique public affairs consultancy assisting clients with regulation and policy throughout the APAC region.

You have experience of working at the Office of Fair Trading (now the Competition and Markets Authority), the Australian Competition and Consumer Commission and currently the Competition and Consumer Commission of Singapore (CCCS). What attracted you to a career in competition law regulation?

The intersection between how law regulates economic markets for me is an inherently interesting exercise given the nature, breadth and diversity of different markets. Competition law being integral to ensuring markets work well means it must balance a number of sometimes competing interests in a framework that needs to be sufficiently flexible to apply to different contexts. This generates new and interesting challenges where complex issues arise regularly, so it's a continual learning process that provides a great deal of satisfaction.

What do you see as the key challenges and opportunities for a competition regulator? How might these differ depending upon the relative evolutionary stage of the regulator and the competition laws they enforce?

A key challenge is to strike the right balance in a regulatory approach between ensuring anticompetitive behaviour is dealt with and addressed, while encouraging and fostering competitive behaviour, and not stifling business development and innovation through over-regulation. In terms of opportunities, a competition regulator has the opportunity to create an environment which allows businesses and markets to flourish and thereby contribute to the economic wellbeing of society.

In terms of the evolutionary stage, the right regulatory balance depends on the context of the markets it regulates, including the size of an economy, the level of economic development and competition within a market. For example, in smaller economies, merger threshold levels that indicate competition concerns may arise may be set at a higher level than those that apply in a larger economy.

In September 2018, the CCCS issued an infringement decision against Grab and Uber in relation to the sale of Uber's South East Asia business to Grab for a 27.5% stake in Grab in return. The CCCS imposed both remedies and financial penalties on the parties to the transaction, noting that "the Parties had the option to notify the Transaction for CCCS's clearance prior to its completion. However, the Parties proceeded to complete the Transaction on 26 March 2018 and began the transfer of the acquired assets immediately, thus rendering it practically impossible to restore the status quo." What impact, if any, do you consider this decision might have for voluntary merger notification regimes, in both Singapore and other voluntary regimes such as Australia and the UK?

The *Grab/Uber* merger is CCCS's first investigation against a completed merger that resulted in an infringement decision.

Under Singapore's voluntary merger notification regime, the parties had the option to notify the transaction for CCCS's clearance prior to its completion. However, the parties proceeded to complete the transaction on 26 March 2018 and began the transfer of the acquired assets immediately, with the consequence that restoration of the status quo (i.e. pre-transaction) was not possible. CCCS found that the parties had committed the infringement intentionally, or at the least, negligently, and imposed a penalty of SGD 13.1 million on Grab and Uber.

The impact of CCCS's actions to impose interim measures to keep the market open and contestable, and then impose financial penalties, sent a clear message that parties must comply with the law regardless of whether notification of the merger is voluntary.

While there is no effective way to return to the pre-transaction market landscape in this particular case due to the intangible nature of the affected business, this should not be generalised across all M&A activities in all industries. A voluntary regime, coupled with the powers to investigate mergers and impose financial penalties and other remedies, serves to reduce compliance costs for mergers that do not raise competition issues, while deterring businesses from completing anticompetitive mergers.

The financial penalties imposed by the CCCS in the above-mentioned *Grab/Uber* decision amounted to a combined amount of just over SGD 13 million on the parties. Recent years have seen a trend of increasing levels of financial penalties imposed for breaches of competition laws by competition authorities around the globe. Do you see this trend continuing and, if so, why? Is there a risk that increasingly high financial penalties may have the effect of eliminating certain industry players or reducing investment available for innovation, thereby ultimately reducing choice for consumers?

Financial penalties are only imposed on companies that infringe competition law intentionally or negligently. CCCS's financial penalties serve two objectives, namely to reflect the seriousness of the infringement and to deter parties from engaging in anticompetitive behaviour. The level of penalties imposed on a party are calibrated to meet these objectives in light of the infringing conduct by that party.

Increased penalties may be due to a number of factors, including the turnover of the infringing parties, the duration and scope of the conduct, as well as how egregious the conduct is. The level of penalties will depend on the nature of the cases being investigated. For example, while CCCS issued a SGD 13.1 million penalty in the *Grab/Uber* case, in its most recent decision on hotel information-sharing, the penalty was SGD 1.52 million which was, on average, less than previous infringement decisions in the last two years.

Competition law serves to prohibit conduct that is harmful to the smooth functioning of markets. The development of new products or innovation through R&D are in themselves procompetitive and can give rise to more efficient outcomes. Should a business's conduct result in a net economic benefit, such conduct will be excluded from the Competition Act in Singapore. Penalties are only imposed where a firm engages in conduct that prevents, restricts or distorts competition. This serves as a deterrent for such behaviour and consequently ensures competitive markets, which encourages innovation.

To date, the CCCS has issued only one infringement decision in relation to a breach of section 47 of the Competition Act concerning abuse of a dominant position, namely that against Sistic. Subsequent cases have been closed following the provision of commitments by the relevant entities. In your view, is the increased prevalence of commitments a positive development? What are the key elements that commitments should contain in order for them to be most likely to be acceptable to a regulator in order to reach a resolution of an investigation?

Under the Competition Act, commitments may be offered not only to address competition concerns under section 47, which prohibits the abuse of a dominant position, but also for the section 34 prohibition that prohibits anticompetitive agreements, and the section 54 prohibition that prohibits mergers which may lead to substantial lessening of competition within any market in Singapore. Commitments are, in my view, a positive development as an added tool that can be utilised by CCCS to address the competition concerns it identifies.

Commitments can result in competition concerns being addressed in a more effective and efficient manner, with the shape and form of the commitments being offered by the business concerned. The use of commitments, however, needs to be assessed on a case-by-case basis, and to be balanced with the deterrence an infringement decision can bring. Where a commitment is accepted under the Competition Act because it addresses the concerns identified, there is no finding of an infringement against a business that is willing to change its behaviour to address those concerns.

In accepting commitments, CCCS's key consideration is whether the commitments remedy, mitigate or prevent the competition concerns that it has identified during the course of its assessment. Any commitments proposed by parties, whether structural or behavioural, are carefully considered by CCCS on a case-by-case basis. Besides considering whether the proposed commitments are sufficient to address the competition concerns identified, CCCS will have regard to whether the proposed commitments are proportionate to the concerns raised. CCCS will also consider whether the commitments can be effectively and readily implemented, as well as whether they are easy to monitor. To assist in its consideration of these factors, CCCS conducts a public consultation on proposed commitments from businesses for feedback as to whether the commitments will sufficiently address all competition concerns identified.

In the CCCS's recent infringement decision, in January 2019, concerning the exchange of commercially sensitive information between competing hotels, the CCCS's evidence reportedly included various WhatsApp chats. How does a regulator ensure continued awareness of new platforms that may facilitate the illegal exchange of competitively sensitive information? What practical challenges do such new forms of evidence pose within existing enforcement frameworks and how can these be overcome?

Rapid technological developments are changing business models and our forms of communication; these bring both opportunities and challenges for regulators. In view of this, CCCS has embarked on studies that examine these developments in the light of the existing competition enforcement framework in Singapore. In 2017, CCCS published a paper with the Personal Data Protection Commission and the Intellectual Property Office of Singapore entitled "Data: Engine for Growth – Implications for Competition Law, Personal Data Protection, and Intellectual Property Rights" that examined the landscape of big data in Singapore and explored the proliferation of data analytics and data-sharing on competition policy and law. CCCS also published, in 2017, a Handbook on Competition and E-Commerce in ASEAN (Association of Southeast Asian Nations). Such work ensures an awareness by CCCS of developments and the impact these can have on how an assessment is conducted. It also demonstrates the usefulness of a multidisciplinary perspective to examining such issues.

New forms of communications and the multiplicity of platforms available pose challenges in respect of evidence-gathering and how conduct within these markets should be assessed. Regulators employ a range of methods to detect anticompetitive conduct, including programmes that incentivise persons and businesses to come forward to alert CCCS to the conduct, and CCCS has a variety of powers to compel the provision of information; these tools all remain relevant today. For the assessment of conduct, such as information exchanges utilising new technology, the conduct may differ in form, but the existing framework still serves to delineate conduct that is anticompetitive and so provide regulatory boundaries that businesses need to be mindful of when operating in a market.

Continuing with the theme of new technologies, the potential anticompetitive impact of algorithms is an ongoing focus area for a number of competition regulators. How do regulators address the potential challenges of regulating price-setting algorithms, within existing competition law and policy frameworks?

The use of algorithms by digital platforms may bring about efficiency gains and promote market transparency to the benefit of consumers. Businesses are able to use monitoring algorithms to collect and analyse real-time information concerning their competitors' prices, business decisions and other market data, and thereby more easily adjust their prices to offer more competitive prices to consumers.

Algorithms, however, can potentially make it easier for businesses to collude and fix prices. The ease and speed with which competitors' actions can be monitored can facilitate the alignment of prices and reduce the incentive for deviations, making collusion easier and more attractive. Algorithms can also prevent the breakdown of a collusive arrangement through their ability to predict and distinguish between an intentional deviation from a collusive arrangement, a natural reaction to changes in market conditions or even a mistake when supporting a more collusive outcome.

There are consequently inherent challenges that regulators face with the advent of big data and the use of algorithms. There is no settled position on the issues involved at present, and it is an evolving field that has been the subject of study by a number of regulators. Based on the CCCS's enforcement experience, the current suite of enforcement tools has hitherto been sufficient to deal with competition issues arising from digital platform cases. Where the use of algorithms by businesses is to support or facilitate any pre-existing or intended anticompetitive agreement or concerted practice, such cases fall squarely within the existing enforcement framework. Where algorithms are used in classic "hub-and-spoke" scenarios that involve competitors colluding through a third-party intermediary, this would equally be caught by the prohibition against anticompetitive agreements. Such a scenario could arise, for example, where there is an industry-wide use of a single algorithm to determine prices, and competitors use and rely on that same third-party owned "hub" (a pricing algorithm) to coordinate their pricing strategies. That said, the CCCS is continuing to do more work in the area of algorithms and artificial intelligence, as the technologies develop and evolve.

With effect from 1 April 2018, the Competition Commission of Singapore took on the additional function of administering the Consumer Protection (Fair Trading) Act (Chapter 52A) and was renamed the CCCS. At the time, Dr Koh Poh Koon, Senior Minister of State, Ministry of Trade and

Industry and Ministry of National Development, highlighted the close and complementary relationship of competition and consumer laws. Has this relatively recent expansion of the scope of the CCCS had an impact on the overall enforcement priorities of the CCCS? How has the wider overview of both competition and consumer protection influenced how the CCCS conducts its investigations to take advantage of relevant synergies and ensure the protection of Singapore's markets?

Competition and consumer protection share a close and complementary relationship.

For competition law, the focus is on markets. Measures to enhance competition in markets can bring about benefits for consumers in the form of more choice, lower prices or improved quality. For consumer protection, the focus is protecting consumers from the unfair trading practices that businesses may engage in within a market. The enforcement of the Consumer Protection (Fair Trading) Act (CPFTA) against errant retailers for egregious business practices ensures a more level playing field for law-abiding businesses. The addition of the consumer protection function to CCCS's remit consequently represents an expansion in its range of tools to achieve its mission of making markets work well to create opportunities and choices for businesses and consumers in Singapore.

For example, in 2017, CCCS conducted a market inquiry into the supply of formula milk in Singapore. In the study, CCCS found that an insufficient understanding of the nutritional content of formula milk and the dietary requirements of infants and young children, had led parents to perceive that more expensive or premium brands of formula milk were of a higher quality. To facilitate greater price competition, recommendations, such as a review of importation rules for formula milk to allow consumers to enjoy a wider range of formula milk products at more competitive prices, were proposed. In addition, CCCS also suggested strengthening education efforts with consumers to help consumers better understand the nutritional content of formula milk and the dietary requirements of infants and young children.

Last year, CCCS concluded and published the results of its market study on the online travel booking sector in Singapore. The study examined various commercial arrangements and practices adopted by industry players, and the competition and consumer protection issues that can arise. The study identified four common practices of online travel booking providers that give rise to consumer protection concerns: drip pricing, pre-ticked boxes, strikethrough pricing and pressure selling using false or misleading claims.

In the market study report, CCCS has set out its recommendations regarding how online travel booking providers should conduct themselves to address these concerns. The recommended positions are intended to encourage online travel booking providers to adopt transparent pricing practices, such that prices and their accompanying terms and conditions are communicated clearly. This will enable consumers to make an informed choice and allow businesses to compete on a level playing field.

Following from the study, CCCS has developed a set of guidelines on price transparency to assist businesses in their display and advertisement of prices to consumers to avoid misleading consumers and infringing the CPFTA. These guidelines apply to both online and offline transactions. A public consultation on the guidelines was conducted in 2019 and the finalised guidelines will be published in due course.

In October 2018, the CCCS hosted the 22nd ASEAN Experts Group on Competition (AEGC), following which a press release highlighted a number of key initiatives by the AEGC, including an ASEAN Regional Cooperation Framework. Has this initiative, in practice, led to enhanced cooperation among ASEAN competition regulators? Where do you see continued opportunities for regulators to achieve efficiencies from such cooperation? Are these initiatives also expected to result in benefits for entities subject to the different competition law regimes across multiple ASEAN jurisdictions?

The AEGC is the official platform in ASEAN for competition agencies to discuss and cooperate on issues relating to competition policy and law. At this stage, the objective of the AEGC is to facilitate cooperation among member states. It has therefore focused on creating an environment that supports discussion and consensus building. For example, under CCCS's chairmanship of the AEGC in 2018, the AEGC implemented the ASEAN Regional Cooperation Framework, which is a set of guidelines to facilitate cooperation in ASEAN on a broad range of issues such as enforcement, information exchange, resource sharing, and capacity-building. Another initiative was the ASEAN Competition Enforcers' Network to facilitate cooperation on competition cases in the region and serve as a platform to handle cross-border cases.

These initiatives serve to strengthen the enforcement of competition law in ASEAN and build on the cross-linkages and environment of cooperation that already exists between competition agencies in ASEAN. I would expect such cooperation to continue into the future with further connections being forged and deepened in relation to both technical capabilities and in the area of enforcement. The *Grab/Uber* merger case was a practical example of how cooperation on actual cases may arise within ASEAN and be of benefit to ASEAN competition regulators, even though the competition framework may differ between jurisdictions.

Apart from initiatives to support enforcement action, work is also being done in other areas to benefit and support competition law and policy in ASEAN. For example, an ASEAN Competition Compliance Toolkit was developed to provide guidance to ASEAN member states on promoting business compliance with competition law. Further, to stimulate research, a Virtual ASEAN Competition Research Centre was established which aims to promote competition research collaboration and which hosts a repository of research articles on regional competition policy and law as well as profiles of researchers/academics with an interest on competition policy and law in the region. In short, work continues apace in ASEAN on competition law and policy with the body of material in this area commensurately growing, providing opportunities for enhancing the technical capabilities of regulators and their ability to cooperate.

Finally, in your view, what does success look like for a competition law regulator?

A key measure of success for a competition regulator is, in my view, where a culture of competition is embedded in the market, facilitated by a strong legal framework that is complied with by market players and is understood by consumers, overseen by a regulator that is respected for its role and functions.

Amelia Fletcher
University of East Anglia
Iona McCall

Amelia Fletcher is Professor of Competition Policy at the University of East Anglia. She currently holds positions as Non-Executive Director at the UK Competition and Markets Authority, the UK Financial Conduct Authority and the Payment Systems Regulator, and is a member of the Enforcement Decision Panel at the UK energy regulator (Ofgem). Amelia was previously Chief Economist at the UK Office of Fair Trading (OFT) (2001-2013), where she also spent time leading the OFT's Mergers and Competition Policy teams. She was appointed Most Excellent Order of the British Empire (OBE) in the 2014 New Year's Honours list for services to Competition and Consumer Economics. Amelia holds a DPhil and MPhil in Economics and a BA(Hons) in Philosophy, Politics and Economics from the University of Oxford.

Iona McCall is a competition economist with over 17 years of experience advising clients on competition and regulatory matters. She is currently acting as an expert advisor to a global bank in relation to foreign exchange manipulation, a leading European bank on an EC investigation into an alleged infringement in the bonds market and for an international car company in relation to the bearings cartel. Prior to joining AlixPartners, Iona acted as an expert advisor on the trucks class action and for the Department of Health in relation to antitrust violations in the pharmaceutical sector. In 2019 Iona was named by 'Who's Who Legal' as a Future Leader in the field of competition economics. Iona holds an MSc Economics from the London School of Economics and a BSc (First) in Economics and French from the University of Birmingham. Iona also spent a year studying economics at the Sorbonne in Paris.

Behavioural economics is becoming increasingly relevant for competition policymakers and enforcers alike. Recent decisions by the European Commission and CMA, and judgments in UK Courts have highlighted the importance of economic analysis that reflects the realities of the case. Consumer biases have been key aspects of the recent Google cases in the European Union as well as the 2016 retail banking and energy market investigations in the UK. Amelia has written and presented widely on competition and consumer policy and has a particular interest in the implications of behavioural economics and online markets.

Behavioural economics has been a point of focus in competition policy for the last 10 years. When did you first start thinking about behavioural biases and what they might mean for competition policy?

The publication of *Nudge* by Thaler and Sunstein in 2008 was really the trigger point. I was Chief Economist at the UK Office of Fair Trading (OFT) at that time. While I had personally learnt some early behavioural economics at university, I had not kept up with academic developments in the area and had never thought about how it might relate to competition policy.

When that book came out, UK government departments and arms-length bodies were all encouraged to think about what behavioural economics might mean for policy. The then Prime Minister (David Cameron) even had a direct interest in the issue and round-table discussions were hosted at Number 10. At the OFT, we created a small behavioural economics team and set about considering this question.

The OFT had and its successor, the Competition and Markets Authority (CMA), has both competition and consumer enforcement powers. What do you see as the differing roles for behavioural economics in consumer protection versus competition policy?

When we first started thinking about behavioural economics, the implications for consumer policy were more obvious, but we were convinced that there would also be implications for competition policy.

Consumer policy is to an extent already based on psychological insights, such as that consumers tend not to read small print or that they can be misled if information is presented to them in particular ways. The biggest contribution of behavioural economics in this area is probably providing a more formal framework for consideration of these effects, including enhanced empirical methods for testing them.

For example, an early OFT laboratory experiment looked at the impact of "drip pricing", that is, the practice of only showing some elements of price towards the end of the sales process. There was some scepticism as to whether this pricing practice might be misleading, since consumers do know the full price before making their final transactional decision. The lab experiment was valuable in showing how drip pricing led participants to make substantially worse decisions. Interestingly, it also found that it led them to search less, which may in turn harm competition.

In competition policy, I think behavioural economics has had two key implications. The first is that it has raised awareness of the importance of the demand side (consumers) in the effective functioning of markets. This has blurred the lines between competition and consumer policy and has shown how the two are complementary tools in making markets work well for consumers. Take the drip pricing example I just mentioned. If drip pricing reduces search and therefore harms competition, then using consumer policy to address this practice will also help to promote competition.

The second implication is that understanding consumer behavioural biases can be crucial for understanding the behaviour of firms and how it can be anticompetitive. It is noteworthy that the European Commission *Google Shopping*[1] and *Google Android*[2] cases are both essentially underpinned by the existence of behavioural biases. In the *Google Shopping* case, the key factor is saliency bias, whereby consumers are heavily influenced by the relative salience or prominence of information. In simple terms, they are disinclined to scroll down a search page or click for a new page. This means that prominence on a search page is a key driver of consumer decision-making, and that denying access to prominent positioning can thus be exclusionary.

In the *Google Android* case, the tying case is underpinned by the existence of status quo bias. Users who find search and browser apps pre-installed on their devices are likely to stick to these apps, and this can restrict the ability of rivals to gain customers. To my knowledge, this latter case is noteworthy for being the first time that the Commission has employed a formal behavioural economics term (status quo bias) in a press release announcing an antitrust decision.[3]

---

1   Case AT.39740 *Google Search (Shopping)* Decision of 27 June 2017 C(2017) 4444 final. Available at: <http://ec.europa.eu/competition/antitrust/cases/dec_docs/39740/39740_14996_3.pdf>.

2   Case AT.40099 *Google Android* Decision of 18 July 2018 C(2018) 4761 final. Available at: <https://ec.europa.eu/competition/antitrust/cases/dec_docs/40099/40099_9993_3.pdf>.

3   "Commission fines Google €4.34 billion for illegal practices regarding Android mobile devices to strengthen dominance of Google's search engine" press release of 18 July 2018, available at: <http://europa.eu/rapid/press-release_IP-18-4581_en.htm>.

The discussion around behavioural economics focused initially largely on demand-side biases and the implications for the design of remedies. One of the earliest and most high-profile of these was the Microsoft Internet Explorer web browser case where DG Competition used behavioural insights to design the on-screen ballot box remedy. What do you think have been the most significant changes the consideration of behavioural biases created in the design of demand-side remedies?

Demand-side remedies sometimes arise in the context of competition enforcement, as the *Internet Explorer* case exemplifies. However, they are arguably more often imposed through other legal tools. For example, in the UK they might result from a CMA Market Investigation, from sector regulation, or through specific legislation.

In 2016, I was commissioned by the consumer body, Which?, to carry out a detailed review of demand-side remedies that had been put in place over the previous 10–15 years. I observed clear changes in the design of such remedies after 2008–2010, following the publication of Nudge, with behavioural economics starting to have a clear influence over the later period.

One simple example relates to disclosure. Prior to 2008, there was an assumption that giving consumers more information was always good. But a very basic finding in behavioural economics is that consumers can suffer from "information overload". So, providing more information may not help and can even make consumer decision-making worse. There is now a greater focus on considering how to make any information disclosures smart, so that they genuinely help consumers.

Another example relates to the greater use of empirical testing of remedies, in particular through randomised controlled trials (RCTs). These are valuable in helping to design demand-side remedies that will best enhance consumer decision-making and therefore competition. UK sector regulators, in particular, are increasingly carrying out RCTs as a core part of the remedy design process.

The UK Financial Conduct Authority has been active in testing remedies. This is more challenging for the CMA given the timeframes involved. Do you think it is better to do nothing than get it wrong, or go ahead even if untested?

I am fully supportive of the CMA carrying out its market investigations expeditiously. However, I personally think it is would be useful if legislation could be altered to allow the CMA more time for remedy design, to allow for robust remedy testing.

I am also supportive of a proposal recently put forward by the CMA's Chairman, Lord Tyrie, that the CMA should be able to revisit and refine remedies that are not working effectively for a given period following a market investigation, and to rely on the findings of that investigation without having to carry out a new one. This is how the sector regulators already work, following their own market studies, and it facilitates a more mature and robust approach to testing out remedies and considering what will really make a difference. Not only would this be beneficial for consumers and competition, but it may also be beneficial to the firms involved if it avoids the imposition of costly but ineffective remedies.

That said, there will always be an extent to which remedies cannot be tested *ex ante*, either due to a lack of time or because of the nature of the remedy. It would, for example, not have been possible to test the CMA's Open Banking remedy through an RCT. I certainly don't think the CMA should do nothing in such circumstances, given the potential for such remedies to have substantial benefits in practice. However, I do think it supports the importance of *ex post* evaluation of remedies, to assess their effectiveness in practice, and potentially also the formal use of sunset clauses.

Do you think that the application of behavioural economics to demand-side remedies has fundamentally improved outcomes for consumers? Where do you think that they have worked well and what examples are there of them working less well or creating (potentially less desirable) unintended consequences?

An enhanced understanding of behavioural economics can only help in the effective analysis of how markets are working and the design and implementation of remedies. However, there can certainly be difficult trade-offs to strike.

For example, an issue which has received particular focus over recent years is the higher prices that are often charged by firms to their long-standing, less engaged, customers. In 2018, Citizen's Advice labelled this a "loyalty penalty" and made it the focus of a super-complaint to the CMA. The CMA is now overseeing a cross-regulator programme of work to address the issue.

One potential solution to this problem is to try and enhance engagement amongst these inert customers, and a number of interventions have been made to this end. To the extent this is successful, we might expect to see these newly engaged customers receive lower prices. However, we might also expect to see suppliers adjusting their prices in response. This may result in prices increasing for those customers who were already engaged. Perhaps more problematically, it could also result in prices increasing still further for those customers who remain disengaged despite the intervention. This doesn't mean that such engagement interventions should be abandoned, but it does mean that authorities need to give thought to the wider distributional implications when imposing them.

Further complexity arises from the fact that it can be very difficult to engage inactive consumers at all. Where this is the case, there may be a need for more intrusive measures if inactive consumers are to be protected.

These may be voluntary, such as the pricing commitments that three UK mobile companies recently gave Ofcom in relation to out-of-contract consumers, or they may need to be imposed.

More recently there has been increased discussion about supply-side biases. Fundamentally, firms are run by people, all of whom have their own biases as well as facing incentives created, for example, by their contracts, work environment, remuneration structure and wider business environment. As we saw in the recent Competition Appeal Tribunal judgment in the *Pfizer/Flynn* case on prescribing practice, what people are supposed to do does not necessarily reflect their actual behaviour. What do you see as potentially key supply-side biases?

While demand-side biases are becoming well understood, and even mainstream, the application of supply-side biases remains more controversial. There is a reluctance, in competition policy and more generally, to think of firms as anything other than profit-maximising.

This is understandable. However, I think it has to be recognised that behavioural biases may not be restricted to the demand side of markets. For small firms, this is hardly surprising, with the smallest of firms constituting just one or two people. It would perhaps be more remarkable if such individuals were able to behave so very differently in their business activities from their personal life.

However, even within larger firms, there is an extensive and growing literature on the tendencies of executives to engage in a variety of behaviours that are not necessarily profit-maximising. These include over-optimism, empire-building, maximisation of stock market valuation, focus on the relative performance of the firm (rather than its absolute performance), and even protection of market share in order to protect jobs (perhaps to avoid difficult conversations with staff being made redundant). The implications for risk-taking can go both ways. Some individuals may seek personal admiration – to "stand out from the crowd" – by taking big risks. Others may seek a quiet life and wish to protect their position by acting conservatively. The old adage "Nobody ever got fired for buying IBM" is relevant here.

In some cases, these behaviours may in fact be individually rational for the executives involved, given the reward structures they face, including recruitment and promotion processes, the perceptions of shareholders and wider capital markets, all of which may themselves be hard to fully rationalise.

Whether individually rational or not, these apparent biases can potentially lead to anticompetitive behaviour (or indeed procompetitive behaviour) which is not apparently profitable for the firm.

Indeed. For example, if firms compete on relative performance, then competition between them may actually be stronger than if they compete on absolute performance. At the same time, if the CEO of a dominant firm wishes to protect market share in order to save jobs, then it may choose to engage in exclusionary behaviour even if this does not appear to be profit-maximising.

Some of these effects are well understood and are already incorporated into policy thinking. For example, in the audit market, the concern that firms may be risk-averse and conservative and thus give heavy weight to key suppliers with a strong brand, has been identified as a factor limiting the development of the smaller audit companies.

In the context of mergers, the fact that potential entrants into markets tend to be over-optimistic about their own likely success means that authorities tend to give particular scrutiny to the purchaser approval process for assets which are divested in order to gain merger clearance.

Should these supply-side biases be incorporated more strongly into competition policy and less weight be placed on profit maximisation?

Antitrust has traditionally included a strong focus on considering the profit incentive of firms to engage in the behaviour in question. This emphasis has perhaps been stronger in the US, where the influence of the Chicago School has been stronger. However, such thinking is present in many EU cases too, with authorities seeking to demonstrate in their decisions that the dominant firm is likely to profit from the abusive behaviour.

If we take supply-side behavioural biases seriously, though, it is less obvious that this is still a sensible question to ask. Would it be so outlandish for competition authorities to allow for the possibility that a firm may engage in a course of abusive conduct simply because its CEO wants to preserve market share for personal reasons, and irrespective of whether the behaviour will be profitable?

Likewise, in the context of mergers, if some mergers are driven not by pure profitability motives but by executive reward, empire-building incentives, or potentially over-optimism or over-confidence bias, then would it be unreasonable for competition authorities to allow for this when assessing likely merger effects and, indeed, possible efficiency justifications?

Supply-side biases may also affect the likelihood of anticompetitive agreements being formed and remaining stable. For example, collusion may be facilitated by strong trust and social links across cartel members. Whistleblowing and leniency incentives may not work if parties don't want to breach this social trust. Anecdotally, I have been told of one individual who backed out of a whistleblowing offer when he realised he would be sitting down at an industry dinner later that week with the very people he was accusing of collusion. I have also heard about a leniency applicant that lost its protection because the CEO breached the requirement not to inform fellow cartel members about the application until dawn raids had been undertaken. He apparently told them on the basis that he couldn't hide the truth from what were some of his oldest and dearest friends.

On the more positive side, collusion may be inhibited by a non-profit-related human desire to be a law-abiding member of society. This suggests that a successful strategy to reduce collusion might usefully focus on changing culture and social norms, not just penalising illegal cartels. The fact that individuals may be more likely to focus on their own career prospects than on the profits of their firms also helps justify the use of individual sanctions for cartel infringement, such as director disqualification orders, criminal sanctions or individual fines. The last of these is not currently available as a sanction in the UK, but has been recently been proposed by the CMA's Chairman as a potential reform.

Another factor worth highlighting in the context of cartels is that, in the presence of demand-side behavioural biases, firms may be able to engage in an alternative form of collusion: collusion to dampen competition. For example, it may be in the joint interest of two rival firms to agree to set their price structures very differently, or to make their pricing highly complex, in order to limit comparability between them. By disincentivising consumer search, this can dampen competition and enhance firm profitability.

As we have explored here, behavioural economics highlights the distinction between how we expect people and firms to behave, and how they actually do behave. In antitrust enforcement, what is the difference between incorporating insights from behavioural economics and simply grounding the economic analysis in the facts of the case?

I agree that authorities do already incorporate behavioural insights to some extent, by focusing on the empirical facts of the case. The key question is what other assumptions are being made in such cases, and the basic economic underpinnings of competition policy often involve implicit assumptions about firm and consumer rationality.

It is worth noting that behavioural factors can also influence empirical analysis. For example, standard demand estimation techniques do not typically allow for the fact that consumer purchasing behaviour may be strongly affected by framing effects. For example, a price reduction from £2 to £1.50 may have a very different impact on sales if the price label specifically states "Was £2, now £1.50", as opposed to the price simply changing without such labelling. Similarly, consumers who exhibit loss aversion may have very different reactions to a price change depending on the direction of the change, with many more switching away on the basis of a price rise from £2 to £2.20 than would switch to the product on the basis of a price reduction from £2.20 to £2. Again, most demand estimation techniques implicitly assume symmetric reactions. I think more work could usefully be done on how to make allowance for consumer biases within such empirical analysis.

In a recent article you suggested that the application of behavioural economics in the recent Google cases may only be the "tip of the iceberg". Clearly digitalisation, and the increasing ability for firms to collect and interrogate large datasets and merge structured and unstructured data, all create new opportunities for firms. In this context, where do you see behavioural economics raising further questions for competition policy or challenging current thinking around the use of economic analysis in antitrust enforcement?

Digitalisation has a number of implications in this area. Many of these are positive, such as the fact that digitalisation enables the development of better information and choice tools for consumers, which should actually enhance consumer decision-making and help drive competition.

However, I would highlight two potential areas of concern. First, the huge amount of data that digital companies can collect about individual consumers potentially facilitates highly targeted marketing and, potentially, also pricing. This can have benefits. I would personally rather receive marketing that genuinely reflects my interests than more generic marketing. And on the pricing side, to the extent that price differences reflect true willingness to pay, there may well be benefits in terms of widening market access to consumers. For example, if price discrimination makes lower prices available to more vulnerable customers, or to customers with lower willingness to pay, then this may on balance be beneficial.

However, the situation becomes substantially muddier if such pricing or marketing also reflects behavioural biases, and especially if the higher prices end up being charged to the more vulnerable consumers, or if the targeted marketing is more obfuscatory than informative.

Targeted pricing may also have implications for the practical implementation of competition policy. In a world with limited consumer information and no price discrimination, the switching of marginal consumers creates competition between firms which benefits all consumers, and markets can be defined relatively broadly. This may no longer be true in a world with individualised pricing. While there may continue to be intense competition for marginal switching consumers, there will be far less competition for the disengaged consumers, who arguably now comprise a separate market or even myriad individual markets.

This relates to the "loyalty penalty" issue I mentioned earlier. So far, this concern has typically been addressed in the UK through market investigations and sector regulation. There remains an open question as to whether antitrust could also have a role to play. It does not seem a huge conceptual leap to suggest that firms are dominant in the market for their own disengaged customers, that behaviour designed to hamper them switching away is exclusionary and that high pricing is exploitative.

Fairness may also be relevant here. A key behavioural insight is that people care not only about their own treatment in absolute terms but also about the fairness of outcomes. In recent years, the UK regulators have given substantial thought to how they should address these complex fairness issues, and I suspect this debate will continue.

The second area I would highlight relates to the fact that online sellers have very close control over how they present information to consumers, and indeed can easily experiment with this over time. Again, this could be beneficial in terms of helping improve consumer decision-making. But equally it could facilitate the ever more effective obfuscation and confusion of consumers, or the exploitation of biases such as saliency bias, default bias and status quo bias.

I already mentioned the role that such biases played in the Google abuse cases. Default bias was also key in the Microsoft Internet Explorer case touched on in an earlier question. I think this is a point with potentially far wider implications, though. Such biases may be an important factor enabling digital platforms to leverage their strong position from one market into related markets, and as such we may expect more abuse cases relating to such leverage, which are underpinned by such behavioural biases.

You were recently part of a Digital Competition Expert Panel set up by the UK Treasury that brought together academics from the fields of public policy, law, economics and computer science, led by the US economist Professor Jason Furman. You were given the task of considering whether competition policy was working effectively in the digital economy and, if not, to make recommendations for change. Perhaps the most significant of your recommendations was the suggestion that the UK should put in place ex ante regulation in the form of a Digital Markets Unit to oversee the development of competition in markets involving digital platforms. What role did behavioural economics take in your consideration of the challenges generated by the digital economy and the development of this recommendation?

The recommendations of the Panel were based on the fact that there are a number of economic factors which tend to lead to digital platform markets both "tipping" towards being highly concentrated and to this market position then being extended into related markets. We discussed the key relevance of trans-global economies of scale and scope, network effects, and the role of data, but we also emphasised the important role that behavioural biases play in these markets.

A very simple point in this regard is that competition in platform markets, and even their tendency towards tipping, is strongly affected by whether users single-home (use only one platform for a particular activity) or multi-home. In many digital markets, multi-homing is theoretically very simple and costless for consumers. I can easily switch between the Apple and Google Map apps on my phone for example. However, in practice, we seem to see a very strong tendency by consumers to single-home, and indeed to exhibit strong default or status quo bias in their choice of single-home. This is important for understanding the likely development of competition in this sector.

The control that digital platforms have over how information and choices are presented also has important implications for consumer behaviour and thus the nature of competition. It is, of course, a key difference between the online and offline worlds that the former involves no direct face-to-face human interaction between a seller and a consumer. Consumers are typically fairly good at reading their interactions with other humans and can usefully be guided by them (albeit they can certainly also be conned in person too). In an online environment, these usual human interactions are effectively replaced by informational tools, which seek to provide similar guidance, such as rankings, reviews and star ratings. Consumers frequently put great weight on these tools in their decision-making.

The fairness, consistency and transparency of such tools is thus crucial both for ensuring that consumers are not misled and for ensuring that competition between business users of a platform is not distorted. The Panel proposed that this should be an important area of focus for the new Digital Markets Unit, building on the EU Platform to Business Regulation, a view which was influenced by our understanding of the role that consumer behavioural biases play in digital markets.

Effective consumer law is also crucial in digital markets and will help to address the risks arising from consumer biases. An early example was the development online of pre-ticked boxes for add-on products, which exploited default bias to distort competition and unduly expand sales of such add-ons. EU consumer law has now been revised to ban this practice.

The CMA is currently heavily active in bringing consumer law to bear more widely on digital platforms, in particular to ensure that consumers are not subject to misleading sales practices. For example, the CMA has recently taken action relating to how information is presented online by secondary ticketing agents and hotel booking sites.

Consumer policy in this area is, however, complex and ever-developing. While existing tools are currently being applied successfully, there may well be a need for further legislation in this area in the future. A number of potentially valuable options were outlined in the CMA response to the "loyalty penalties" super-complaint. For example, a particular problem online is that it can be exceptionally easy for consumers to sign up to a new service, but rather more difficult to cancel it. Of course, the service may then "auto-renews" and its price may creep up over time. Saliency and status quo bias, and potentially also myopia, could all play a role in consumers being susceptible to being exploited by this form of practice. It is not clear whether such practices can be fully addressed under existing consumer (or competition) law.

The future holds a number of challenges for competition authorities, do you think that the ongoing development of our understanding of behavioural biases will continue to play a key role in tackling them?

I think it has to. The more we learn about the implications of behavioural economics for how markets work and for the effectiveness of remedies, the more it seems perverse to ignore them. When I speak on this topic, I get a full range of responses from "this is dangerous thinking, which could undermine the rigour of competition policy" to "this is obvious and it is not new; we do it all already". Of course, I think the truth lies somewhere in the middle. A greater focus on behavioural economics will change things, of course, but it can also be seen as just the latest step in bringing a more economic approach to this area of law.

Beatriz De Guindos

Spanish National Markets and Competition Commission

Pia de la Cuesta & Irene Moreno-Tapia

Beatriz De Guindos is the Competition Director at the Spanish Competition Authority since June 2018. She belongs to the Spanish elite civil servants in the economic field since 2003. From the beginning of her career at the Public Administration, she joined the Spanish Competition Authority, holding various positions until her appointment as Competition Director. In 2014 was appointed for a 2-year term as Alternate Executive Director at the World Bank Group. In 2017, she was awarded by W@Competition and PaRR Global as one of the '30 in their 30s' Notable Women Competition Professionals in the Enforcement Category.

Pia de la Cuesta has been Regional Compliance Officer Europe Africa for thyssenkrupp Elevator AG since January 2020, being the first point of contact for antitrust, anticorruption, data protection and anti-money laundering matters. Previously she served as Regional Compliance Officer Iberia for thyssenkrupp AG. Prior to joining thyssenkrupp in 2015, Pia served as local in-house counsel for Holcim (today LafargeHolcim) before becoming Corporate Compliance Counsel at the Holcim's Swiss Headquarters in Zurich. Before Holcim she worked as an antitrust and commercial lawyer for Garrigues and CMS Albiñana & Suárez de Lezo. Pia holds a Degree in Law from the Salamanca University and a Master's Degree in European Law from the Free University of Brussels (Université Libre de Bruxelles).

Irene Moreno-Tapia, head of the Competition and EU Law Practice at Cuatrecasas Barcelona office, specialises in all areas of competition law, with particular expertise in vertical agreements and abuse of dominant positions. Also, she regularly advises national and multinational companies on the control of concentrations – both at Spanish and EU level – and represents them before the administrative courts. She has successfully represented many clients on competition cases before the Spanish and regional authorities, in both administrative and litigation fields. She also has ample experience in other areas of EU law, such as pharmaceuticals and chemicals, and has participated in many cases before the EU courts.

Your professional life has been devoted for its major part to competition law. What do you think a female leader can bring to an institution like the CNMC?

I have been part of the Spanish Competition Authority for more than 15 years now, and during this time I've had the opportunity to work in many different capacities (case handler, head of unit, special adviser) and in all areas (mergers, antitrust, cabinet of the president). This previous experience allowed me to know well our roles and responsibilities and, above all, the teams, what makes things much easier. I fully believe in meritocracy and that elements of correction should only be put in place when there is a situation of discrimination, which has not been my case.

One of the main virtues of women is our ability in multitasking, which is extremely useful for jobs in institutions such as competition agencies, where we have to deal with many different cases and sectors at the same time, and our deadlines are very tight in both mergers and antitrust procedures. Our ability to work in teams and address very different issues simultaneously can play a notable role in those circumstances.

What are, in your opinion (as a competition expert and as Director of Competition in the CNMC), the challenges that we are currently facing in this field, globally and in Spain in particular?

At a global level, our main challenge is clearly dealing with digital markets in a coherent and consistent way across the globe. Our challenge is not only addressing the dynamism of these markets with the appropriate instruments, but also doing it jointly between all competition enforcers and in a coherent way, since digital markets tend to be global and have no frontiers at all.

Another subject emerging strongly at a global level is the debate about national champions. It is probably due to the geopolitical context that we are living in right now, but experience has taught us that we should keep industrial policy apart from antitrust rules, which are based on a rigorous and objective assessment. That said, I certainly share the opinion that additional instruments (industrial policy, commercial policy) must play their role in achieving a level playing field. However, competition policy tools, namely antitrust and merger rules, by their nature, must be left out of any influences that could put at risk the impartiality of the assessment.

Regarding Spain, one of our immediate challenges is the amendment of the Competition Act to transpose the ECN+ Directive. The Competition Act, approved in 2007 and modified in 2013, has been a complete success, but some minor improvements are considered necessary by many stakeholders in order to increase effectiveness. In this sense, we are considering the possibility of introducing a settlement procedure. We are also proud of our unique 18-month statutory deadline for antitrust investigations, which brings together effectiveness and legal certainty, but it might be necessary to increase this deadline in particularly complex cases to be able to deal with big amounts of information in the files and effectively ensure the rights of defence when we have many parties in a case.

Finally, there is a challenge that remains relevant at both national and global levels: advocacy on competition rules. It is our duty to enhance compliance, work jointly with all stakeholders in the detection and eradication of competition infringements and help unleash the potential of market competition.

The concentration of supervisory bodies under the CNMC and its efficiency have been heavily discussed. The arguments for the integration of the former CNC (Comisión de la Competencia) together with the sectoral regulators were, inter alia, based on an alleged efficiency in the supervision of market competition and on the risk of regulatory capture by both the private and the public sector. Some consider that this goal has not been achieved. Seeing your long experience in the national competition authority under both systems, which format would you say best serves the goals of the antitrust policy?

To understand the differences between both models and the origin of the CNMC, I believe that we have to go back to the previous situation and make a critical and objective analysis of the coordination between the competition authority and the pre-existing regulators. If we do this retrospective exercise, we will see that there was a lot of room for improvement in coordination, despite the mandatory meetings and reports that were foreseen in the former legislation.

The current model, at least theoretically, should be able to eliminate the legal uncertainty raised from the potential different positions of the regulator and the competition authority, for example, regarding a merger in the telecommunications or the energy sector. In addition to consistency of decisions, the integrated model can bring synergies for competition enforcement in the form of improved access to information, better regulation and enhanced *ex officio* detection of anticompetitive behaviours in regulated sectors.

The experience of these six years has shown that these synergies are possible (the joint work of the different Directorates in merger control in the fuel sector or in the process of liberalisation of passenger rail transport are some clear examples). This does not mean that it is easy or that the institution's potential is always fully exploited, especially considering that our integrated model has been very challenging, for instance, when combining labour and civil servants that came from very different working cultures and with different job promotion perspectives. The new institution also faced some resistance and criticism from law firms and consultancy boutiques dealing separately with competition and regulatory issues that had to adapt to the new model too. However, I think it is fair to recognise that the integrated model, if existing synergies are successfully achieved, can be more effective than simple coordination between regulators.

Some national competition authorities in Europe (e.g. France, Italy, UK) also have competences in the field of consumer protection, which is at the heart of competition law. Do you think this would be feasible in Spain?

Competition policy is about the competitive process and the consumer, as the end beneficiary of a healthy effective competition in the market. Therefore, it is not surprising that more and more competition authorities assume very effectively consumption protection policies among their functions. In the case of Spain, consumer protection policies are decentralised, that is, regional governments have the competences in this area. Therefore, it seems neither possible nor probable that the CNMC could assume these powers.

In any case, the CNMC has made considerable efforts for years to keep a fluid communication and collaboration with consumer authorities and associations. To this end, we have recently signed an agreement with the Council of Consumers and Users, which coordinates consumer associations in Spain in order to provide training and information on regulated sectors, such as telecommunications and energy, to help consumers understand their rights and detect any breaches of consumer protection and/or competition rules.

The US and EU approaches with regard to individual liability for competition law infringements have traditionally been significantly different. US antitrust authorities are well known for their use of criminal sanctions against individuals, from fines to imprisonment. EU Member States have started to introduce criminal penalties for competition law infringements, mainly by means of administrative fines but also with prison sentences for individuals in case of bid-rigging. Do you think the consideration of competition infringements as criminal offences is a decisive factor to deter antitrust violations? Do you envisage a trend change in Spain in this regard?

In Spain, unlike the EU regime, we do have fines on natural persons but these are only economic fines, not criminal sanctions, except for bid-rigging cases where criminal law may also be applied to individuals. Moreover, in our jurisdiction, individuals can also benefit from leniency. This can create the necessary incentives for companies to apply for leniency if they suspect one of their executives might apply for leniency on their own behalf. In fact, we have had experience on individual applications.

The culture of competition law is growing fast among Spanish society in the last few years, especially following the high number of cartels dismantled under our leniency programme (more than 100 applications and almost 40 cartels sanctioned since 2008). Following a very active communication strategy and transparency policy by which all our decisions are made public, consumers and undertakings better understand their right to effective competition in the markets and are able to identify the existence of competition infringements that they can bring before the CNMC.

But I am afraid we are still far from criminalising competition infringements. This is something that eventually will have to be introduced in our system, especially taking into account its enormous deterrent effect, but for the time being it seems to me that the legislator is focused on ensuring the necessary tools and powers for an effective enforcement under the administrative regime.

In the last decade, the CNMC has been mainly focused on cartels (driven by leniency applications) with minor enforcement in other type of restrictive agreements (horizontal or vertical) and abuses of a dominant position. This trend may continue now that the ECN+ Directive allows national competition authorities to set priorities and dismiss complaints on that basis. How do you think this will impact the activity of the CNMC?

Indeed, our leniency programme has been very successful and these big cases have driven much of our efforts in the last 10 years. Nevertheless, we have had several abuse cases in relevant markets such as railways, energy, telecoms or the postal sector, to name a few. It is not surprising that these are regulated markets, which have been opened to competition, and incumbents have not always adapted to the new market conditions in a lawful way.

The ECN+ Directive will not much change our way of dealing with restrictive agreements and abuse cases in such markets, since these remain relevant for competition authorities. However, ECN+ does bring a very useful power for those very few authorities, such as the Spanish Competition Authority, which are still today unable to prioritise their investigations and make an efficient use of their scarce resources.

The transposition of the Directive will allow us to release some of those resources from cases which, even if there are no evident grounds of infringement, have to be assessed and investigated under the current law before filing them away. The new provision will also force national competition authorities to draw clear guidelines on their annual priorities, bringing more transparency on our strategic plans to ensure, once again, the necessary legal certainty regarding this new power to file away complaints.

Digitalisation is changing the competition world. These changes influence how competition works in the markets, i.e. price algorithms, big data, manufacturers competing with distributors through platforms, two-sided markets, and how competition authorities investigate. A recent report commissioned by DG COMP ("Competition Policy for the Digital Era") pleads for certain changes in the competition rules to adapt to the new times. Do you have any thoughts on this?

The role of competition policy in digital markets has been a hot topic in the competition arena for a long time. We are more than 10 years away from the first mergers and antitrust cases in this sector such *Google/ Double Clickair*, *Microsoft/Linkedin* or the Microsoft interoperability cases. Yet, a vivid debate is still ongoing about whether competition authorities are well equipped to understand and safeguard competition in digital markets. But some of these issues (innovation, network effects, two-sided markets, essential facilities) are not new topics in reality. We have dealt with similar issues in the past. What it is new is the context: the combination of all the previous factors and their relevance lead some markets to being more prone to dominance. Digital markets enhance the natural power of big players very fast because the technological and economic landscape changes very quickly and disruptively.

Under these circumstances, competition authorities need to be especially vigilant and intervene in a timely manner, but always on the grounds of specific evidence in each case and after a careful assessment of the effects of the investigated conduct or transaction. Therefore, more than adapting competition rules, I believe we need to update our focus on dominance and try to find flexible solutions to not-so-new problems such as the access to data. I fact, I recall a case from 2009 in the electricity sector in

Spain (the so-called *Centrica* saga) which dealt precisely with the access to a consumer database from electricity distributors (incumbents) by a new entrant in the retail market that was considered to be an essential facility from a competition assessment perspective.

In merger control, we need to pay more attention to the competitive significance of the acquired firm (dynamic and prospective analysis) versus the more traditional static assessment of horizontal and vertical overlaps. But, again, I don't think it's a question of tools or rules but rather focus adaptation as we have done in sectors such as pharma, where assessing the impact on innovation of a merger plays a key role.

In this sense, the EU Commissioner Digital Experts Report concludes as well that the principles of competition remain valid but we need to reconsider our theories of harm in some cases. It also points out new features in digital markets such as multi-homing, which is key to preserving competition between platforms that may lead to innovation (in fact, this is in line with some of our remedies in recent merger control cases regarding platforms in Spain).

The only question that, in my opinion, remains open in the report is whether we are ready to enlarge the "by object" cases, by shifting the burden of proof under certain circumstances (for instance, requesting interoperability without need of proving indispensability). The report tends to point out that it might be best to err on the side of false positives, and this is something that I believe still needs to be taken with a lot of caution. Competition enforcement has always been fact-based and under a clear evidentiary basis and I truly believe it should remain as such. Our efforts have to be focused on getting up to speed in digital expertise in order to be able to intervene before it is too late, but this prospective and more dynamic analysis should not come at the expense of a solid evidentiary and economic footing of decisions, free of any speculative judgment.

Spain is the only European country in Europe where acts of unfair competition, if affecting the public interest, can become competition law infringements (section 3 of the Competition Act 15/2007 of 3rd July). What is the reason behind this specificity (or its purpose) and don't you think the CNMC is therewith invading competencies belonging to the commercial courts and tribunals?

It is important to clarify first that the use of article 3 is very limited compared with agreements and abuse cases. In addition, the sanctions for an infringement of article 3 are considered "serious" (5% turnover limit) while horizontal anticompetitive agreements and most abuse cases are considered to be "very serious" infringements (10% limit).

That being said, I believe that article 3 can be very useful in some circumstances. The consideration of unfair competition by the CNMC needs a triple requirement: i) the conduct must encompass an unfair act, ii) free competition must be altered and iii) the general interest must be affected. If these requirements are not met, commercial courts are then better positioned for the assessment of the case.

Our experience with unfair competition cases is very positive in sectors where companies do not have a dominant position, but where there is still a high degree of concentration or there is an incumbent with a relevant position (for example, in the markets for electricity or gas supply or the market for elevator maintenance). A relevant operator's behaviour leading to confusion, deceit, competitor's denigration or even non-compliance with regulation can place competitors at a disadvantaged position. When such conducts affect a relevant number of consumers, competition in the market can be largely distorted, affecting the general interest. It is in those cases where the competition authority should intervene, restoring competition in the market and not just limiting action to the parties in the file.

Several of the fines imposed by the CNMC under this legal provision have been recently upheld by the courts, enlarging our case law on article 3, which I am convinced will continue to be an extremely useful instrument. Competition policy can play a relevant role in those cases where there is no dominance but where unfair behaviour by a relevant operator has a massive effect. In those cases, I believe the CNMC is better positioned than the commercial courts to fully address the impact of unfair competition in a given market.

In Spain, the National High Court (Audiencia Nacional) as well as the Spanish Supreme Court have lately revoked various decisions adopted by the CNMC on significant fines imposed, e.g. to the paperboard cartel, the dairy industry, telecoms, to name a few. Some of these annulments were due to formal defects in the handling of cases, while some others reflect an inaccurate or insufficient founding. Which do you think are the reasons for this trend and what measures, if any, is the CNMC taking in order to strengthen public enforcement?

I would like to point out, in the first place, that more than 80% of Supreme Court judgments and 75% of those of the National Court have confirmed the resolutions of the CNMC between 2014 and 2018, as regards the assessment made by the competition authority. This information is collected in the statistics available on our website, which include the list of all sentences, classified by court and by year. However, the media impact given to cases in which the decision of the competition authority is not upheld by the courts is much more extensive. I can assure you that the courts share our assessment in the vast majority of competition decisions.

It is also worth mentioning that our current Competition Act dates back to 2007, but the first final rulings regarding case enforcement under this law are from 2015. The referred annulments of decisions that have taken place between 2016 and 2018 are mainly in reference to decisions taken before 2013, and reveal that the courts are raising the bar in terms of legal, economic and procedural standards of our decisions under the 2007 law, compared with the former.

The CNMC is making a big effort to adapt to these new requirements through several specific measures that were announced two years ago and which have been swiftly implemented since then. Indeed, when courts have not endorsed our actions, we have consequently adapted our decisions to the case law in order to guarantee both an efficient and effective exercise of our functions and the full guarantee of the stakeholders' rights. We have taken measures to improve economic analysis, adapt our fining methodology, prevent procedural errors and reinforce communication and coordination with judicial bodies, among others. We are already bearing some fruits, for example, with the Court of First Instance confirmations on the new fining methodology.

There is an existing debate on the legal defence system of the CNMC, according to which some experts are calling for the current system (where cases are delegated to the State Attorney) to be replaced with an in-house legal defence team including competition law experts. This would be consistent with the requirements of the ECN+ Directive aimed at the improvement of national competition authorities' enforcement tools, to apply EU antitrust rules more effectively. Which is your opinion on this?

According to the Spanish law, the CNMC can bring actions directly before the national courts, which is completely consistent with article 30 of the ECN+ Directive. Thus, there is no need to make any amendments in the Spanish law in order to transpose this article.

Nevertheless, taking into account the scarcity of resources, our competition authority has traditionally made use of the State Attorney for its legal representation before the courts, according to an agreement signed some time ago. This system allows us to save human resources, but also to benefit from the wide expertise of the State Attorney in national and regional judicial procedures. It does not mean that the CNMC delegates its representation completely but, on the contrary, our legal team meets regularly with the State Attorney coordinators, we prepare and review the written response to appeals and, more recently, officials from the CNMC, specifically from the Competition Directorate, assist the State Attorney in the hearings.

Finally, it is also worth pointing out that, in case of conflict of interest (for example, in cases against public entities or when we challenge legal provisions adopted by the government), the CNMC appears directly before the court with attorneys from our staff.

The Spanish merger control system is peculiar, as notification thresholds are based on turnover and market share. You are known to be a strong believer of the market share system, which indeed has proved useful in times of transactions involving technological companies with little turnover but strong positions in new markets. However, the market share threshold is far from being easy to implement, as precedents (if any) may not be available and, in some cases, markets evolve rapidly. How do you think the system can be improved to increase legal certainty? Would a threshold based on the value of the transaction instead (more straightforward) be an acceptable alternative?

Indeed, I strongly believe that our threshold based on market share is a valuable tool to catch mergers that can cause competition concerns in the affected markets, specially taking into account digital markets.

The argument of legal uncertainty becomes invalid if you take into account that the Spanish Competition Act foresees the possibility of making a formal previous consultation (which is formally decided by the board in a short time) and the option of making an informal consultation to case handlers from the Competition Directorate (the so-called pre-notification system). In almost 100% of our merger cases the notifying parties make use of the latter.

In addition to this, all our decisions are published in our website, so it is possible to consult all the definitions of product and geographical relevant markets that have been adopted by the authority through the years, in a lot of different markets and sectors. Precisely due to our threshold based on the 30% market share (which accounts for 60% of the notifications), we need to be especially cautious and meticulous in our market definitions, avoiding open market definitions that do create uncertainty for the notifying parties.

In my opinion, the alternative option of a threshold based on the transaction value is not as effective. In fact, the recent experience with this threshold in neighbouring countries has not proven to be particularly useful to catch digital transactions. On the contrary, mergers like *Facebook/Whastapp* or *Apple/Shazam* did meet our threshold based on market shares and we were therefore able to refer them to the European Commission for the assessment of the effects in the whole European market, and not only in the Spanish market.

In any case, in these fast-changing markets, competition authorities need to remain flexible and resilient and at the same time cautious about changing the rules. That is why international cooperation among competition authorities remains more relevant than ever, to share experiences regarding our future endeavours and work together on the best solutions to understand the structural changes in our economies and how can we address together the new challenges in an effective way.

Maria Jaspers
DG COMP, European Commission
Anneleen Straetemans

Maria Jaspers is the head of the Antitrust Policy and Case Support Unit in DG Competition of the European Commission. The unit is in charge of coordinating the Commission's antitrust and cartel cases and developing competition policy in this area. Before that, Maria spent five years as a head of unit in the Cartel Directorate. She joined the European Commission and DG Competition in 2001 and worked in different units dealing with antitrust policy and enforcement issues before taking over as a deputy head of the antitrust and merger case coordination unit in 2007. Before joining the European Commission, she spent two years in private practice.

Anneleen Straetemans is a seasoned international lawyer with 9 years of private practice and in-house experience. Her background is antitrust, so she has a knack for cracking market dynamics and knows her way around regulators, administrative procedures, litigation, effective compliance programmes and cross-border investigations. In her current role, she focuses more on M&A, IP and data privacy. She strongly believes in the power of big data and AI to solve legal & compliance issues and she likes to believe she understands blockchain. She is a strong advocate for diversity and inclusion and is vice chair of W@Competition.

On European Antitrust Policy

In the last two years, we saw the rise of "hipster antitrust", with politicians on the other side of the Atlantic calling for wide-ranging reforms of antitrust policy. But we have also seen increased political pressure within Europe, with voices in France and Germany calling for an overhaul of merger control. To what extent is antitrust policy in Europe influenced by the political mood of the day?

The discussions regarding the goals and impact of antitrust policy have certainly intensified in the context of globalisation and digitalisation and have expanded beyond specialised competition circles. I firmly believe that the credibility and relevance of the EU competition enforcement system is due to the fact that it is a rule-based system where the evidence and the robustness of our legal and economic analysis determines the outcome – not short-term political goals or political connections. We should, of course, always remain open to necessary adjustments to our rules and practices that could allow us to better achieve our goals in a changing environment. And we also have to be able to explain the underlying rationale of our policy and its application in individual cases to the wider public. Commissioner Vestager has done a fantastic job in that respect. In today's political climate and changing societies, I think that it is more important than ever to recognise how transparent, courageous, evidence-based competition enforcement can strengthen and restore people's trust in fair markets and societies. I am therefore, not least as a European citizen, very concerned about unsubstantiated calls for fundamental changes that could easily undermine the credibility and legal certainty of our enforcement system.

Apart from any shifts in the political landscape, what major trends in European antitrust policy have you experienced in the past five years, and what do you think the future holds for the coming five years?

That would no doubt be the impact of digitalisation. Digital technologies are increasingly transforming all sectors of the European economy, challenging not only old business models, behaviours and structures but also the competition framework used to monitor such systems. As competition enforcers, we are often among the first to be confronted with such changes, since they are immediately reflected in the facts, arguments and theories of harm that we are addressing. The European Commission has by now gained a lot of experience and set directions through the numerous "digital" cases that we have already dealt with, including for example the *Google* and *E-book* antitrust cases and several merger control cases. During the last years, we have also embarked on an intense external reflection process on how to shape competition policy in the digital era. This included a stakeholder consultation with more than 100 contributions, a large conference, followed live by more than 500 participants in Brussels and several thousands in more than 50 countries via the web, and a report from three external academics who had been selected to advise the Commissioner on these issues. Our insights and the solutions that we develop will, be taken into account in pending investigations and will feed naturally into a number of ongoing policy reflections, such as the revisions of the exemption systems and guidelines for both vertical and horizontal cooperation.

Beyond understanding and formulating sensible responses to topics of particular relevance in a digitalised environment, such as the role of data, platforms and innovation, we also need to ensure that we have a framework of analysis that is sufficiently predictable and administrable to allow us to carefully analyse the likely impact on competition while still concluding our cases within timeframes that meet the certainty requirement of the business. Finally, one should not forget that DG COMP is not only a competition enforcer but also part of a wider European Commission with responsibilities for many other disciplines than competition law. We are therefore working closely with our colleagues to ensure that regulation and other public interventions are informed by competition policy and complement our enforcement. These are, in other words, very interesting times for enforcers and policymakers.

What role do you see for antitrust policy to combat division and discord within Europe? Is there a unifying role for antitrust to play as key pillar of the Single Market?

Absolutely. Competition policy has a vital role to play in order to ensure that the diversity, which is inherent in the EU, with many languages, cultural differences and administrative barriers, does not result in segmentation of markets. Targeted enforcement helps to create a more integrated and better-functioning single market, which is arguably the EU's strongest asset. This does not only ensure a level playing field for all companies in the EU. As I mentioned before, I also believe that our independent, rule-based enforcement strengthens and restores people's trust in fair markets and equal opportunities. We therefore have a responsibility to make sure that citizens understand how the decisions that we take impact their lives.

On Global Antitrust Policy

What role do you see for intergovernmental organisations, such as the ICN or OECD, to drive antitrust policy and convergence?

The complementarity of the work undertaken within these well-established multilateral forums is vital in order to promote convergence of policy and practices across jurisdictions, as well as to facilitate case cooperation with competition authorities in other jurisdictions. Both offer opportunities to learn and be inspired by practices and achievements in other jurisdictions and to jointly reflect on policy areas for which there is so far less concrete experience. I would expect that the European Commission will continue to actively contribute to this important work.

There are numerous initiatives and calls for greater convergence among global antitrust enforcers. But do you believe convergence among antitrust enforcers outside Europe should be a goal in itself?

We have already achieved a quite impressive level of convergence in many areas resulting in a level playing field and lower compliance costs for global companies. But we have to recognise that differences in objectives and instruments, economic circumstances, legal traditions or enforcement systems mean that convergence cannot be achieved in all areas. I do not see that as a deficit or an obstacle, as long as the different policies pursue clear objectives and are enforced in a transparent manner, allowing the business to adapt. There is simply no superior worldwide body of antitrust law and differences in enforcement reflect differences in objectives and values. I therefore believe that the much debated divergence between, for example, the EU and the US approach to unilateral conduct is both exaggerated and unhelpful.

On Consumers

Economists tend to use the model of a rational consumer who makes informed and rational decisions. But with what we have learned from behavioural science over the past decades, does that model still hold? Should we continue to model antitrust policy to benefit the theoretical rational consumer or do we know enough about irrational consumer decisions that we should bring these insights into the analysis?

I do not think that antitrust policy has ever been modelled on the assumption that there are consumers that are consistently making conscious choices. More importantly, I think that our enforcement record since at least the *Microsoft Windows Player* case shows that we can and do take framing biases, such as biases towards default options, into account if evidence (including credible behavioural insights) supports the theory that consumers would remain with the default option even when switching might be both easy and not costly. We drew similar conclusions in the more recent *Google Android* decision concerning pre-installed and default apps. Other typical framing biases, such as the tendency to choose the first items on a list (although it will arguably not require much time and effort to scroll down the list) was also part of our assessment in the *Google Search* case.

Likewise, behavioural biases can and should also be taken into account to ensure that a remedy is effective and may, for example, require that consumers are offered an explicit choice to avoid or reduce the bias. This was the solution found in the Microsoft browser commitment case, where a choice screen enabled the users of the Windows operating system to choose, in an informed and unbiased manner, which web browser they wanted to install in addition to or instead of Microsoft's browser.

On Cooperation

We have seen the Commission becoming more open to different forms of cooperation with companies to conclude cases quicker. The successful cartel settlement framework is now finding its way in antitrust cases, as well in the form of cooperation procedures. However, in cartel cases, the policy and rules on cartel conduct are clear, and so is the benefit in concluding these cases quickly and efficiently through a settlement. In antitrust cases, the behaviour at issue may not be as clear-cut, but still the Commission may find these novel cases suitable for cooperation. What is the policy rationale for this? Do you think these decisions will trigger a call for further guidance and would the Commission be responsive to that?

We have during recent years indeed concluded a number of cases where the parties acknowledged their liability for the infringement in exchange for a quicker, more streamlined procedure and a fine reduction. This, that we now routinely refer to as the "antitrust cooperation procedure", is inspired by the leniency and cartel settlement procedure and is meant to complement the choice between a standard prohibition decision and a commitment decision. The purpose was to address cases where the parties have an interest in cooperating but the commitment route would not be suitable, e.g. because the infringement had already terminated or we had an interest in finding an infringement and sanctioning the relevant company. In addition to acknowledging its liability for an infringement, a company can also choose to cooperate by voluntarily providing or clarifying evidence or by helping in the design and implementation of remedies. As in cartel settlement cases, the Commission will assess on a case-by-case basis whether a case would be suitable for this cooperation. The fine reduction will depend on the extent and timing of the cooperation and the procedural efficiencies gained in the particular case.

Our first experiences are very positive, notably for those cases where the parties cooperated before we had issued a Statement of Objection and where we managed to conclude the cases much quicker than we would have done under the normal prohibition route. Although the decisions are less detailed than in a normal procedure, they contain more details regarding the underlying facts and our assessment than cartel settlement decisions. That is a conscious choice, precisely in order to ensure that we give sufficient guidance to other parties in similar situations. Contrary to leniency and cartel settlements, the Commission did not opt for an immediate codification of this procedure, but rather wanted to first gain experience with various case scenarios. We have, however, already issued a fact sheet explaining the basic steps of the procedure.

On Judicial Review

There have been several cases coming out of the courts in Luxembourg that seem to urge the Commission to rethink how it runs and substantiates certain antitrust cases (e.g. the use of market definition in Servier or the object/effect distinction in Intel). Has this led the Commission to re-evaluate how it runs its antitrust cases and, if so, what do you believe will be the result of this?

I think that it goes without saying that a thorough judicial review by an independent court is the ultimate safeguard and guarantee for the credibility of any rule-based system. That role is particularly important for an authority such as the European Commission which has both investigative and decision-making powers. The Commission has overall a good track record in the European courts, despite the in-depth scrutiny of our assessments and procedures. We do of course carefully analyse all decisions and orders rendered by the court, irrespective of whether or not our decisions have been (partially) annulled, in order to see whether the court's findings would call for changes in our analysis, procedures, or the level of reasoning in our Statement of Objections or decisions. One should, however, remember that competition enforcement is never carried out in a static environment. The Commission is therefore regularly adjusting and adapting its investigative techniques, procedures and substantive assessments. Due to the length of the court proceedings, it is not uncommon that the court rules on, for example, procedural aspects that have already been reinforced by the Commission or are no longer representative of the current practice.

On Antitrust Issues

For an outsider, it may seem that the Commission is bringing more and more novel antitrust cases, focusing on algorithms or novel contractual set-up, but is that perception accurate? Has the Commission lost interest in good old-fashioned margin squeezes, ties or refusals to supply?

Not at all, but the cases that we investigate reflect the business models and conduct that the market players apply today. Although the underlying rationale of many strategies engaged in by dominant firms still centres around the wish to protect the core market or use that advantage in order to leverage that position into other adjacent markets, the practices will often take a different form in today's business environment. Many of those practices, therefore, no longer fit clearly into traditional categories of abuses, which does not, however, make them any less serious. The same is true for many Article 101 scenarios. The online environment and digital technologies allow companies to interact in a different manner from in the offline environment. Although the bulk of our cartel enforcement still concerns traditional price- or market-sharing arrangements, we are starting to gain experience with alleged collusions on other competitive parameters, such as innovation or quality.

On Women and Competition

Some voices have argued that gender and antitrust are related issues because market concentration and monopolisation tend to affect women more than men. The argument goes that this is because men remain the vast majority of CEOs, shareholders and investors to whom wealth is transferred in concentrated industries. Women, on the other hand, do not benefit as much from concentration as men. Is this something you consider too when setting out antitrust policy lines?

The European Commission is naturally concerned about the implications of increased concentration for many different reasons. I found the debate on gender awareness and competition policy that has intensified during the last years, not at least driven by discussions in the OECD, very interesting and thought-provoking. There are many actions that still need to be undertaken if we as Europeans want to remain true to the fight against gender inequalities. That ranges from overcoming obstacles (logistic or social) that prevent women from pursuing their careers, to a greater awareness of whether and how gender plays a role in (conscious or algorithm-driven) price-setting or customer differentiation. I do not see how that the number of female managers or board members (pre- or post-merger) should be a factor when assessing the competitive impact of a merger. I do however see a possible scope for taking gender relevance into account when selecting and prioritising cases, i.e. avoiding having a large part of the portfolio of cases concerning products or services that are primarily consumed by men. Although that might not have an immediate relevance for our enforcement, I would also be interested in any research into whether female-led companies are more or less likely to collude and whether they would – in general – position themselves differently from men, once an infringement has been detected.

DG COMP sometimes gets labelled as a bulwark of men, with few women in senior positions – you being one of the exceptions. Do you have any message to young women competition professionals who may be discouraged by this?

A senior position in DG COMP would usually mean director level and above. I am only a head of unit, although with a very interesting portfolio. More than 40% of the heads of unit in DG COMP are actually women and the picture is similar for deputy heads of unit. Although the gender picture is currently less balanced at director level and above, we should not forget that we (still) have a female Commissioner as well as a female-dominated cabinet. More importantly than what any statistics may reveal, I cannot think of a single situation during my many years in DG COMP that I have felt disadvantaged because I was a woman.

I am personally not a strong believer in (short-term) mandatory quota systems, since they will at least create the impression that someone is given an opportunity only due to the fact that she is a woman and not because she was the best pick and happened to be a woman. I am still optimistic enough to think that a modern working environment/leadership and social pressure will ensure equal opportunities to grow and advance, irrespective of gender. I am therefore not concerned by the current lack of female senior managers in DG COMP, as long as the organisation continues to actively search for and push women with good potential in all areas and levels of responsibility. I have been lucky to work with not only interesting cases and projects but also dedicated and talented colleagues that push and inspire you to be at your best. I am fully confident that DG COMP will continue to be a hugely interesting and rewarding workplace for competition experts and that the organisation will ensure that women get the exposure and the experience needed to grow and develop.

Karin Lunning
Swedish Competition Authority
Maria Wasastjerna

Karin Lunning has been practising competition law for over 20 years. She was appointed Deputy Director General of the Swedish Competition Authority in February 2018, having served as Acting Director General for the period of February – August 2017. Prior to this she held the position of department director at the authority for a number of years, heading up the international department and latterly the department for communications and international affairs. Karin has lived for a number of years in Asia, where she worked on various international competition assignments including organising OECD capacity-building events. Lately she was appointed as member of the administrative board of the European Union Agency for the Cooperation of Energy Regulators.

Maria Wasastjerna is a Partner and Co-head of Hannes Snellman's competition practice in Finland. She has extensive experience in competition law and regulatory matters. She advises Finnish and international companies on all aspects of competition law, specialising in regulatory legal and compliance matters, as well as in competition litigation and M&A transactions. Prior to joining Hannes Snellman, Maria gained several years of experience as an in-house lawyer in global corporations, most recently as Nokia's lead competition counsel. Her work experience also includes training at Cleary Gottlieb's Brussels office, the European Commission and the US Federal Trade Commission.

Karin, you have been practising competition law for over 20 years. If we go back in time, could you tell us how you got interested in competition law to start with, and what it is that makes it an interesting area to work in still today?

In 1993, after having competed my legal clerkship at the Stockholm District Court and *Svea* Court of Appeal, I wanted a new professional experience before proceeding with the next step in my career as a judge. I ultimately decided on competition enforcement, which in my view was a particularly exciting niche of the newly emerging area of EU law. In particular, I was attracted to the prospect of dealing with both economic and competition issues, and joined the Swedish Competition Authority (SCA), which at the time was a newly established authority.

I have always been genuinely interested in societal complexities and how legislation and legal frameworks can be used as tools to achieve wider social goals and ambitions. This is what drove me to work as a government official and why I derive a great deal of professional contentment from working with issues – such as competition and public procurement – that contribute to well-functioning markets with increased innovation, which in turn lead to increased productivity and economic growth. Competition law serves an important role in this regard and remains an interesting area to work in today. A strong competition policy will have an important role to play when forming the EU's future industrial strategy. Generally, competition law will always have to develop in concert with society's overall development, and it is indeed professionally rewarding to be a part of this. The international aspects of competition law are also something that I find very stimulating and interesting.

You were appointed acting director general of the SCA in February 2017, having been department director for a number of years. What is the best and most challenging part of your job at the SCA?

The most rewarding aspect of my job is the constant and regular work addressing intellectually challenging and relevant legal and economic issues. Additionally, it is a privilege and highly stimulating to collaborate with talented and dedicated teams of professionals at the SCA. We focus a lot on effective teamwork and it is great to be a part of this.

The most challenging part when it comes to competition enforcement is conducting effective investigations, especially when market conditions are changing so rapidly. It requires utmost professionalism to keep up with the development of certain markets and business models, and to respond swiftly when there is a competition problem. I believe that our task of safeguarding competition to the benefit of the consumers has become much more complicated over the years. It is always a balancing act for us to decide when to engage, and we always strive to use our limited resources in the most efficient way. As a priority, we constantly evaluate our working methods to make sure that they are up to date. It is crucial that we always challenge ourselves and our ways of working in order to make sure that we adapt and endeavour to improve. This is a never ending journey. Trust is a key word and it is important that our stakeholders, the public and, ultimately, consumers have confidence in that we carry out our mission in the best way.

You lived for some time in Asia, where you worked on international competition assignments, including organising OECD capacity-building events. What did you learn from these experiences and how have they been useful at the SCA and in your current position?

I have always had a particular fascination and interest in international issues, probably originating from spending two years in the US in the

1980s. Regarding your question about experiences from Asia, I learned and developed a lot – both privately and professionally – from living almost six years in China and Malaysia. My positive experiences from roles in various OECD capacity-building assignments and ICN projects made me understand and realise the importance of good collaboration and the need for harmonisation in order to achieve efficiency. These things are equally important today in light of the new digital economy. I also learned that you need to understand how other legal systems and institutional models work in order to achieve international convergence. Therefore, it is important to identify the differences and to genuinely understand the rationale behind the systems before starting to harmonise the rules. One way to lay the groundwork for possible harmonisation when looking at unilateral conduct has been to bring economists together. If they speak the same language and understand each other better – and positively even eventually share the same views around economic theories – there is a better chance of reaching agreement and common understanding on different aspects of fostering effective competition law frameworks.

One thing that really made an impact on me from participating in the OECD outreach events was the realisation that our daily work at the different agencies shows a lot of similarities when it comes to both opportunities and challenges. Competition agencies around the world face the same obstacles. It is very beneficial to discuss mutual topics and common objectives. We are all dealing with challenges in trying to detect competition infringements such as cartels and abuse of market power – however in different contexts and different economic and political environments. Our mission is very much the same – to safeguard competition to the benefit of the consumers. It gives you a feeling of inclusiveness and fosters collaboration. With this, the strengthening of due process can also be achieved. I am very impressed how fast some of these younger competition authorities in South East Asia have developed in such a short time.

Since returning to Sweden, I have worked a lot with international affairs and it is very rewarding to be a contributor to various global teams. The international competition community has so much in common and, in some respects, we are like a big family. Many of the senior officials, practitioners and stakeholders have been involved in competition policy and enforcement for several years and know each other well. Over the years, I have made several good professional friends in this field. Good relations are important – they are a prerequisite for efficient collaboration and the sharing of best practices.

Competition in the digital economy is on the agenda of almost every competition authority these days. How has the SCA approached the question concerning the implications for competition law of the transition to the data-driven economy? How has digitalisation possibly affected or changed the authority's internal ways of working?

Even though we constantly need to be on our toes and be extremely sensitive to market development, it is my belief that the transition to the data-driven economy and the digitalisation of markets has not moved the SCA into completely uncharted territory. We have not seen a need for an overhaul of the competition rules, as such. Our recent case experience shows that the existing competition law framework appears to be fit for purpose, whether we are dealing with the analogue or digital economy.

However, the overall pace is higher and we have indeed noticed new business models and new forms of potential anticompetitive conduct emerge as a result of the ongoing digital transformation. We are therefore focusing on adapting and developing our enforcement activities to account for these new challenges. The dynamic nature of digital markets means that we need to be agile and able to work quickly and efficiently, particularly when it comes to digital platforms. We are constantly working on refining our investigative tools and methods and investing in effective technical solutions in order to be able to handle the ever-increasing amount of data we receive.

I would also like to stress the importance of conducting research and constantly building and improving our expertise when it comes to the digital transformation. Digital markets are often complex and sophisticated, and we must fully understand how they function, and how they affect competition, if we want to be successful in our investigations. This is currently one of our key strategic focus areas. We have just launched a market study on the functioning of competition on digital platforms in Sweden, which focuses, for example, on digital advertising, mobile app stores, food delivery, audiobooks, digital payment services and digital marketplaces. The purpose of this study is to illuminate the extent of competition and identify any potential need for measures to promote competition. In addition to this, we are working on a joint Nordic report on digital platforms, which we expect to publish next year.

At the same time and as we all know, not all questions arising from digital markets are pure competition issues. Therefore, we need to make sure that the right enforcement tools are being used for the right situation. In this regard, we need to be mindful and ensure that we apply diligence in a balanced way as regards the actions and initiatives to initiate and pursue. We are also focusing a great deal on effective cooperation with other agencies, such as the consumer and data protection authorities in Sweden, which also deal with various challenges relating to the data-driven economy.

In recent times, competition policy has been visible in public debate and discourse, especially concerning data-driven tech companies and the concern regarding their market power and influence extending to consumer's everyday life. This has also made competition law somewhat political. In your opinion, is competition law political and driven by national preferences and values? Is the situation different in the Nordics compared with, e.g., Brussels?

EU competition authorities and governments are currently engaged in discussions on the importance of providing a level playing field to all market participants in addition to exploring various challenges posed by the data-driven economy. We look forward to continuing to be active participants in this debate.

From our perspective in Sweden, I do not think competition law enforcement is or should be political. We have not experienced any external political pressures on competition law enforcement. However, we need to be aware that there are emerging voices that more broadly question the fundamentals of competition policy and advocate for other policy considerations to be part of the competition law framework. We must be cautious about injecting other policy areas into competition law enforcement.

For many years, we have been careful to separate the discussion about competitiveness from protecting the competitive process. Today it is more difficult to separate them entirely from each other in the debate because of technological developments, globalisation and shifting perspectives on protectionism.

Related to this, I would like to mention a joint article published by the directors of the Nordic competition authorities in June 2019, where we expressed our full support for a strict and politically independent merger supervision regime both at EU and national levels. The article was a response to political moves in France and Germany, who jointly proposed that EU merger supervision rules should be revised to allow the creation of "European Champions". This initiative came in light of the European Commission decision to block the merger between Siemens and Alstom.

Consumer welfare is the central pillar of the successful European competition regime. However, if competition law enforcement becomes politicised, there is a major risk that this hard-won principle might be set aside, especially considering the uncertain nature of political decision-making. I think that promoting competition independent of political pressures is key to creating truly competitive European companies that can produce better products and offer lower prices to consumers.

The resources of the SCA are limited and you have to deal with numerous complaints of customers and competitors, and mergers and acquisitions. How do you go about prioritising cases?

Efficient prioritisation is a key success factor for any organisation in today's world and prioritisation must always be based on set objectives and strategy. For us, merger and acquisitions are handled according to required legal periods, which always gives them high priority. When it comes to complaints from customers and competitors, we select matters for further investigation based on the SCA's prioritisation policy for enforcement. Various factors and circumstances are compared and weighted against each other. We published our first prioritisation policy in 2009 and since then such policies have served us well. We revise the prioritisation criteria on a regular basis after comments from stakeholders. In fact, we are currently in the process of revising such criteria again and we are currently in the phase of seeking guidance and input from stakeholders before finalising them. In general, we focus on investigating matters which are of general interest and which lead to desired, clear results. The prioritisation policy applies to both competition enforcement and public procurement matters.

When it comes to competition enforcement, several factors need to be taken into account. For instance: whether the problem causes harm to competition and consumers; the importance of securing a guiding precedent; whether the SCA is best suited to intervene; if conditions exist to investigate and remedy the issue effectively under the competition rules; or if there are signs of corruption or other behaviour that undermines general trust. The reason why we consider suspected corruption when prioritising tip-offs and complaints received is that this behaviour is severely damaging to competition and consumers. Such negative actions also have the capacity to facilitate and aggravate infringements of the rules we enforce. We aim to be transparent when deciding not to prioritise a certain case. The SCA's decision not to prioritise a specific case cannot be appealed, but the affected parties always have a subsidiary option to bring their own case to court.

And on a more personal level, how do your prioritise your time in your daily work?

We all have major workloads and, as I said, it is key to prioritise efficiently and always do so bearing in mind the set objectives of the authority. Personally, I try to spend time reflecting on the level of importance and urgency when setting my own priorities. That being said, my role as Deputy Director General means that my priorities naturally depend a great deal on Mr Rikard Jermsten. He is the head of the SCA and I act in his place when he is not in service. Those tasks are of course given top priority. Besides that, I have overall responsibility for external relations and am protective security manager with respect to security-sensitive operations, on which I obviously cannot compromise. In addition, I always make sure to find sufficient time to contribute to specific projects where I have a defined role. There can always be a risk that such work ends up lower in the list of priorities in light of more urgent matters, but it is crucial that these projects also progress according to plan, in order to achieve the desired targets and, in turn, the continuous improvement of our work.

The SCA recently hosted the W@Competition Nordic conference in Stockholm, with an impressive line-up of speakers and participants from the Nordic and Baltic regions. In your panel (or "fika talk") the focus was on looking into the crystal ball. Could you share your thoughts on the trends and developments for 2020 and beyond in the competition field?

While I said earlier that competition law enforcement in Sweden is not political, is obvious that competition policy has become more of a political issue because of the ongoing discussions on how to modernise European industrial policy. I believe this discussion will continue for some time, including the question of how a strong competition policy can contribute to enhancing the competitiveness of European industry and the internal market.

It is also undeniable that climate change will have a bearing on the functioning of markets in the future, and we have to consider what impact this will have on competition policy in the future, for example in respect of sustainability agreements.

I believe and predict that the consumer welfare standard will still be the central focus of competition law and policy but, of course, competition policy must keep pace with modern challenges. At the same time we need to be cautious about mixing too many other policy areas into competition law enforcement. It is not clear that competition authorities are always the best placed to make decisions on other policy matters.

As mentioned earlier, digitalisation will undoubtedly affect the types of cases we investigate, and the tools and methods we use when investigating. Even though we do not see a need for an overhaul of competition rules as such, we should not entirely rule out the idea that fast-moving digital markets might call for other means to deal with market power in order to safeguard competition and to intervene effectively. I am aware that *ex ante* regulation has been suggested in some quarters. Typically, we believe that *ex ante* regulation of a market can be appropriate to the extent that the competition rules are not sufficiently effective to deal with problems. We would welcome more empirical analysis in the area.

Looking ahead, what do you want to achieve next in your professional career?

I still much enjoy being active within the competition law arena and appreciate the energy one gets from working in an organisation with important tasks to carry out, and doing this together with professional colleagues. I am very much a team player, and to be a member of a stimulating team – big or small – is very important to me. I have had the privilege of going on leave twice during my career at the SCA and it has worked out very well. This has given me the possibility to experience other cultures and to work with competition policy in a broader, international sense. I also believe this has developed me a great deal as a professional. My experiences living abroad and working in Asia made me realise that I wanted to broaden my focus to include international affairs and broader cross-border issues. I also realised that I did not have to leave the SCA in order to assume new challenges and other responsibilities.

Today there is constant competition for talent, and being flexible as an employer is important to benefit both the employer and the employee. Recently, I joined the board of a governmental network that includes 16 Swedish governmental authorities. The main purpose is to facilitate the continuation of governmental employees' careers within the Swedish government, while still allowing the employees the ability to move between different authorities, thereby providing flexibility and opportunities for additional professional development.

Being a competition professional and a competition enforcer for more than 25 years has taught me a lot about due and efficient process, diligence, general professionalism and how to identify key elements of a well-functioning competition agency.

In general, I look forward to continuing using my experiences in this regard, outside the pure competition field. I was recently appointed by the Council of the European Union to be a member of the Administrative Board of the Agency for the Cooperation of Energy Regulators (ACER). This side assignment will start in 2020. ACER's overall mission is to complement and coordinate the work of national energy regulators at EU level, and to work towards the completion of a single EU energy market for electricity and natural gas. ACER plays a central role in the development of EU-wide network and market rules with a view to enhancing competition. It also coordinates regional and cross-regional initiatives, which favour market integration, and it monitors the work of European networks of transmission system operators and their EU-wide network development plans. Finally, ACER monitors the functioning of gas and electricity markets in general, and of wholesale energy trading in particular. In 2020, the Agency will strongly focus on the implementation of the Clean Energy Package and on its enhanced tasks and responsibilities. The Agency will also contribute to Europe´s decarbonisation efforts and the goals of the European Green Deal.

I hope that through my experiences as a governmental official and competition lawyer I will be able to contribute to this important work, and I am really looking forward to learning more about the European energy sector.

Teresa Moreira
UNCTAD

Margarida Rosado da Fonseca

Teresa Moreira has been Head of the Competition and Consumer Policies Branch of UNCTAD since 5 October 2016. She previously served as Consumer Director General of Portugal from January 2010 to September 2016 and as a member of the board of the Portuguese Competition Authority (March 2003 – March 2008) when it was first established. She also served as Portugal's Director General and Deputy Director General for International Economic Relations, and held senior positions at the former Directorate General for Competition. She worked for 20 years as a teaching assistant at the Faculty of Law, University of Lisbon, in the areas of International Economic Law and European Law as well as in European Competition Law and European Economic Law (graduate studies). Teresa Moreira holds a law degree and a Masters degree in European Law (European Competition Law) from the Faculty of Law, University of Lisbon, Portugal.

Margarida Rosado da Fonseca heads the EU and Competition practice of CS Associados and has more than two decades of experience. Her professional career includes acting as an EU and competition (and regulatory) lawyer and, in the public sector, she was Merger Director at the Portuguese Competition Authority and a specialised jurist in the ESAME Team (XIX Government) during the Financial and Economic Assistance Programme to Portugal, notably participating in the working group for the reform of the competition legal framework. She is Secretary General of the Portuguese Association for European Law and of the Association of Portuguese Competition Lawyers.

Teresa, could you tell us a bit about your background?

I started as a competition case-handler in the Directorate General for Competition of Portugal in 1986. I moved to International Affairs (participating in the European Commission's Advisory Committee on Restrictive Practices and Dominant Positions; attending the OECD), and later became Head of the Legal Service and then Deputy Director General. In 2003, I was appointed a member of the board of the recently established Portuguese Competition Authority (PCA), an independent and fully-fledged public body.

Previously, I dealt with international trade, bilateral economic relations and the coordination of European Affairs, and cooperation for development issues within the vast remit of the Ministry of Economy of Portugal. It was a very special period that broadened my areas of interest and work, since it covered all trade issues and investment as well as sectoral policies such as competitiveness, energy and tourism.

For several years I also taught graduate studies in European Competition Law and European Economic Law at the Faculty of Law in Lisbon. The establishment of the PCA encouraged young lawyers and economists to take a strong interest in competition law, which led to larger, highly motivated audiences.

Consumer policy was surprisingly interesting: it is a cross-cutting topic, covering issues as diverse as contract terms and conditions, product safety, education and information, advertising and dispute resolution. Actions and initiatives have an almost immediate impact, which is gratifying in the civil service.

I worked closely with sector-specific regulators; discovered new topics such as alternative dispute resolution and behavioural insights for policymaking; and coordinated with municipalities, consumer associations and small non-governmental organisations as partners. Working with a small, hard-working and very committed team, I had the opportunity of asserting Portugal's experience at regional and international levels, within the EU, the OECD, UNCTAD and other networks (including the Iberoamerican Forum of Consumer Protection Agencies (FIAGC) and the International Consumer Protection and Enforcement Network (ICPEN)).

In 2003 there was a reform of the competition rules and enforcement agencies which consisted in the creation of the first independent competition authority and the enactment of a Competition Act influenced by the 2002/2003 developments at EU level. Besides being a single purpose authority, the PCA had an innovative means of financing and interactions with sectoral regulators as some of its main features. You were one of the three members of the board of the PCA (and the only woman) in a country with incipient competition awareness in both the public and private sectors. Could you please comment on this and share with us some highlights of your experience?

Portugal adopted its first competition law in 1983: investigations were conducted by the Directorate General of Competition which sent the proceedings for decision by the Competition Council.

Despite some important cases throughout this period, there was no general awareness of competition law and policy. The establishment of the PCA as an independent public body, responsible for law enforcement against anticompetitive practices and also entrusted with full merger control responsibilities, and the adoption of a new Competition Law in 2003, played a major role in the dissemination of competition culture.

The initial PCA team combined senior civil servants with enforcement experience from the previous Directorate General and young highly qualified lawyers and economists, some with little work experience, others arriving from the academic world. This proved to be a very successful combination of skills, strengths and commitment, and a real *esprit de corps* gradually developed thanks to intense sharing of knowledge and teamwork. The first years of activity of the PCA were very exciting: it was a unique experience to contribute to the shaping of a new powerful institution and to establish its reputation in the market and society.

Advocacy initiatives with media and business associations – non-traditional stakeholders – were launched, cooperation arrangements were concluded with sectoral regulators to facilitate coordination, and a good working relationship was gradually developed with the judiciary and competition practitioners, seeking to improve awareness of the role of competition law and policy and of the PCA's mandate.

There was a deliberate investment in training to encourage good performance, and academic lectures open to the public were organised regularly.

It was a privilege to have been a member of the PCA's first board and to have played an active part in the PCA's launch. I have always followed the PCA's performance and I am impressed by its achievements.

Considering each of the areas of competition enforcement during your mandate and the most important cases, which would be considered the main takeaways? How did the board experience the beginning of the application of EC Regulation no. 1/2003 and the cooperation with the European Commission (Commission) notably concerning collaboration in surprise inspections?

The Competition Law of 2003 had already benefited from reference to EU Council Regulation 1/2003, but the launch and the first years of the European Competition Network (ECN) brought challenges, adding to the new PCA's powers to decide enforcement cases and to impose fines and ancillary sanctions.

Regulation 1/2003 raised questions regarding completely new issues, such as the application of both national rules and the Treaty rules, the share of competences within the ECN, the role of the Commission, the Commission's new powers to inspect other premises and the foreseen cooperation with national courts. DG COMP provided for extensive training of NCAs at different levels in order to ensure a functional network and to instil confidence. This would build close cooperation between PCA staff, the DG COMP team and other NCA experts.

From my point of view, the merger control experience, which included some high-profile cases in regulated markets and two hostile takeover cases in key sectors (electronic communications and media, and banking services) was probably the most fulfilling: during the first five years of activity, the PCA commissioned and undertook economic studies, developed and consolidated the procedural framework, dealt with interesting legal and economic issues, interacted with different sectoral regulators, drafted guidelines after public consultation and closed a considerable number of cases. Although several important anticompetitive cases were launched during this period, due to the depth and length of these investigations, the enforcement record was not comparable. Nevertheless, the internal discussions on investigative tools, on leniency, on sanctions and on private enforcement brought together different units and experts and led to a clearer line of action for the PCA. The extensive work developed in the energy and telecoms sectors was well justified as these sectors remained critical in the following years. The opinions and recommendations issued on liberal professions and State aid measures contributed to open markets and create a fairer level playing field.

Looking back on your own experience as member of the first board of the PCA, how could you summarise the main developments achieved since 2003 and the challenges that lie ahead? To what extent can we expect a surge of private enforcement of competition rules and, if not, what are the main factors to be addressed if such an aim is to be pursued in parallel with the public enforcement of competition?

The first years of the PCA's activity clearly established the authority and highlighted the importance of competition in Portugal. The President of the PCA was extremely active in the media and the PCA publicised its decisions, which increased its visibility and raised its profile to public opinion. Together with regular advocacy initiatives, a competition culture was gradually disseminated and enhanced.

Developing an independent public body with strong investigative and sanctioning powers, particularly vis-à-vis well-established and respected sectoral regulators, was a challenge. The main development to highlight is the wide recognition by market players and public opinion of the high-level mission of the PCA, its capacity to promote and protect competitive markets in Portugal, and its performance. Effective enforcement of competition law requires deterrence as business compliance, so the recognition was a remarkable achievement. Another relevant development was the Government's understanding of the horizontal and instrumental nature of competition policy, which led to regular consultations and increased the PCA's involvement in the drafting and assessment of legislation and regulation. A third development was the awareness and interest of relevant stakeholders such as the judiciary, consumer associations, academics, and legal and economic practitioners in the field.

I believe that the groundwork for private enforcement of competition law to flourish in Portugal has been established, even though some public perceptions of the length of judicial proceedings may discourage it. It is of the utmost importance to draw the attention of consumer associations and other non-governmental organisations, as well as SMEs and micro-companies' representatives, to this powerful tool to claim damages.

On the topic of data contents and digital, in 2010 you mentioned that the defence of the rights and interests of consumers (and of the public interest) required determined and sustained intervention on the part of the public authorities involved, and also highlighted the urgent need to strengthen enforcement, which represented a joint effort of various national authorities, taking advantage of European and international cooperation networks. One of the priorities of the European Commission for 2019–2024 is, "A Europe fit for the Digital Age" and the recently appointed European Commissioner for Competition is also the executive vice president for that area. How can we optimise interdisciplinary enforcement in the data economy (consumer, data protection and competition law)?

Consumer policy can only be achieved through a deliberate public policy that (i) ensures legal rights and protection against unfair, misleading and fraudulent business practices through law enforcement and accessible dispute resolution and redress mechanisms, and (ii) promotes consumer empowerment through information, education, the creation of consumer associations and their involvement in public policy. Business engagement is also indispensable for increased consumer protection, so self-regulation initiatives that go further than legal obligations should be strongly encouraged and supported.

Despite the number of cross-border practices and market integration, consumer law enforcement tends to remain confined at national level, although a European Consumer Protection Cooperation Enforcement Network was established in 2006 to facilitate collaboration and coordinated action. This framework was modernised in 2017,[1] and it increases national authorities' powers and improves cooperation towards a more effective enforcement of European consumer law.

---

1   In force from 17 January 2020 (Regulation (EU) 2017/2394 of the European Parliament and of the Council on cooperation between national authorities responsible for the enforcement of consumer protection laws, and repealing Regulation (EC) No 2006/2004, published in the Official Journal of the European Union, L 345, pages 1-26.

This is undoubtedly an important step to raise the bar of the "high-level of consumer protection" within the European single market in the digital era. Regional cooperation strengthens the position of enforcers and gives them leverage vis-à-vis the big players, being decisive for successful law enforcement.

In recent years there have been several calls for joint efforts by NCAs, consumer protection agencies, data protection authorities and sectoral regulators to effectively tackle abusive behaviours in digital markets. Coordination and cooperation need to be improved and all relevant stakeholders should be involved to build a safe and reliable marketplace for consumers where innovative start-ups and SMEs have business opportunities. The UNCTAD Digital Economy Report 2019[2] recommends an holistic approach involving different policy areas (including competition), "… to make the digital economy work for the many, not just the few".

Can you explain to us the aims and scope of the UN body you are heading and its ultimate goals?

UNCTAD – the United Nations Conference on Trade and Development[3] – is the focal point for both competition and consumer protection within the UN system, as the custodian of the only two internationally agreed instruments in both fields: the UN Set of Principles and Rules on Competition (1980),[4] which sets out the core of competition law and policy, including for international cooperation in this area; and the UN Guidelines for Consumer Protection (1985, revised in 1999 and 2015),[5] which were extensively modernised in 2015 to address emerging

---

issues (e-commerce, financial services, consumer data privacy, tourism, energy, dispute resolution and good business practices). Each instrument established an Intergovernmental Group of Experts (IGE) as the UN forum for consultations in each area, under the auspices of UNCTAD.

The UN Set on Competition recommends the adoption of competition law and policy to fight against anticompetitive practices and abusive market power, recognising a "development dimension", that is to say, the legitimacy of developing countries to adopt and implement it according to their own specific circumstances (including public interest clauses and temporary exemptions, for instance) and promoting international cooperation. The UNCTAD Model Law on competition[6] was agreed upon in by competition experts in the early 1990s, and comprises 13 provisions on the "substantive possible elements for a competition law", including commentaries with case-law references and bibliography that are regularly updated.

The UN Guidelines for Consumer Protection address the "legitimate needs" of consumers in the general principles, which are commonly recognised as the consumer rights of the twenty-first century and highlight the main features of successful national consumer protection policies, including recommendations on physical safety, dispute resolution and redress, sustainable consumption, electronic commerce, financial services, good business practices and international cooperation, among others.

UNCTAD advises developing countries and countries with economies in transition, which represent most of its membership (totalling 195), to adopt and implement competition and consumer protection laws and policies. UNCTAD has a unique role to play in both areas, disseminating international best practices to its large membership in cooperation with other international and regional organisations and networks.

---

6   https://unctad.org/en/Pages/DITC/CompetitionLaw/The-Model-Law-on-Competition.aspx

The number of new competition law frameworks and competition agencies has been increasing significantly in the last decade in the various regions of the globe, together with the consolidation of efforts by international organisations and networks aimed at strengthening cooperation in this field of law. Considering market concentration in technology-intensive sectors and the rising importance of online commerce, there have been calls for amendments of the existing competition policy and tools. How could the rising international cooperation be streamlined and enhanced so as to effectively address concerns arising from the dynamics of the (globalised) economy?

The generalisation of competition law and policy across the world (almost 140 jurisdictions have adopted legislation) is a very positive outcome of the work undertaken by several international organisations and networks, including the ICN, OECD and UNCTAD, and of regional organisations such as the EU, whose external economic agreements highlight considerably the need for competition rules to complement trade liberalisation.

The EU and US models influenced competition, legal and institutional frameworks in all continents, and this led to a convergence of laws and enforcement structure. Competition authorities tend to have an independent status and expert nature, although several developing countries face resources constraints.

The introduction of competition provisions at regional level or the commitment to develop work within the legal frameworks of regional economic organisations of developing countries and countries with economies in transition (ASEAN;[7] CARICOM – Caribbean Community; CEMAC – Economic Community of Central African States; COMESA – Common Market for Eastern and Southern Africa; EAC – East African

---

7   Within ASEAN there is work on competition law enforcement and regional cooperation, although there are
     no regional competition rules.

Community; ECOWAS – Economic Community of West African States; Eurasian Union; MERCOSUR – Common Market of the South; WAEMU – West African Economic and Monetary Union) is an interesting recent development[8] that supports less experienced countries in overcoming challenges while allowing a stronger stance against cross-border infringements by global companies. Of course, the interaction between national competition laws and regional rules raises coordination issues and needs to be appropriately addressed, but the emergence of regional competition provisions is extremely valuable for developing countries, while complementing international cooperation.

Moreover, there is a wide and lively international competition community that encourages formal and informal cooperation between authorities from developed and developing countries. Since 2009, the biannual meetings of the BRICS competition authorities illustrate impressive achievements of these emerging countries' competition authorities. The African Competition Forum, launched in 2011, provides an informal network of competition authorities engaged in joint work and raising awareness. In 2012, UNCTAD, in partnership with the Competition Commission of Bulgaria, launched the Sofia Competition Forum as a platform for the exchange of experiences and discussions with the West Balkans countries, which produced relevant reports and guidelines on enforcement issues.

New initiatives have also been launched, the latest having been discussed and agreed in 2019 (Guiding Policies and Procedures under Section F of the UN Set on Competition[9]) in UNCTAD IGE meetings on competition, following the 2016 proposal from the Federal Antimonopoly Service of the Russian Federation for a "toolkit" to facilitate international cooperation in cross-border cases under the UN Set on Competition.

---

8   The African Continental Free Trade Agreement of 2018 also includes a Protocol on competition policy.

9   https://unctad.org/meetings/en/SessionalDocuments/ccpb_comp1_%20Guiding_Policies_Procedures.pdf.

This document benefited from contributions of experienced and less experienced competition authorities and is intended to serve as a guide to assist young and small competition authorities in developing countries in need of cooperation, foreseeing a more active involvement of the UNCTAD secretariat in assisting them during consultations. It is expected to be formally approved by the Eighth Review Conference that will take place under the auspices of UNCTAD in July 2020, thus reaffirming the UN Set as a relevant instrument to foster international cooperation.

The rise of the digital economy underlines how international cooperation is crucial to effectively tackle challenges and opportunities both for consumers and business in a global setting. Global challenges need global solutions: competition and consumer protection authorities should take the lead in advocating for a healthier, fairer and more competitive digital economy. Through inter-agency coordination and cooperation at national, regional and international levels, knowledge and tools will be accessible and assistance available to overcome resource constraints and limited experience.

There are different degrees of competition awareness and enforcement in various regions of the globe, despite the positive developments that occurred in the last decade. What could be useful guidelines to attenuate such differences? What are the features you would identify as typical of jurisdictions where the enforcement of competition rules faces more hurdles, and what are the ways to successfully overcome them?

Effective enforcement of competition law remains a challenge in several developing countries due to market structure, incipient competition culture, limited resources, and lack of understanding of the policy's contribution to achieve economic growth development.

The early focus of UNCTAD's technical assistance on the adoption of legal frameworks and the set-up of the respective institutions, usually combined with the strengthening of capacities of competition authority staff, already widened some years ago to target a larger audience of relevant stakeholders – governmental bodies, sectoral regulators, the judiciary, business and civil society organisations. Without their engagement it is not possible to mainstream competition law and policy, and that is crucial to achieve progress. We always bring together experts of experienced and young authorities to share experience and foster mutual learning, and we involve other international and regional organisation colleagues in our technical cooperation activities to promote synergies.

Due to its wide membership and expertise, UNCTAD is well placed to advise Member States to make full use of competition policy within their development strategies. Policy advice should be supported by sound research to evidence policymaking. The positive impact of implementing competition law and policy in a jurisdiction also needs to be assessed and measured to enhance public understanding and support and to make a more compelling case for this important public instrument. This is one of the issues to further explore in UNCTAD's future work.

What do you think is most difficult goal to achieve when pursuing the public interest in the context of competition law enforcement, and what advice could you give to younger generations?

Communication of the benefits and of the impact of competition law enforcement is essential for market players and public opinion to understand its contribution for consumer welfare. It is necessary to improve the message and to tailor it to the target audience to achieve wider support.

Competition law enforcement is very demanding as it requires strong legal and economic analysis. Investigations of anticompetitive cases can take a long time, differently from merger control cases. It is important to have experience of both anticompetitive cases and merger cases to have a comprehensive view. I also recommend attending judicial proceedings to understand the role of the judiciary when reviewing competition authorities' decisions.

Furthermore, competition law and policy goes beyond law enforcement and should spread to the legislative domain and regulatory frameworks, to have a more significant impact. So, there are other close areas of interesting work to be explored as well.

My final suggestion refers again to the importance of collaboration with other public bodies – sectoral regulators, consumer protection agencies, data protection authorities – to gather knowledge and skills so that it is possible to fully grasp the profound changes that economies and markets are undergoing and to be able to design the most appropriate measures.

Siún O'Keeffe
Academy of the Netherlands Authority for Consumers & Markets

Claudia Koken

Siún O'Keeffe is Manager of the Academy at the Netherlands ACM. ACM's Academy organises training courses for ACM's employees, and advises the Board on learning and development. From 2013 to 2018, Siún was Senior Strategy Adviser at ACM. She coordinated ACM's international network, and advised on corporate strategy, speeches and communications. From 2008 to 2013, Siún was Senior International Adviser at the Netherlands Competition Authority (NMa). From 2003 to 2008, she worked as case handler at the authority. In 2003, she worked as interim référendaire at the European General Court. An Irish lawyer, Siún lectured European and Competition law from 1993 to 2002 at the Universities of Limerick in Ireland and Nijmegen in the Netherlands. She studied Law at University College Cork, College of Europe, Bruges, and King's Inns, Dublin.

Claudia Koken is the founder of C-law Competition Lawyers, a boutique law firm in competition law based in Amsterdam. With some 20 years of experience Claudia worked as an associate and partner specialising in competition law at Baker McKenzie, Norton Rose Fulbright (Amsterdam and Brussels) and Dutch law firms. Claudia started her career in 1998 at the Netherlands ACM. She features in Chambers Europe, The Netherlands as a leading individual in EC competition law. She is also a guest lecturer in competition law at Tilburg University. Claudia is co-founder of W@CompetitionNL.

How did you get involved in W@Competition?

In February 2017, I was invited by the intrepid Evelina Kurgonaite to speak at the Inaugural Conference of W@Competition in Brussels, on "The E-Commerce riddle". As a multifunctional authority, the Netherlands Authority for Consumers and Markets (ACM) was, at that time, keen to underline the links between consumer protection and competition when it comes to dealing with digital platforms. We were conducting a study on online advertising from a competition perspective, and had also fined a number of online stores for breaching consumer rules. Two years on, ACM continues to combine its enforcement efforts in competition, sector regulation and consumer law in the digital world. We have an investigation running on Apple's App Store and are working on improving terms and conditions in the contracts used by online platforms, while also running consumer awareness campaigns targeting fraudulent online stores.

I found the W@ conference format unique and very appealing. I had already joined a smaller networking group, "Women and Competition", run by an ACM colleague, Anke Prompers. In June 2017, I spoke at a W@ symposium on the Commission's final report on the e-commerce sector enquiry. This led to my writing a chapter with a colleague, Bart Noé, in *Digital Markets in the EU*, a University of Nijmegen publication. That probably wouldn't have happened without the impetus provided by W@.

I think W@ is an excellent initiative. I have been involved in conference organisation for many years through my work at the former NMa,[1] the ACM and the International Competition Network. We have so often had problems finding female speakers. It is hard to believe that it should be so difficult, in this day and age, and that change should creep so excruciatingly slowly. It's marvellous to have had Margarethe Vestager as Competition Commissioner, and as even the OECD is putting gender

---

1   Precursor to the ACM.

and competition on the agenda, it seems like a good moment to advance the issue. Now, I am working on launching W@CompetitionNL in the Netherlands together with co-founder Claudia Koken. I know that conference organisers and recruiters are already making use of this platform of information on female competition professionals.

Why do you think it is so important to work on improving the visibility of women in competition?

When I first started lecturing in Ireland, in 1993, we were proud to have equal numbers of men and women studying law, but then saddened to see that when it came to professional success, the women appeared to have so much difficulty in advancing their careers. This waste of talent can only be to the disadvantage of the decisions made by competition professionals, which have a considerable influence on the shape of economic development. I firmly believe there are solutions to these difficulties.

We need to ensure that there are women at the table when project leaders for important cases are being chosen, or we will never get diversity. We need to make sure that the timing of our in-company courses does not exclude employees with family commitments – scrap the 8 o'clock breakfast meetings and the late dinners. Bonding can also be done over coffee, and lunches are easily organised. Ensure that when you advertise for a chief economist, you refrain from adding a long list of "essential requirements" – experience tells us that the women will disqualify themselves from applying, and the men will overlook the criteria they don't meet and apply anyway. Ensure that we have sufficient role models within our organisations, so that people are brave enough to be seen to employ childminders and cleaners to conduct domestic tasks, rather than somehow pretend to do it all themselves. Ensure that we put women professionals forward as speakers in panels, and provide them with the support in their preparation, that they may not seek as easily and automatically as their male counterparts. The tone at the top is crucial. I have seen very often, that once the head of the organisation insisted that a female speaker/candidate be found before proceeding, this was successful. W@ can help, but support from the top is still necessary.

Since 1 September 2018 Martijn Snoep has been the chairman of ACM: a former De Brauw partner and a highly experienced competition lawyer with over 25 years of private practice experience. What can you say about his influence in day-to-day practice at the ACM? Any specific changes in policy?

There are some issues on which Martijn has strong views. He has spoken in the press on his views in relation to the application of competition law to the self-employed – he sees a danger of over-enforcement there, which may have contributed to harmful competition in labour standards and the rise of the working poor. Also, he believes it important that we do not overlook smaller transgressions when deciding which investigations to prioritise. Sometimes what competition specialists see as a small transgression, is a major issue in the public perception. To retain public trust, we need to be mindful of such mismatches. He also sees a danger of under-enforcement in the application of competition law to vertical price-fixing. In cases where the effect on inter-brand competition may appear to be limited, intra-brand or retail competition may be affected. That can have a significant negative effect on consumers and, as such, falls within our mandate. In short he is a proponent of what he calls "impactful enforcement".

Martijn is very supportive of attempts to improve diversity of all kinds within ACM, as was his predecessor. At ACM, we have a "pink network" of LGBT colleagues who run a social network. We are running courses to promote diversity, for example, we had a workshop on autism last year; we are actively hiring people with disabilities and are currently participating in a course to further unbiased screening in the recruitment of new employees. ACM has women at board level and at management level. So I find things are easier now than they were in my earlier years working in the Netherlands.

Do you see a cultural difference in how competition problems are approached in the different jurisdictions?

I found it strange adjusting to a civil law system, when I first came to live in the Netherlands. I had studied law at University College, Cork, received a masters in EU Law in Bruges, and was called to the Irish bar in 1996. I lectured in European and competition law from 1993 to 2002 at the Universities of Limerick in Ireland and Nijmegen in the Netherlands. EU law applies in both jurisdictions, and competition law rules are fairly standard. There are differences in how the law is implemented. The Dutch authority is free to conduct on-site inspections of undertakings without a warrant, and can impose fines directly on companies and on individuals, while the Irish authority cannot. I think public enforcement is more challenging in Ireland.

On the other hand, the Irish authority is very good at working behind the scenes, and facilitating changes in government policy so as to refrain from market distortions in the first place, which has led to liberal commercial trading rules in Ireland over the years. In many ways, the Dutch have a more formal, structured system than the Irish. Many pharmacies are closed in the Netherlands on Saturdays. Primary schools are closed half-days on Wednesdays. The Irish workforce is arguably more flexible, with more service-directed policies. Of course, in Ireland, where there is an island economy, with a smaller population, it is probably easier to build a dominant position and to abuse it, than it is in the Netherlands.

However, as authorities, we struggle with many similar dilemmas. We are both dealing with complicated market changes in sectors such as health and energy, both dealing with the revolutionary changes brought by online trading. It can be difficult in both jurisdictions to convince the court of the severity of an infringement. Both the Irish and the Dutch authorities have to contend with a demanding judiciary, strict on the rule of law. The European Commission's Director General of Competition Johannes Laitenberger spoke recently of the need for a focus on "evidence-based antitrust". This approach has arguably been visible for some time in the Dutch courts, where there has been an emphasis on demanding empirical studies, a thorough investigation and a determination based on facts and data. Demanding standards are not bad for an authority – as Judge Collins of the General Court likes to remind us, "he who asserts must prove". However, it means the employees of the authority have to develop a very high standard of detection and analytical skills if they are to be successful enforcers. This demands that we are a step ahead of the game when modelling our courses. So I am learning a lot in my new job.

Diversity and inclusion are important subjects for the ACM as authority. As stated in the ACM's Annual Report 2018, the ACM helps us to broadly detect problems in the market, to understand them and subsequently chose the best solution. It's important for ACM that all employees feel "at home", regardless of background and gender. As an employee with a foreign background and law training outside the Netherlands, what you can say about your first years of working in the Netherlands, and at the ACM? Was it easy to adapt to the Dutch ways of working? Any particular differences? How is that after so many years of working and living in the Netherlands?

I have been very lucky with my colleagues in the Netherlands. In most European countries, it would not be possible for a non-national to work within the Competition Authority. Following a brief period as interim référendaire at the European General Court, I started as a case handler at the Netherlands Competition Authority (NMa) in 2003, just in time to witness the modernisation of competition law enforcement, with the introduction of Regulation 1/2003, which coincided with the Dutch

Construction Cartel investigations. Then from 2008 to 2013, I coordinated the authority's international network, which gave me extensive experience of working with other competition authorities within the ICN and ECN. A few other authorities have foreigners working within their ranks, but not many. The advantage of the ICN is that it allows authorities to benefit from each other's experience, both in case work and in the development of legislation.

I was very pleased to be part of the strategy team at the time of the establishment of ACM in 2013. While in this role, I advised on corporate strategy, speeches and communications within the ACM. I'm very proud of the success of the multifunctional authority in the Netherlands. When it comes to joined-up thinking, we have, I feel, proven the synergies in combining energy, telecommunication and transport regulation with consumer protection and competition enforcement, in a way that not many states could have achieved. There are cultural differences, of course, between the different disciplines, but the trick is to find the richness in the differences, rather than seek some kind of cultural superiority. That thinking applies to different disciplines and areas of expertise, but it applies equally to different nationalities and different abilities. We have a natural tendency to seek out those with whom we agree and who share our interests, but if we just dare to think outside the box, we see that diversity is enriching.

Since March 2018, you have been Manager of the Academy at ACM. A new role, compared with your previous tasks and responsibilities at ACM. What do you like about your new role?

The ACM Academy is a unit responsible for organising training and educational courses for ACM's employees, and advises the board on learning and development. My new role allows me the opportunity to use my knowledge of the organisation to help improve its performance. The Academy is working to change courses, to suit the employees. For example, we are trying to move away from a rigid scale classification, whereby only employees on a particular scale have access to a particular course, so that also promising employees on a lower scale may be allowed to develop their talents – you can grow grey waiting for a civil service scale to change! Similarly, we are trying to alter the build of some courses, so that they allow people with family commitments, caring for small children or elderly parents to participate. This means not organising courses that extend too long into the evening hours. It means facilitating working at home and dialling-in to meetings.

In 2004, when the enforcement of competition law was modernised, many speculated that enforcement would become more challenging – authorities would no longer have access to a range of "notified" agreements from which they could work-up leads. However, the authorities followed with leniency programmes and sharpened on-site inspection tools. Again today, with the growth of private enforcement of competition law, we hear commentators asserting that leniency will decline and that public enforcement will be threatened. Again, as authorities we will have to retrain our employees, to educate them in *ex officio* enforcement, including digital search and analysis, to hone their detection skills in a world of big data and sophisticated algorithms. Training and education are central to such change management and it is very satisfying to be playing a part in engineering these changes.

It must be great to coach and help colleagues in their career paths, development and making the right choices in work – life balance. You have four (young) children. Do you see any overlap between managing a big family such as your own and managing the ACM Academy? Does it help you in any way? How is your work – life balance? How do you manage it all?

I feel there are many professionals active in competition who firmly believe that they owe their position solely to merit, and are unaware of the privilege they enjoy, be that due to their background or their gender or their native language. At the end of the day, everyone has advantages as well as talents. It is great to be in a position to assist colleagues in developing those talents. I don't believe in right or wrong choices when it comes to work – life balance, that's something everyone has to figure out for themselves. As for combining domestic and professional tasks, I think it is important to be selective in who you work for, and in who works for you. I have an excellent team at work, and another excellent team at home: plus a resilient husband and four capable, independent children who bring themselves up more or less. They show me no mercy, and when recently, I bemoaned the complexity of my life, I got the brilliant response – "just manage it, Mum!". I hope that in launching W@Competition in the Netherlands, Claudia and I, with our top team and board, will be able to help people to manage, and to make full use of, their talents as competition professionals.

Alejandra Palacios
COFECE

Karina Flores &
Laura Méndez Rodriguez

Alejandra Palacios is the Chair of Mexico's Federal Economic Competition Commission (COFECE) is the first woman to head the Mexican antitrust authority. Alejandra was appointed by Congress in 2013 and was reelected in 2017 for a second four-year tenure. She is Vice-President for the International Competition Network (ICN), Member of the Bureau of the Competition Committee of the Organisation for Economic Cooperation and Development (OECD), and member of the International Women's Forum, Mexico chapter. In 2019 the W@Competition organisation included her in its list of "40 in their 40s" as one of the 40 most notable women in competition in the Americas, Asia and Europe.

Karina Flores is a Mexican qualified lawyer specialized in Competition Law. Her experience has been developed both in private sector and public service. Her past experience includes private practice (civil, corporate, and maritime litigation) while her experience in public service includes practices at the Ministry of Economy, in the International Commercial Negotiations area and in COFECE at the Legal Affairs Office. Devoting the last nine years to the Cartels Division in the Investigative Authority of COFECE, where she is the Deputy General Director and the first woman in Mexico leading dawn raids. Currently she is studying an LLM specialized in competition law with the support of the Mexican Competition Authority.

Laura Méndez Rodriguez is a Mexican qualified attorney. She holds an LLM in Competition Law at King´s College London. Experienced in regulation, anti-corruption compliance and competition law. She has devoted her career to the Mexican public service for the last thirteen years, including the Presidential Office and the Federal Consumer Protection Agency. She worked at the Federal Economic Competition Commission occupying many positions, including Deputy Director General in the Cartel´s Division and Director General of Market Investigations. She is currently the General Comptroller at the Institute of the National Fund for Workers' Housing (INFONAVIT). Additionally, Laura is part-time professor at ITAM.

How do you think competition law, and specifically COFECE (Comisión Federal de Competencia Económica) can help to reduce inequality and poverty in Mexico?

Studies have shown that market concentration has a negative effect on inequality: lack of competition creates and intensifies market power, which allows companies to extract more income from consumers.

A recent study commissioned by COFECE from Professor Andres Aradillas-Lopez, an economist specialised in industrial organisation and antitrust, in its assessment of market power, found that, on average, Mexican households pay a 98% surcharge due to market power in 12 selected markets (tortilla, bread, poultry, beef, processed beef, dairy, fruit, vegetables, non-alcoholic beverages, medicines, passenger air transportation, passenger ground transportation, and construction materials). Mexican families allocate about 16% of their income to pay this surcharge. Likewise, the author observed that the impact of market power is larger in lower income households, whose loss is 4.4 times greater than that suffered by families with more resources.[1] In its study he also estimates that in the absence of the price distortions generated by the presence of market power in the selected markets, the *Gini* coefficient, and therefore the income inequality in the country, would be reduced by around 7.3%. The presence of market power through monopolistic practices is one of the several causes of wealth concentration.

Hence, competition policy is a governmental tool to alleviate inequality, and to constrain highly concentrated economic privileges that result in the loss of purchasing power of income. By eliminating structural,

---

1   Andres Aradillas-Lopez & José Nery Pérez Trujillo, *Poder de Mercado y Bienestar Social* (COFECE 2018). The full document is available in <https://www.cofece.mx/wp-content/uploads/2018/10/Libro-CPC-Podery-Bienestar-ver4.pdf>.

behavioural or regulatory restrictions that limit the intensity of market competition, we are promoting the welfare of society, although this is not a job that competition agencies can do on their own.

Which do you think are the main areas of opportunity to harmonise competition policy and the fight against corruption in Mexico?

Within COFECE's powers there is no a strict mandate to fight corruption. However, our constitutional mandate is to guarantee competition in the markets, *including those related to public procurement*. Considering that the lack of competition in public procurement may be the result of acts of corruption between individuals and public officials, the power to sanction collusive agreements between competitors (some with the help of public servants) with the intention of coordinating their bids and illegally predetermining the winner in a public tender, certainly helps diminish or eliminate corruption.

Another related issue regarding public procurement and competition that is out of the scope of COFECE is that in Mexico public tenders are not always the preferred procurement mechanism. In this sense, an area of opportunity exists in encouraging procurement units to privilege public tenders and/or fully justify the decision to use direct adjudications. Likewise, COFECE has found that, often, procurement procedures are directed to a specific bidder even before the tenders begin – which is a type of corruption. For example, when undertaking preliminary market investigations (or failing to do so), the lack of transparency in the rules of participation, including unjustified or discriminatory requirements, and the selection of the evaluation mechanism. Hence, the design of public procurement procedures should seek the greatest possible concurrence to generate intense competition among participants and thus reduce the space for collusive agreements among bidders and/or with public officials.

In this regard, COFECE has worked with the Ministry for the Public Service and other public institutions to carry out training sessions for personnel in charge of procurement processes in federal entities and to private sector suppliers participating in these processes.

How has it been dealing with the fact that in Mexico COFECE has no powers in telecommunications and broadcasting matters, as there is another institution (IFT) in charge of their regulation and competition enforcement? Do you think the coordination has been difficult considering technological convergence?

During the past five years, COFECE and IFT have worked as parallel competition authorities with clearly defined competencies, the former focusing on all markets except broadcasting and telecommunications, which are jurisdiction of the latter.[2]

COFECE and IFT have cooperated closely in advancing competition policy and culture. For example, through the organisation of joint events, such as the forum "Competition, Motor for Inclusive Economic Growth"[3] carried out in the framework of the 25th anniversary of Mexico's Competition Authority in October 2018.

Regarding the division of powers, to date, a few cases involving a dispute on these entities' powers regarding merger cases have come up. Nonetheless, and in accordance to the Federal Economic Competition Law (to which both authorities abide), these cases have been solved quite rapidly by the courts. They have noticed that mergers are acts in which the firms' activities can fall in the competencies of both authorities, thus ruling that both entities by analyse a specific merger, each in their

---

2   Both COFECE and IFT are autonomous constitutional bodies of the Mexican State, created as a result of the Reform to Article 28 of the Political Constitution of the United Mexican States, published in the Official Gazette of the Federation on 11 June 2013.

3   The event record is available at: <https://www.cofece.mx/wp-content/uploads/2018/12/Memoria-Competencia-Motor-de-crecimiento-incluyente-.pdf>.

respective markets. This was the case of the merger between AT&T and Time Warner, and most recently example of the *Disney/Fox* case, solved in 2019 by both authorities, in which each analysed the operation in the markets under their established jurisdictions.

I have to say we haven't had disputes regarding investigations for anticompetitive conduct. I guess some will come because of technological convergence.

The international environment is at a critical historical moment and poses great challenges for Mexico. Although it has 12 free trade agreements with 46 countries, restrictions on direct foreign investment in the country are greater than those recommended by the OECD, mainly in sectors such as transportation, real estate and construction. In other sectors, such as agriculture and manufacturing, they have lagged behind due to too-stringent local regulations, weak legal institutions, entrenched informality, corruption and insufficient financial development. In this context, which concrete actions has COFECE taken to foster free market competition?

The Mexican legal framework, as in other countries, permits the use of measures such as tariffs, anti-dumping quotas and technical regulations, among others, as part of the country's trade policy. However, these instruments could restrict trade in some circumstances. Therefore, our view is that the adoption of these measures must be justified, on a case-by-case basis, by public objectives. In this sense, COFECE has consistently sought for Mexican trade policy decisions to include economic competition considerations, which imply analysis of market players and concentration and consumer welfare when considering any of these trade measures. Regarding this issue, we produced an advocacy document in July 2017, *Trade Policy from a Competition Perspective*, that highlights the constraints to competition that could come about when using foreign trade instruments. One of the main findings of the document was that Mexico's network of foreign trade agreements does not guarantee the supply of products and services at competitive conditions, specially shoes and textiles that are mainly imported from Asia. A sign of this is the fact that the proportion of imports coming from commercial partners has seen a reduction over the past years. In these cases, importers (and consumers) must either pay high tariffs or stop importing, which causes price rises or reduced supply in national markets.

Moreover, COFECE identifies the lack of competition at the local level as one of the main explanations of Mexico´s crony capitalism. We have carried out multiple investigations at state and even municipal levels. Many markets that lack competition have an anchor on local barriers that protect incumbents, foreclosing markets to new entrants (gasoline, natural gas, transportation in all its types, among others). This is a cultural issue that must change in the sense that local governments see themselves as the protectors of local businesses. In this regard, COFECE has used its advocacy tools to generate awareness of the importance of competition at local level and to foster it. In 2016, COFECE published a Miscellany of Regulatory Obstacles to Competition, a state-level analysis[4] which reviewed over 413 laws and bylaws in five main sectors – agri-food, transportation, urban development, public procurement and professional practice – to identify the main barriers to competition and make recommendations to diminish their negative effects.

It is worth noting that COFECE has issued 54 opinions on possible restrictive regulation since its creation,[5] during the public consultation stage of these norms before they come into force. These *ex ante* analyses by COFECE have stopped, on several occasions, for these anticompetitive norms to be published as initially proposed. In line with this, in 2016,

---

4   The document is available at
     <https://www.cofece.mx/cofece/images/Promocion/Miscelanea_Estatal_210916.pdf>.

5   Article 12 of the Federal Law of Economic Competition grants COFECE the faculty to issue opinions, which are documents that propose changes/amendments to norms enforced by authorities with the aim to foster competition in markets by eliminating regulatory barriers. It is worth noting that the recommendations included in these opinions have a non-binding character; nevertheless, COFECE's recommendations have been adopted regularly.

COFECE published the Guide for the Evaluation of Regulation from a Competition Perspective[6] with the objective of providing practical and technical orientation to public authorities and law-makers so they can identify anticompetitive regulation, whether in draft or in force. During 2016 and 2017, COFECE carried out training sessions with authorities based on the content of this document.

In this same line of work, in 2018, the Commission implemented the *COFECE Award for identifying the most absurd regulatory obstacle to competition and entrepreneurship*[7] with the objectives of increasing COFECE's knowledge of possible regulatory obstacles to competition and disseminating the costs associated with anticompetitive regulation. The Commission received 615 reports, of which 53% referred to barriers at municipal and state levels. The first and second place reports have been used by COFECE to develop further analysis and recommendations in the sectors of notary public services and freight transportation in the state of Nuevo León.[8]

Digital markets and big data are key themes in the antitrust enforcement agenda for many jurisdictions. In your view, what are the main competitive concerns surrounding these matters in Mexico, and what is the Mexican approach in the digital era?

In October 2017, COFECE issued an Opinion on the draft decree to amend several articles pertaining the draft of a Mexican law to regulate the financial services provided by Fintech companies (Draft Decree). The decree's objective was to regulate their organisation, operation and functioning, as well as any other financial service offered or carried out by "innovative means".

---

6   The guide is available at <https://www.cofece.mx/cofece/images/Promocion/Guia_EvaluacionRegulacion__vonline_170516.pdf>.

7   The award record is available at <https://www.cofece.mx/wp-content/uploads/2017/11/Memoria_obstaculo.pdf>.

8   The opinion is available at <http://cofece.mx/CFCResoluciones/docs/Opiniones/V51/22/4432090.pdf>.

COFECE's Opinion recommended that the Draft Decree contemplate a provision that required traditional credit institutions to grant Fintechs their banking services under non-discriminatory conditions, since these are necessary for the provision and development of fintech products. If credit institutions do not grant such services under non-discriminatory conditions, COFECE considered that the Draft Decree should allow for the imposition of appropriate sanctions. COFECE also stated that user information is essential so that new entrants, such as Fintechs, can compete on equal terms with traditional banking and credit institutions, recommending that the Fintech Law included the obligation for traditional financial institutions to provide such information to other market participants. Otherwise, Fintechs would not be able to assess the risk level of potential clients and generate products that respond to their needs, presenting themselves as a viable alternative to traditional banking. Moreover, the Commission recommended establishing, explicitly, in the Draft Decree, that Fintechs could adopt any infrastructure and make use of any technology necessary they deemed fit to provide their services. On March 2018, the Law was published and several of COFECE's recommendations were adopted.

In October 2017, COFECE hosted its annual event with the theme "Mexico: Competition-related challenges in the digital economy". This forum set the stage for COFECE to initiate the debate and analysis on the way companies contest market share in digital environments. Experts and key stakeholders shared their understanding on the matter with the objective to better comprehend: (i) the characteristics of digital markets, (ii) the need (or not) for regulation, and (iii) the challenges and scope of competition legal frameworks to prevent and correct firms' conducts and anticompetitive market structures in this context.

With input gathered from the event, COFECE presented the document *Rethinking Competition in the Digital Economy,*[9] the first document of this type written in Spanish.

In terms of enforcement, as of today, there is only one investigation in the Mexican digital economy related to e-commerce platforms. As such it will set a precedent for investigations to come. In addition, COFECE is presently analysing a merger notification between Walmart, a traditional retail supplier of diverse products, and Cornershop, a two-sided digital platform for delivering groceries – a first merger analysis involving one merging party pertaining to the digital economy. Foreseeable analytical challenges will relate to understanding the underlying network economies at work and their impact.

There are changing times in Mexico regarding energy markets (gasoline, diesel and electricity). How is the Commission promoting competition in these markets and what have been the main challenges?

The structure and operation of the energy sector in Mexico changed dramatically with the 2013 Energy Reform, opening up the markets to gradual liberalisation and more competition in all steps of the production chain of the gas and oil and electricity markets. In the months that followed the Reform, COFECE issued many opinions on the related legal framework that was being designed, in order to promote that secondary laws would indeed be procompetitive: for example, the "Opinion on the liberalisation calendar for gasoline prices" and the "Opinion on state and municipal regulations applicable to the construction and operation of service stations", among others. Most recently, COFECE issued the "Opinion on the exclusivity maintained by Airports and Auxiliary Services (ASA, in Spanish) in storage, retail and sale of aircraft fuels".

---

9   The document is available at
     <https://www.cofece.mx/wp-content/uploads/2018/03/ECEconomiaDigital_web_ENG_letter.pdf>.

At the same time, COFECE has produced three advocacy documents to date, with the objective of identifying bottlenecks in the successful implementation of the Reform and issuing recommendations to the corresponding authorities to foster more competition in each step of the energy value chain. The documents, available on COFECE's webpage, are the following: *Transition to Competitive Energy Markets: Gasolines and Diesel* (May 2016),[10] *Transition to Competitive Energy Markets: LP Gas* (June 2018),[11] *Transition to Competitive Energy Markets: Gasolines and Diesel* (February 2019).[12] Additionally, through 2017 and 2018 COFECE carried out a dissemination strategy in hand with the Energy Regulatory Commission (CRE, in Spanish), to explain to the private sector their rights and obligations when competing in the new context.

COFECE's main challenge and responsibility is timely enforcement when anticompetitive conducts arise in this new scenario. In recent years, COFECE has initiated investigations for possible cartelisation in the gasoline and diesel retail market in Baja California, as well as in the LP gas market in Mexico. In both markets, the Commission is also investigating possible abuse of dominance conducts (four ongoing investigations in total).

In your view, what is the main challenge in competition enforcement for COFECE nowadays?

COFECE's current investigation portfolio points to one of the main challenges for competition and anti-corruption enforcement in Mexico today: competition, or lack thereof, in public procurement

---

10   The document is available at
      <https://www.cofece.mx/wp-content/uploads/2018/01/DOC-GASOLINAS-FINAL.pdf>.

11   The document is available at <https://www.cofece.mx/wp-content/uploads/2018/06/Libro-GasLP_web.pdf>.

12   The document constitutes a follow-up to the previous one with a similar name and is available at
      <https://www.cofece.mx/wp-content/uploads/2019/01/CPC-GasolinasyDiesel-30012019.pdf>.

processes. In recent years, COFECE has solved and sanctioned public procurement-related cases in the latex condoms markets, the media monitoring services market and the surgical and auscultation latex glove markets, and at least four more investigations are on their way. Public procurement is one of the priority sectors established in COFECE's Strategic Plan for 2018–2021.

In general, I would say that the main challenge we face when conducting investigations is making sure that our investigation tools (mainly dawn raids) continue to be effective under the new scenarios we have recently encountered. On the one hand, we have faced technological advances that allow investigated parties to store great amounts of information in diverse digital systems, such as the cloud. This has obliged us to adapt the techniques we use during dawn raids to obtain these sorts of files. Also, as a result of the developing digital economy, we tend to receive massive amounts of information that need to be processed in a timely manner.

On the other hand, just recently in a great number of investigations, economic agents from whom information has been obtained through dawn raids, have been pointing out that the obtained documents are protected under client – attorney privilege. They have therefore requested their safeguard and that access to other parties, including COFECE, be forbidden. This is really a new matter in Mexico, not just in antitrust. Consequently, the Commission issued a technical criteria related to this matter which seeks a balance between the optimum exercise of COFECE's investigation tools and guaranteeing the rights of economic agents.

What do you consider will be your main legacy to the competition authority and to competition policy in Mexico once your term as President of COFECE is over?

COFECE was born as an autonomous body from the executive branch in 2013, and since its creation it was necessary to build a strong institutional design, which would allow it to become a solid competition authority, as part of a new generation of institutions in Mexico whose autonomy was granted to act with greater specialisation, streamlining, control and transparency.

The institutional model that COFECE has built begins with a strategic approach, which allows it to optimise the allocated resources; ensure an effective and efficient operation; and above all, to maintain sight of where the institution must go in the short and long terms. Through this strategic approach, COFECE has been able to prioritise its operations, monitor its activities, evaluate its results and adjust the course when required. One of the main pillars in the construction of a vanguard institutional model has been the task of providing legal and technical certainty about the development of its procedures through the preparation of handouts, guides, criteria and guidelines.

COFECE's model is centred on strengthening the growth of its most important asset: human capital. Since 2013, COFECE has worked on the construction of a Talent Management System, to recruit, develop, retain and evaluate the performance of the staff, in an ethical, respectful, egalitarian and discrimination-free work environment. This system has allowed us to retain and develop high-performance personnel, with the technical knowledge, the vocation of public service and the necessary skills to perform their functions in the best way possible. We have earned some international recognition in this matter.

While it is true that the process of building and consolidating a cutting-edge institutional model is a long-term project, which requires constant self-criticism, review and recalibration of internal projects, analysis to distinguish areas of opportunity that merit adjustments, and continuous improvement, it is also true that the COFECE has managed to impact the wellbeing of families with its resolutions.

This institutional strengthening is what I am most proud of and believe will be my legacy. I can proudly state that COFECE is recognised as one of the top governmental institutions in Mexico.

Knowing that your staff is limited in number, compared to the wave of antitrust investigations and mergers that you must analyse, how does the Commission find a balance?

The resources of any institution are limited and COFECE's are not the exception. To achieve a good balance between the available staff and the cases that are processed annually, strategic planning exercises are carried out. These planning exercises are based on two terms: long-run through a four-year Strategic Plan, and short-run with the implementation of Annual Work Programmes.

The Annual Work Programme stems from long-term strategic planning, in which projects with specific goals are defined to advance in the fulfilment of the objectives of the institution. The actions or projects to be included in this programme must be: relevant (fundamental and transcendental); specific (there is clarity about its scope and the expected result and time frame); challenging (require efforts additional to operational or routine activities); and achievable (the results reside fundamentally in the efforts of the areas).

It is important to point out that the definition of specific projects of great scope does not exempt COFECE from compliance with the rest of the activities and actions of operational nature, subject to demand. However, these planning documents facilitate the prioritisation of the activities carried out by the Commission. Thus, for example, the Annual Work Programmes include activities for the initiation, development and/or conclusion of investigations on anticompetitive conducts, to organise the resources, especially if the overlap in their work is considered.

How important has been the professionalisation of the Commission's personnel in order to achieve your goals? What has been the main action you have undertaken in this context?

As I previously mentioned, human capital is COFECE's most valuable asset: it is our people who apply their technical knowledge to carry out the substantive and adjective processes of the institution. Accordingly, to implement competition policy, COFECE's staff require permanent training in order to improve their skills and keep their specialised technical knowledge up-to-date.

Therefore, as mentioned, from the beginning of its operations, COFECE undertook the task of building a professional development system for its public servants by strengthening the processes of recruitment, selection, professional development, training and retention of personnel. Likewise, it has carried out actions that allow for improving the balance of personal and work life.

The main tool available to COFECE for the professionalisation and retention of its staff is the Talent Management System – we strive for high performance. This system comprises six elements: (i) normative provisions, issued by the Board of Commissioners, that govern the functioning of the system; (ii) general and specific objectives, which incorporate the aspiration towards the excellence of the institution, based on the technical specialisation of human capital; (iii) critical processes, which range from the incorporation of people to the institution, until their separation from work; (iv) the Talent Management Committee, a collegiate body chaired by me, responsible for monitoring the progress of the system and deciding on its evolution; (v) annual planning through Training Programmes; and (vi) accountability through semi-annual reports on Committee activities brought before the Board.

Finally, this system has several instruments such as the Annual Training Programme, the Training Needs Detection Surveys, the Work Climate

Survey (through which personnel feedback is provided), and the Individual Staff Performance Assessment, which helps to focus the efforts of every individual who works in COFECE.

Most importantly, the Talent Management System has yielded results. To mention an example: staff turnover rate decreased from 39.4% in 2014 to 9.7% in 2018. This in turn supports an increase in the level of specialisation and the technical rigour required for the analysis and implementation of competition policy.

Bitten Thorgaard Sørensen
Danish Competition and Consumer Authority

Rasa Zaščiurinskaitė

Bitten Thorgaard Sørensen is Deputy Director General at the Danish Competition and Consumer Authority. Prior to joining the Danish Competition and Consumer Authority as Deputy Director General in 2013, she worked 10 years in private practice with the Danish law firm Gorrissen Federspiel where she advised clients on all aspects of EU and Danish competition law. From 2007 to 2008, Bitten was a foreign associate with Davis Polk & Wardwell in New York. She was also an external senior lecturer in competition law at the University of Copenhagen for several years.

Rasa Zaščiurinskaitė is a Partner and Head of the Competition Practice Group at COBALT Lithuania. For over 15 years, she has concentrated her practice in competition law and has substantial experience in Energy, Pharmacy, Aviation and other regulated areas of law. Rasa has a Master's degree in Law from Vilnius University and a Master of Laws (LLM) degree in EU Competition Law from King's College London. She has also gained valuable knowledge of EU competition law through attendance of numerous international and national conferences. Rasa also delivers presentations at local and international EU law conferences and has been contributing articles on EU competition law to various publications.

Introductory Question

Prior to joining the Danish Competition and Consumer Authority (DCCA) in 2013, you worked in private practice with a Danish law firm where you advised clients in all aspects of EU and Danish competition law. What were the main reasons to switch to the DCCA instead of staying in the private practice? How has your experience as a private practitioner helped you in your work at the DCCA?

I thoroughly enjoyed working in private practice so it was very much an opt-in, and I remember that the decision was a hard one because of the interesting work and the great people I worked with . But, in the end, it was just too big an opportunity for me to pass up. I believe there were three main reasons that I decided to make the move: one, the prospect of being part of the political process and thus cultivating my interest in the public policy side of the legal work; two, the chance of being part of deciding the strategic direction and policies of the DCCA; and three, the chance to develop as a leader and, I hope, playing a positive part in developing the DCCA's very talented employees.

Some of the inspiration for making the move came from my period working in the US where moves between private practice and government service is much more frequent than in Denmark. Having been on different sides of the table has hopefully helped me better understand the different perspectives.

General Questions about the DCCA and ECN+ Directive

What has been the main focus of the DCCA in public enforcement of competition in recent years? What are the current main challenges and priorities for the DCCA?

When deciding whether or not to pursue a certain case, we look at the expected effects on competition. More precisely, when taking into consideration the expected effect, we look at the seriousness of the case with respect to the alleged violation; the expected significance of the case with respect to the market, the competition culture and the economy as a whole; whether or not the case deals with an issue of novel nature; and the resources required to decide on the case, including the strength of the evidence.

We prioritise cartel cases, including bid-rigging, which continue to be an area of concern. We also focus on issues related to abuse of dominant position, where we have had some quite interesting cases within recent years. Focus is also given to cases involving trade associations and we have seen a number of cases regarding anticompetitive agreements involving trade associations.

Not surprisingly, one important focus area for us is digitalisation. With the purpose of increasing our focus on the implications of digitalisation, we have established a new unit, which is responsible for the enforcement of competition rules in cases concerning digital platforms. Besides enforcement, the new unit will conduct analysis on different aspects of platforms and digitalisation.

Denmark is one of the few EU Member States to have a criminal liability for severe competition law infringements. The ECN+ Directive empowers the competition authorities of Member States to be more effective enforcers: Article 13 sets out clearly that competition authorities must have the power to apply administrative sanctions in non-criminal proceedings for the infringement of EU competition law violations. What are your expectations on the possible changes, in general, on the work of the DCCA due to implementation of the ECN+ Directive?

Aside from the area you mention to a large extent, Denmark already fulfils the requirements of the ECN+ Directive, but it is true that the adoption of the directive implies that Denmark will have to introduce changes to our fining system.

The design of a new system is part of a political process and, at different options must be considered. In the end, it is a political decision how such system should look but I do hope that the new system will be efficient both in terms of quality and time.

In autumn of 2017, Denmark and other Nordic countries signed the Nordic Cooperation Agreement. As stated, the purpose of the agreement is to improve cooperation between the Nordic competition authorities, inter alia by reducing obstacles for effective cooperation on enforcement, by obliging the countries to coordinate efforts in cases relating to the same practice or merger and by ensuring that the countries support each other in their enforcement activities by providing each other with investigative assistance when appropriate. How does this agreement supplement the European Competition Network? Have you already noticed the actual effect of this agreement? What are the main gains from such an agreement for the Nordic countries? Do you believe such practices could or should be extended to other regional cooperation of Member States, for instance, Nordics + Baltics?

The Nordic countries have a long tradition of cooperation within this area that goes back 60 years and it is an important forum for informal exchange of experiences regarding current competition law issues, case handling, project management and investigation methodology. Recently, we have also introduced an exchange programme where employees are offered an opportunity to work at another authority for up to six months. This provides valuable experience in case handling and contributes to maintaining a good network between the Nordic competition authorities.

The Nordic Cooperation Agreement from 2017 is an extension of an agreement that Denmark acceded to in 2001. The intention behind the updated cooperation agreement is to strengthen the ability of the Nordic competition authorities to efficiently investigate cases under their respective competences in order to improve the functioning of markets to the benefit of consumers and businesses The revision of the agreement was initiated by Norway that due to its non-EU member status cannot apply the provisions in Council Regulation 1/2003. In addition to exchange of information, the new agreement allows us to assist each other with requests for information and with carrying out inspections. The agreement constitutes a supplement to Regulation 1/2003 as it applies in national cases as well as in EU/EEA cases and in merger cases.

With regard to the Baltic countries, we are fortunate in that Regulation 1/2003 provides us with the tools to cooperate the same way as we do with other EU countries. Whether and to what extent further cooperation with other agencies would be necessary will also depend on whether specific cases arise which cannot be dealt with through the current tools. And as some of our cases and challenges are similar in nature, I believe it is fair to say that we do see a rise in our informal cooperation.

Joint Bidding

The DCCA has been very active in safeguarding competition in the public procurement proceedings, not only fighting bid-rigging but also preventing unlawful joint bidding by companies. In 2018, the DCCA published new guidelines on how to assess joint bidding under competition law with concrete advice for companies that are considering entering into joint bidding agreements with other companies, especially their competitors. What effect of these guidelines do you see in practice? Do you see a tendency to fewer joint bids in general?

The fight against bid-rigging have been a priority for the DCCA for a long time and still is a very important part of our work. In addition to enforcement action, we have also published guidelines to municipalities and other contracting entities on how they can detect bid-rigging.

Joint bidding has been a hot topic in Denmark, as well as in other Nordic countries, in recent years. In addition to the enforcement action we have taken, the guidelines on joint bidding were issued in order to assist companies in knowing what to consider when entering into such forms of collaboration. From the feedback we get, there is certainly increased attention on the rules in this area. Recently, the decision by the DCCA in 2015 in the so-called "Road Marking Case" was confirmed by the Supreme Court. Based on that we will update our guidelines.

Cartels and Leniency

According to surveys ordered by the DCCA for the year 2017, 36% of companies believe that other companies break the law by entering into cartels. As we know, the disclosure of cartels, especially of secret cartels, highly depends on tips and information from companies, e.g. through leniency procedures, among other things. Nevertheless, the majority of the Danish companies interviewed indicated that they would not report a violation if they became aware of it because of the fear of revenge from those who had been reported, and because they are not 100% sure that it is possible to file a report anonymously. How do you think it is possible to enhance the willingness of companies to cooperate and enhance the disclosure of the cartels, and improve the efficient enforcement of competition rules?

The survey correctly shows that well over a third of Danish companies estimate that other companies in their industry breach Danish competition rules by entering into cartels. However, this is slightly fewer than in 2012 when we made a similar survey.

According to the survey, the risk of bad reputation was one of the main arguments for complying with competition rules. There is, however, no doubt that efficient sanctions also constitute an important means to enhance the willingness to comply with competition rules and to enhance the incentive apply for leniency. In 2013, the possibility of imprisonment was introduced in the Danish Competition Act. Even though no one has been sentenced to prison yet there is no doubt that the risk of imprisonment has a deterrent effect. When it comes to fines, they have traditionally been low in Denmark, but we see the courts impose higher fines as a result of the increase in the level of fines that was also introduced in 2013. As a follow-up on the above-mentioned survey, we carried out a leniency campaign.

Another important point to make is that under certain conditions, it is possible to keep the identity of a tipper anonymous if the tipper risks retaliations (both physical and business-related). It is also possible to send information anonymously to the DCCA through our whistleblower tool, which uses an encrypted connection. By using this tool it is possible to submit information and to engage in anonymous two-way communication with the DCCA.

Abuse of Dominance

The DCCA is only of the few national competition authorities which has recently tackled excessive pricing as abusive practice in the pharmaceutical sector. By a decision from January 2018, the Danish Competition Council found that CD Pharma (a pharmaceutical distributor) abused its dominant position in Denmark by charging Amgros (a wholesale buyer for public hospitals) unfair prices for Syntocinon. On 29 November 2018, the Danish Competition Appeal Tribunal upheld the decision made by the Danish Competition Council. Following the appeal of CD Pharma, the case is currently pending before the Danish court. Please share what were the main reasons for the DCCA to investigate this case and what were the main challenges for the DCCA in finding the excessive pricing?

When deciding whether to pursue a possible infringement, the DCCA always considers the expected effects in relation to improving competition and creating better-functioning markets and the expected use of resources to investigate the case. A key element in this is the gravity of the possible infringement.

When it comes to cases concerning excessive pricing, intervention should be approached with caution, since the markets in many cases will correct themselves. However, in some markets this is not necessarily the case. In particular, the dynamics of pharmaceutical markets can make it relevant for competition authorities to prioritise cases on unfair prices. When deciding whether to pursue the CD Pharma case the DCCA considered a number of elements, such as the very significant price increase (2,000%); that the product in question was no longer patented; that CD Pharma was a distributor and consequently no apparent need for protection of innovation was present; there were no generic or substitutable pharmaceuticals available on the Danish market; demand was price-inelastic. In addition, barriers to entry were high, and due to the size of the market, the market was less likely to attract new entrants.

There were two main issues of the appeals case. The first was whether the relevant period of dominance – of one and up to two years – constituted a "significant period of time". The Danish Competition Appeal Tribunal confirmed the DCCA's assessment that there is no general minimum period of dominance.

The second main aspect was the assessment of CD Pharma's profit margin on Syntocinon (the first step of the United Brands test). This is often a challenging part of the assessment in cases concerning excessive prices, since it requires knowledge of the relevant costs, e.g. access to internal information about actual costs of producing or selling the specific product in question. The DCCA was unable to obtain documentation of the relevant costs and therefore had to rely on cost estimates based on other information. The Danish Competition Appeal Tribunal upheld the estimated profit margin of 80–90% made by the DCCA.

Digitalisation and big data pose specific challenges for competition authorities. Ongoing debates on the questions include when and how to intervene in the dynamic digital economy markets, whether the competition tools are the right tools to tackle some unfair practices, e.g. the Facebook case in Germany, are among those challenges. What is your view on the public competition enforcement in this area? Whether the competition enforcement is the right and sufficient tool to tackle digitalisation and big data – related unfair practices concerns?

Whenever I discuss this subject, I try to remind myself and others that first and foremost digitalisation is a great opportunity for all of us and for competition, as it brings new business models, new and disruptive competitors, and more effective production methods, which all bring better products and lower prices.

That being said, network effects, big data and the use of algorithms all raise a number of potential challenges to competition, to competition enforcement and to competition law.

As is the case for most other authorities, this is an area of high priority for us and, against this background, a new unit within the authority will be established which will strengthen our efforts within digital platforms. The main areas of focus for the unit will be enforcement of the competition rules vis-à-vis digital platforms, market studies in respect of digital platforms, big data, machine learning, artificial intelligence and algorithms, and analysis of the behavioural instruments of the digital platforms.

We will be following up on the analysis and the enforcement action which the new unit will be taking, however, at this stage, I personally do not believe that we have seen enough evidence to support a change in the core elements of competition law, however, there may be a need for adjustments of some elements.

Also, the question of whether competition law is the right and sufficient tool to tackle the new challenges is not necessarily binary. In some cases, competition law will be both the better and more adequate tool, whereas in other cases, (sector-) specific regulation may be the better tool to solve the relevant issues, e.g. in terms of barriers to entry. However, *ex ante* regulation should always be considered carefully and be well-founded.

Mergers

The DCCA has been active in gun-jumping cases including the *EY/KPMG* case in 2014, and the *SEAS-NVE Holding/Syd Energi Holding* case in 2018. On 31 May 2018, the Court of Justice issued its much anticipated preliminary ruling in *EY/KPMG*, where the court clarified that the termination of the cooperation agreement between KMPG Denmark and KPMG International did not violate gun-jumping rules. What are the main takeaways for you from the *EY/KPMG* case?

I once said of this case – with a slightly adjusted Kennedy quote – that it is well-known that victory has a thousand fathers, but defeat is an orphan, yet I will gladly be the mother of this case. Both EU and national case law in this area is sparse. The standstill obligation is an important element in securing an effective merger control. However, we know from companies and their lawyers (and this was also my own experience working in private practice) that this is also an area that is extremely important for the merging companies and where there has been little guidance. As said, it is one of the priorities of the DCCA that we take on cases that raise novel questions, in order to clarify the legal position..

The preliminary ruling from the European Court of Justice did provide more clarity as to the scope of the standstill obligation. However, there are still areas which are not fully clarified by the ruling. Hopefully, the *Altice* ruling will provide further guidance.

Public Authorities and Competition

Most Member States face the initiatives from the public sector to offer goods and services in competition with the private sector which usually also raises concerns about how to ensure fair competition, avoid conflicts of interest and other misuse of state power. The DCCA has also issued recommendations for the Danish government in order to ensure clearer rules for public sector participation in the market. How are these concerns of public authorities' participation in the business in competition with the private sector tackled in your jurisdiction?

Back in May 2016, the Competition Council issued a report on public sector activities in commercial markets, which included recommendations in respect of the current rules.

Based, inter alia, on this report, in March 2019 a draft bill was in public hearing but never decided on due to the general election in June 2019. The current Minister for Industry, Business and Financial Affairs has also shown interest in and is contemplating actions within this area, however, the exact embodiment of this is not finalised. So this is certainly an area of great interest.

Rose Webb
New South Wales Department of Customer Services

Felicity Lee & Amelia McKellar

Rose Webb is the Deputy Secretary, Better Regulation Division in the New South Wales Department of Customer Services and Commissioner for Fair Trading. Rose has a wealth of Australian and international experience in regulation including a three-year period working as Senior Executive Director and then Chief Executive Officer of Hong Kong's Competition Commission from 2014 to 2017. Between 2001 and 2008, and again between 2011 and 2014, Rose worked for the Australian Competition and Consumer Commission (ACCC), including serving as Executive General Manager, Mergers and Acquisitions.

Felicity Lee is a senior associate at Ashurst specialising in competition and antitrust matters, with particular experience in contentious merger clearance applications, competition litigation, regulated industries/ infrastructure access, and consumer law. Before joining Ashurst, Felicity worked as a competition, consumer and regulatory lawyer at the Australian Competition and Consumer Commission, and as legal counsel specialising in competition law at two large food and beverage companies.

Amelia McKellar (née Ho) is a senior lawyer in the competition and regulatory team at Gilbert + Tobin with extensive international competition and consumer law experience both from her time practising in Australia and when working abroad at Freshfields Bruckhaus Deringer, based in London. Amelia has particularly significant experience in multi-jurisdictional mergers and behavioural competition matters, having coordinated multi-jurisdictional matters both overseas and from Australia, as well as having acted many times in a local counsel capacity. Prior to Amelia's time in London, she was a senior associate in the competition team of another leading Australian firm.

Tell us about the path that led you to being the CEO of the Hong Kong Competition Commission (HKCC).

I did two stints at the Australian Competition and Consumer Commission (ACCC) – from 2001 to 2008, mostly working on enforcement cases, and from 2011 to 2014, working on mergers. (In between I went off to Australia's federal environment department to set up a new compliance and enforcement function.) When I "boomeranged" back to the ACCC, I had every intention of staying there for a long period.

However the call from the headhunter for the HKCC was hard to resist. I had always regretted not working overseas earlier in my career, and I knew I was unlikely ever to get the chance to be part of a "start-up" competition agency again.

I started at HKCC as the Senior Assistant Director working with Dr Stanley Wong, the first CEO. Unfortunately he became ill quite early in his term and I was asked to take on the CEO role when he resigned in early 2016.

What did you find most rewarding about your role as CEO? And what did you find most surprising?

The most rewarding was starting from pretty much nothing – four people and an office when I arrived in 2014 – and within three or so years growing to a fully-fledged competition agency that had filed its first enforcement cases and won a number of awards for its competition advocacy. Seeing a whole bunch of people with disparate backgrounds and experiences form together as a team was inspiring.

One surprising aspect was finding myself in a jurisdiction without a competition law for my first 18 months in Hong Kong (I arrived in April 2014 and the Competition Ordinance commenced in December 2015). Australia's competition law started in 1974, and I hadn't really appreciated how important competition law was to making an economy work efficiently and fairly until I was suddenly living somewhere without it. Equally amazing to me was how quickly people in Hong Kong grasped the benefits of the law and were able to identify anticompetitive conduct.

Do you recall a case that sparked your initial interest in competition and consumer law? And what is it about competition and consumer law that has kept you hooked for all these years?

Not so much a case but more a realisation that competition and consumer law met my interests in both economics and law (I studied a combined economics/law degree at university). The Australian law and the predecessor to the ACCC (the TPC) were all still pretty new at the time I was studying. In contrast to the English case law you typically study at an Australian law school, we discussed lots of US cases in competition law class and it all seemed very modern!

Since then it has been great to be a part of not only the gradual development of competition and consumer law in Australia – ranging from international cartels (like just about everyone at the ACCC at the time, I worked on air cargo matters) to mergers in emerging markets. It has also been fascinating to be part of the spread of competition law across the Asia-Pacific region.

What do you hope will be your legacy and do you have any particular focus for your term as NSW Fair Trading Commissioner?

I hope that my overall legacy will be fairer markets in New South Wales (NSW) for consumers and businesses. In addition to being responsible for the implementation of the Australian Consumer Law in NSW, Fair Trading is also responsible for a large number of specific regulatory and licensing schemes (more than 70 statutes). These range from licensing paintball markers to regulating real estate agents to enforcing the state's biofuel mandate. It is easy to get caught up in the detail of all this regulation. I hope that we can ensure we don't lose sight of our primary mission of protecting consumers from harm and ensuring a level playing field for business.

What advice do you have for fellow women competition professionals and what guidance has played a critical role in your career?

My experience in Australia has been that competition law has had a relatively high representation of women, both at the regulator and in the profession. One theory is that it is because it is a newer branch of law and so maybe isn't as traditional as other areas. Another view is that women have been quick to realise how interesting it is!

Particularly in relation to regulators, we have seen quite a few women leaders in the Asia-Pacific region. Both the Malaysia Competition Commission and HKCC had women as their inaugural chairs, and the first CEO in Singapore was also a woman. The examples of other women carrying out these senior roles has always been an inspiration. Some good advice I have received is to back your own judgment. Sometimes competition law issues can sound very complex and technical, but if your own analysis tells you a situation is probably anticompetitive then you should rely on that, no matter how many complicated economic and legal theories are being thrown at you.

What are your views on the relationship between regulators in Australia and other Asia-Pacific regions?

One of the great things about being involved in competition law in the past 20 years has been the changes in the Asia-Pacific region. It has been part of the experience during my lifetime of much of the Asia-Pacific moving from "developing" to "developed". I think having the opportunity to engage on competition issues with countries with different political, economic and legal backgrounds has strengthened Australia's competition law regulatory system. It's great that some Asia-Pacific agencies, like Hong Kong, have been able to actively recruit staff from Australia, or alternatively have ACCC and other Australian staff work and train with them.

Tell us about your path back to Australia as NSW Fair Trading Commissioner, including what it was about this role that drew you back and how you have found transitioning into the role and resettling back in Australia.

I really enjoyed my time in Hong Kong, but as my contract period was coming to an end I decided that I would come back to Australia, mainly due to having elderly parents in Sydney who were not so well. I didn't really have a plan as to what I would do next, but literally a few days before I left Hong Kong a head-hunter called to see if I would be interested in this role. In addition to being Fair Trading Commissioner, I am responsible for a range of other regulatory activities, including work health and safety, and liquor, gaming and racing. I think it was the opportunity to work across a range of regulatory schemes that all have the object of protecting the community while allowing business to thrive at their heart that was the main attraction of the position.

I still miss Hong Kong – although Sydney is a big city, the streets seem strangely quiet and subdued compared with Wan Chai. And, as every Australian knows, you are a long way from everywhere else here. No one is ever just "passing through" Canberra, whereas we had lots of visitors, including heads of major agencies, visiting us regularly in Hong Kong.

How have your roles at the HKCC and NSW Fair Trading impacted your views of and relationship with the ACCC and vice versa?

After so many years sitting on the "central government" side of the table at the ACCC looking at things from the position of a large well-established regulator, it was a bit strange to be in a "small and new" regulator in

Hong Kong, and then being in the state regulator (versus the centre) in NSW. However, it's great to have so many ongoing connection with the ACCC in my current role. They have even been kind enough to invite me back to participate in some of their training for Asia-Pacific agencies, which has been great for maintaining connections with many agencies.

Meng Yanbei
Renmin University
Susan Ning

Meng Yanbei is Professor and Doctoral Tutor at the Law School of Renmin University of China, focusing on competition, industry and foreign investment law. In addition, she is Vice-Dean of the Asia-Pacific Institute of Law of Renmin University, Director of the Centre for Digital Economy and Competition Law and Executive Director of China-Korea Market & Regulation Law Centre (MRLC). Ms Meng is also a member of the Expert Advisory Group of the Antimonopoly Committee of the State Council. She has published 92 papers, authored or co-authored 50 books and has spearheaded over 32 research projects in China.

Susan Ning joined King & Wood Mallesons in 1995. She is a partner and the head of the Compliance Group. Ms Ning's main areas of practice include cybersecurity and data compliance, and antitrust and competition law. In addition, Ms Ning also practices in international trade and investment law. Ms Ning holds a Bachelor of Laws from Peking University and a Master in Law from McGill University. She was admitted as a Chinese lawyer in 1988.

How do you enjoy your job as member of the Expert Advisory Committee of the State Council's Anti-monopoly Commission?

As a scholar engaged in the teaching and research of anti-monopoly law for many years, I am very honoured and fortunate to be appointed a member of the Expert Advisory Committee of the State Council's Anti-monopoly Commission (Expert Advisory Committee) and to have the opportunity to participate in the work of the Expert Advisory Committee. For me, it is a mission, as well as a responsibility, and I look forward to being able to contribute to research on China's antitrust theories, legislation and practice.

As we all know, the Expert Advisory Committee is entrusted by the Anti-monopoly Commission or its member units to provide a consultation service, which mainly includes advising on the study and formulation of competition policies; advising on research and development of antitrust guidelines; advising on the status quo report, which is to provide an assessment of market competition; participating in ad hoc research projects on major issues for the Anti-monopoly Commission and its member units; advising on major antitrust matters; keeping abreast of and studying anti-monopoly priorities and hot issues both at home and abroad; and providing timely advice and information. Such research activities are rare opportunities for scholars to get access to the forefront of issues concerning anti-monopoly legislation and enforcement, and allow contemplation of the challenges facing Chinese competition legislation, theories and practice from a more macroscopic perspective. In my case, I think if I work sufficiently diligently, the job could broaden my academic horizons and improve my research ability.

What are your competition law training experiences?

I started to learn competition law in 1992–1995, when I graduated from Southwest University of Political Science and Law, and then went to Renmin University of China (RUC) to pursue a master's degree in economic law. Those years were also of great importance for the construction of China's economic system, as Deng Xiaoping proposed to establish a "socialist market economy" during his visit to South China in 1992. In October 1992, the 14th National Congress of the Communist Party of China (CPC) formally confirmed that the goal of China's economic system reform is to establish a socialist market economy. In 1993, the third plenary session of the 14th CPC central committee made decisions on several issues concerning the establishment of a socialist market economic system, and promulgated and implemented the anti-unfair competition law of China (AUCL) in 1993. The AUCL of 1993 not only prohibited typical unfair competition behaviours, but also regulated the restriction of competition behaviours are now regulated under the Anti-Monopoly Law (AML), such as the abuse of exclusive status by public enterprises or enterprises entrusted with exclusive positions, the restriction of competition behaviours by the government and its subordinate units, predatory pricing behaviours, tying or the imposition of unreasonable conditions, and collusive bidding behaviours, etc. RUC Law School was a pioneer among the law schools in China in setting up a course on competition law, where I systematically studied domestic and foreign competition laws. I got a job with RUC in 1995 and began to pursue my PhD in economic law. Competition law is one of my major research areas, and the title of my doctoral thesis is *Research on Joint Behavior of Restriction Competition*. In my subsequent research career, I also studied and visited Georgetown University Law Center in the United States to study antitrust law and economics, from 2007 to 2008.

With more than 20 years of competition law teaching and research, I have set up the curricula on anti-monopoly law, anti-unfair competition law, Asia-Pacific competition law, case analysis of competition law and others. So far, I have published over 92 academic papers, including "Study on the Application Scope of Antitrust Law in China's Monopolistic Sector", and published *Anti-Monopoly Law*, *China "Oil and Gas Law" Theoretical Research and System Construction* and another 50 books or textbooks. I presided over the study of "Research on Antitrust Enforcement in Monopolistic Industry" and I presided over or participated in 32 other research projects. The process of teaching and studying competition law is, for me, also a process of continuous learning and contemplation on competition law.

How do you enjoy your job as a professor in the competition law field?

The Chinese competition law academic community is very active. There are elders who are eager to lead and support their students and talented youngsters. There also exists an independent and free academic atmosphere and tradition of solidarity and fraternity, which is an excellent academic environment for Chinese competition law scholars.

As regards my competition law teaching activities, as I said in my speech at the 2016 Competition Policy Forum to discuss the training of competition law talent, it is a very happy thing to teach competition law at RUC Law School.

First, RUC Law School was the first university to offer a course in competition law, and has established a history of competition law teaching and training. This is what I have greatly benefited from.

Second, the teachers of RUC Law School have relatively free autonomy in the setting of the curriculum. I set up anti-monopoly law and anti-unfair competition law as selective courses for undergraduate students, competition law and Asian-Pacific competition law for the masters course, and a compulsory course on competition law for the LLM. A seminar on competition law was also taught to PhD students majoring in economic law.

Third, there are good platforms and conditions for the training of anti-monopoly law talent in RUC Law School. For example, perhaps because of geographical convenience, we can invite excellent antitrust scholars, officials, judges and lawyers, from home and abroad, to the RUC classroom to give lectures. Therefore, our students can keep abreast of the frontier theories of antitrust law, with close-at-hand summaries of practical experiences of anti-monopoly law and theoretical thinking.

Moreover, RUC attaches more importance to internationalisation. Our teaching syllabus for the summer vacation session has a special international semester, which includes disciplines at the forefront of international projects. We occasionally invite internationally renowned anti-monopoly law professors and scholars to RUC to set up an anti-monopoly law course in English. This coincides with the internationalisation (convergence) of anti-monopoly law itself, and is also conducive to the cultivation of anti-monopoly law specialists.

To give another example, the economics discipline at RUC is famous, and anti-monopoly law is a discipline that integrates legal analysis with economic theory. Within the same campus, and even in the same Mingde Building, the cultivation of RUC anti-monopoly law talent represent a good combination of the Law School with the advantages of the School of Economics. So, as a professor of competition law, I enjoy the life of teaching competition law and studying competition law on my campus.

What are your comments on the development of China's AML so far? In your view, what are the biggest challenges for China's AML enforcement.

China's AML has achieved remarkable results for over 10 years. It has played an important role in protecting fair competition in the market, improving economic efficiency, safeguarding consumer and public interests, and promoting the healthy development of the socialist market economy. The status and the role of China's competition policy have been continuously enhanced, the level of anti-monopoly legalisation has been continuously improved, and a market system with a unified, open and competitive order has been gradually achieved. At present, China has become one of the most important anti-monopoly jurisdictions after the United States and the European Union.

The legislation and practice of China's anti-monopoly law have constantly confronted challenges. These challenges can be divided into two categories: one is that China, together with other countries around the world, is confronting challenges on how to deal with emerging issues, such as platform enterprises, big data usage behaviours algorithm collusion, algorithmic discrimination, and data-driven consolidation. In the context of the digital economy, we must consider whether the legislative objectives and basic analytical framework of the AML have changed, and what changes have occurred in assessing elements of anti-monopoly law and analytical tools. Agencies also face challenges in regulating the exercise of rights in the field of intellectual property, especially the regulation of standard essential patents. The other challenge is characteristically Chinese, such as the implementation of the AML in monopolistic industries, the regulation of administrative monopolies, and whether and how the fair competition review system is to be embedded in the AML. All of these challenges require the competition law community to explore answers from China itself.

What are your comments on each of the specific antitrust enforcement areas, i.e. merger review and antitrust investigation?

Since the establishment of State Administration for Market Regulation (SAMR) and the consolidation of the three antitrust enforcement agencies, it is very important to amend the AML supporting regulations. At present, SAMR has revised seven guidelines relating to the merger notifications, and has published "Interim Provisions on the Procedures for Administrative Penalties for Market Supervision and Administration" and "Interim Measures for the Hearing of Administrative Penalties for Market Supervision and Administration". The original three antitrust law enforcement agencies issued a series of AML enforcement regulations and rules in their respective areas of concern. With the completion of institutional reforms, speeding up the pace of formulating regulations that meet law enforcement needs has become an urgent task for SAMR. In order to establish a unified protocol for AML enforcement, to prevent and suppress monopolistic behaviours, SAMR issued a draft to solicit public comments on 3 January 2019 – draft Provisions on the Prohibition of Monopoly Agreements; on 14 January 2019, SAMR issued draft Provisions on the Prohibition of the Abuse of Administrative Monopoly; and on 30 January 2019, draft provisions on the Prohibition of Abuse of Dominant Market Position. On 26 June 2019, SAMR formally issued Provisional Provisions on the Prohibition of Monopoly Agreements, Provisional Provisions on the Prohibition of the Abuse of Administrative Monopoly, and Provisional Provisions on the Prohibition of Abuse of Dominant Market Position. At the same time, the Supreme People's Court is also revising the judicial interpretation of Antitrust Civil Litigation, and the 13th National People's Congress Standing Council has put the amendments to the AML on its legislative agenda. All these legislative efforts are important topics in the study of China's AML.

In these specific areas of AML-related regulation, namely, the rules concerning monopoly agreements, abuse of dominant market position, concentration and administrative monopoly behaviours, there is also a large number of emerging and hot topics, worthy of our in-depth study:

1. On the regulation of monopoly agreements, the main issues to be studied are: the logical analysis framework for determination of illegality of horizontal monopoly agreements and vertical monopoly agreements; the regulation of hub-and-spoke cartels; the regulation of the algorithm conspiracy; and the construction and implementation of the safe harbour system for monopoly agreements.

2. On the issue of the determination of abuse of dominant market position, the main topics to be studied are: the importance of the relevant market definition in determining dominant market position; whether and how the principles of essential facilities can be applied in the circumstances of the platform economy; big data applications and intellectual property rights; enforcement attitudes towards issues of digital economy and abuse of the collective dominance; and proportionality to regulate the foregoing issues in anti-monopoly laws.

3. For merger review, the main topics to be studied are: against the background of digital economy, whether filing standards shall include other new standards apart from turnover; how to effectively regulate "gun-jumping" behaviours; whether merger review remedies shall be more likely to include behavioural remedy in the context of the digital economy; and the integration issue of combining economic analysis, legal analysis and industry analysis in the assessment of competition effects.

4. On the issue of the regulation of administrative monopoly beha- viours, the topics to be studied are: the relationship between the fair competition review system and the AML; the relationship between realisation of the competition neutrality principle and the AML; the relationship between effective regulation of administrative monopolistic behaviours, government regulation and supervision of economic activities; and the coordination of anti-monopoly law and administrative litigation law.

5. On the effective implementation of the AML, the topics to be studied are: the relationship between AML enforcement and the judiciary; the confiscation of illegal income in AML enforcement; the distribution of burden of proof in anti-monopoly justice; competition advocacy and the spread of competition culture.

What do you think that competition law contributes to the development of the Chinese market economy?

China's economy has shifted from a high-speed growth stage to a stage of quality development. In order to continuously improve the quality of economic development, China needs to confirm the foundational status of competition policy. Only by establishing the basic status of competition policy can we truly establish an economic system with "effective market mechanism, incentivised microscopic individuals and proportional macro-control".[1] The path of strengthening the basic position of competition policy is multi-layered, and one of the paths is legislative perfectionism and effective implementation of the AML. At present, the main work carried out in China's antitrust field includes: the formulation and improvement of the AML supporting regulations; the revision of the AML; antitrust enforcement and justice; competition advocacy; and antitrust compliance review.

The second path is the proposal for the strengthening of the competition neutrality principle. The principle of competition neutrality creates a fair competition environment for different subjects of market ownership, and requires equal treatment of all types of ownership enterprise, including private and foreign enterprise, in the aspects of factor acquisition, entry permission, management and operation, government procurement and bidding. Strengthening the principle of competition neutrality has drawn most attention in China because of two major issues: government behaviour and state-owned enterprises.

The third path is the promotion of the fair competition review system. China's fair competition review system continues to promote measures for strict review of forthcoming documents. Before the end of 2019, it will have achieved full coverage at national, provincial and municipal govern-

---

1   Report of the 19th CPC National Congress.

ment level; it will further reform and improve the fair competition review system, amend the implementing rules, establish regular assessment and clean-up mechanisms, carry out third-party assessments, strengthen the supervision mechanism for fair competition review, conduct regular spot checks of documents, and incorporate fair competition review into the relevant credits assessment system.

The fourth path is the promotion of policy reform. At present, competition-friendly foreign investment policy, industrial policy, fiscal policy and investment policy are being established in China. Competition policy is in the process of achieving the realisation that "the market plays a decisive role in the allocation of resources and plays a better role in the government", which will promote the development of China's economy.[2] Among such policy reform, the perfection and effective implementation of competition law plays an indispensable and important role.

What career/personal achievement are you most proud of? What is your favourite moment during your time as AML professor or AML Commission member?

The proudest achievement of my career is that I have published and co-authored 14 textbooks, among which there is a series of competition law teaching materials. Those textbooks have played a role in promoting the teaching of competition law in Chinese colleges and universities, especially law schools, and have also produced a certain academic influence. The *Anti-Monopoly Law* textbook, published by Peking University Press in 2011, is one of the earliest teaching materials on anti-monopoly law published in China, and has a certain innovation in chapter arrangement, style design and content of teaching materials. After it was widely praised, the publishing house published *Anti-Monopoly Law* (second edition) in

---

2   Decision of the Central Committee of the CPC on several important issues concerning comprehensively deepening reforms, adopted at the Third Plenary Session of the 18th CPC Central Committee.

2018. In view of the different needs of competition law teaching, I have also published a series of teaching materials such as "Competition Law" and "Competition Law Case Analysis" with Renmin University of China Press. The publication of these teaching materials has played a role in the cultivation of Chinese competition law talent.

I have not been a member of the Expert Advisory Committee for a long time, and I am keen to exercise my duty and contribute my best efforts.

How much law, how much economics and how much politics should there be in competition law enforcement?

I'm sorry that I don't have a very accurate statistic or number to answer this. But as far as I can see, most officials in China's antitrust law enforcement agencies have very good educational backgrounds as well as legal experience, and some have a good background in economic education or training, which is in line with the requirement for the professional competence of law enforcement officials in antitrust enforcement.

How do you balance work life and family life as a Chinese antitrust expert? Would you teach your daughter competition law at home?

The basis to balance work and family mainly lays that how we view the relationship between work and family, and perhaps different people are positioned differently. As for me, both work and life are very important. I love my work, and I love my family life too. I think they are equally important, and there is no way to rank as primary and secondary. They should not be in conflict. Instead, both should be in a relationship of mutual achievement. When you assign your time not only to work but also to the family, it may seem that that allows less time for work, which it may slow down progress a little bit, but life is a marathon: peace and good family life may allow you to work more quietly, calmly and rhythmically, allowing you to move forward more steadily and farther.

My daughter is currently a freshman student at the School of Economics of Peking University, and so far she has not shown any interest in competition law, or even economics. What she is interested in is art and history. She has a nodding acquaintance of competition law, mainly because that she was raised on the RUC campus, and there are so many competition law books on my office and home shelves for her to occasionally flick through, but I never seemed to tell her about competition law, not to mention any training for her. Maybe one day she'll invite me to tell her something about competition law. I would be very much looking forward to it, but maybe she will never make such an invitation.

What are your suggestions to young AML practitioners, especially female practitioners?

My suggestion is for reference only, specifically:

1. Love/interest is the best teacher, we need to discover the inherent charm of competition law. Because of the highly professional nature of competition law, irrespective of researchers or practitioners, it requires the investment of more effort, through the process of learning, research and application, and love/interest can make us happy.

2. Practising in the competition law field requires us to maintain the habit of lifelong learning. Working in this field requires not only rigorous professional training, but also continuous learning and uninterrupted reading and thinking, so can we identify, solve and deal with the emerging theoretical and practical challenges in the field.

3. Practitioners should have a broad vision and comprehensive professional ability. The competition law field not only needs the integration of theory and practice, but also a relatively deep understanding of economics, industry and market. Only in this

way can we make a relatively accurate judgment on the market competition situation and the impact of market behaviours. This will help us to have a better understanding, study and application of anti-monopoly law.

4. It is very important for women competition law colleagues to be confident. With the increasing number of female students at university law schools and schools of economics, there is a growing number of outstanding female judges, lawyers, legal advisers and academics in international and Chinese competition law. As long as we work hard enough, we will be confident enough about our professional abilities.

5. Of course, together with all these efforts, please also love your life.

Part II
In-house Counsels

Jeannine Bartmann
Allianz

Katrin Gaßner

Jeannine Bartmann is the Chief Compliance Officer of the Allianz Group and its parent company Allianz SE. Before taking over that position in April 2019, she was Deputy General Counsel and Head of Antitrust, IP, IT law and Digital Initiatives at the legal department of Allianz SE. In that capacity, she has written various publications and held numerous seminars and speeches on antitrust law in the insurance sector. Before joining Allianz in 2003, Jeannine was a salary partner in a German-based international law firm advising clients on competition and IP law matters. She is a German doctor of law and holds an Executive Master of European and International Business Law degree from the University of St Gallen, Switzerland.

Katrin Gaßner is a member of the Freshfields Bruckhaus Deringer LLP antitrust, competition and trade practice group. Her practice includes work on complex mergers (merger control and foreign investment reviews), international cartel cases, internal investigations and compliance management. She has developed particular experience in setting up worldwide compliance systems and audit procedures over many years, adapting them to the specific needs of the individual, in most cases multinational clients. She is also an active member of Freshfields' Global Investigations Group, advising in a number of current high-profile investigations in Germany. She also advises clients in the context of the EU Commission's sector inquiry into e-commerce topics and related follow-up investigations.

You joined Allianz in 2003. Tell us a little bit about your career at Allianz.

I joined the legal department of the parent company of the Allianz Group from an international German-based law firm, where I was a junior partner and competition law expert, and together with some of my colleagues had opened the firm's Brussels office. At Allianz, I was principally tasked to build up the Group's antitrust compliance programme. Three years after joining, I was given the leadership of a team in charge of competition, IP and IT law. In the years to come I took over a broader set of topics and responsibilities ranging from regulatory topics like outsourcing to advising digital initiatives as well as talent management in the legal function, while continuing to lead the Group's antitrust law practice and compliance programme. In 2017, a new General Counsel took over and I became his deputy. Very recently, I joined the compliance department at Allianz SE to assume the role of the Group Chief Compliance Officer.

Which incisive trends have you observed over the past 16 years, and what has had the strongest impact on the way you work?

Digitalisation has significantly impacted the way we work, in particular the way and speed legal advice is sought from and provided to the business. Whereas when I started we used to still write memos on specific legal questions, legal advice nowadays is much more solution-oriented and very often an integral part of the end product. At the same time, our internal customers' expectations regarding responsiveness and ability to understand the underlying business and IT processes have significantly risen.

Antitrust compliance is a major concern in all large organisations, and probably will always be. Risks have changed over time though. What are the main risks you observe currently, and how can global organisations make themselves fit for all challenges?

The growing antitrust scrutiny of competitors exchanging information, in particular in hub & spoke and signalling scenarios, has significantly increased the risk of non-compliance in the past, requiring additional training efforts and advice to be provided to various parts of the business. With digitalisation and the platform economy, we have now entered a new area of competition law challenges, which we need to address by closely following enforcement as well as legal trends, and by translating them so they can be appropriately considered by the business when developing new products or ways of operating. Enabling the first line of defence is key to addressing what lies ahead.

Authorities around the globe are subjecting digital transformation to increased scrutiny. E.g. in merger reviews, they try to predict the impact of consolidation on competition in general and on innovation in particular. Is this something you experience as well, and if so, how can an organisation prepare to manage this?

In Europe, this trend is clearly noticeable. In the US, however, not so much, so it seems that the transatlantic gap could be growing again. However, in European merger control assessments the innovation theory of harm is not limited to the digital economy but also affects more traditional industries, like seeds and pesticides. This development impacts on the predictability of merger decisions by the companies involved and illustrates the need for a holistic assessment of the innovation incentives for the merging parties as integral part of the feasibility study for a contemplated transaction.

Digitalisation has changed customer expectations in all business sectors. On the Allianz home page it says that there is much happening around Allianz in terms of digitalisation. What are the most important digital solutions Allianz is offering to its customers?

It does not seem appropriate for me to single out particular solutions, as Allianz is driving digital transformation throughout its entire business. A good example, in my view, is the Allianz Customer Model that strives for simplified, intuitive, comprehensive and harmonised insurance products, or Allianz Direct, the new European Direct Platform that has started selling harmonised online motor insurance products in different European countries, or Allianz X, that is identifying and investing in digital growth companies that are part of the ecosystems related to insurance.

As the economy becomes more digitised, companies increasingly manage large data sets, which of course also include personal data. Companies are more and more aware of the existence and the requirements of the new General Data Protection Regulation (GDPR), but many are still having troubles with the actual implementation within their company. Which aspects of the GDPR present the greatest challenges for your industry?

There are quite a few challenges, in fact. For me, one of the most complex ones is the right to be forgotten, whereby full deletion of personal data can be requested once it is no longer needed for the purposes it has been collected. In order to fulfil a corresponding demand of a data subject, a company needs to put processes in place that enable it to locate the data and delete it wherever it has been stored. Another one is the deadline for notifying the authorities of data breaches. Again, processes need to be set up that allow companies to identify the affected data and to get a full understanding of the circumstances of the breach, its consequences and appropriate remediation measures within this short period of time.

Finally, in a compliance context, a new challenge seems to develop regarding the interplay of the right of access to data and the company's confidentiality obligation towards whistle blowers under the new EU Whistleblowing Directive.

As an insurance company, Allianz of course deals and has always dealt with lots of personal data. Has the adoption of the GDPR generally raised the bar in terms of data security even for companies that have long been accustomed to dealing with personal data that customers trust them to keep safe?

In fact, the bar for data security is always rising. Whereas regulation (including data privacy laws and rules on critical infrastructures) is a major factor, the main driver for me still is cyber risk driven by digital transformation of businesses. However, investing in data security is not only about technology but also about education, as one of the top risks to data security in my view is social engineering.

Although data security generally provides the means to achieve proper data protection, the two may occasionally be at odds with one another. If a public cloud for example, ensures higher data security than a proprietary network of a company, storing personal data in the cloud would make perfect sense from a data security perspective but could give rise to concerns under applicable data privacy laws.

Coming back to the digital solutions Allianz is developing in a time of digitalisation, we assume that protecting trade secrets becomes increasingly important for Allianz also. According to the Trade Secrets Directive, which entered into force last year, a company will have to show that it has actively taken steps to identify and protect its trade secrets. If it is unable to show that such steps have been taken, the information may lose its trade secret status. Has this regulation and its upcoming transformation into national law changed Allianz's approach to the protection of business secrets?

I would not say that the directive has changed our approach but it has certainly triggered the review of the adequacy of existing processes in terms of the relevance of different types of information and know-how, adapting them where necessary, as well as documenting the overall concept of contractual, organisational and technical measures, in order to be in a position to evidence proper protection in case of violation.

The brand "Allianz" is listed in the 100 Best Global Brands Ranking with a brand value of US$10,059 billion, which means Allianz has doubled its brand value in the last 12 years. Could you tell us a bit about the legal steps Allianz takes to protect its brand in a sector where counterfeiting and product piracy would at first glance not appear to be everyday threats?

In fact, there are regular attempts by third parties to exploit the Allianz trademark when selling their products or services, in order to benefit from the trust that our customers vest in us. To protect Allianz and its customers against such abuse, we closely monitor the use of our trademark and consistently and vigorously defend it with available legal means. We also monitor trademark registers for applications that may create a risk of confusion and actively oppose such applications, as well as any use of confusingly similar trademarks. On the other hand, we make sure that, where possible, we obtain protection for our trademark wherever we do business.

What advice would you give outside counsel aspiring to better serve in-house clients with regard to digital services and digital work products?

I personally appreciate legal counsel with an in-depth understanding of the underlying technical processes combined with a thorough grasp of our industry and products, who provide solution-oriented – not just abstract – legal advice and are able to accommodate agile working environments.

And what general advice (if any) do you give junior lawyers starting at Allianz? Is it the same for female and male employees or is there a benefit in giving some "special" tips to either of them?

When starting as an in-house lawyer at Allianz, male or female alike, it is crucial to be genuinely interested in and truly understand our business. Therefore, I encourage young colleagues to ask questions until they have a good grasp of the matter at hand, even beyond the pure legal aspects. On that basis, they are expected to provide legal advice in form of feasible solutions, unmistakably stating what does not work while at the same time outlining available alternatives that do work.

Martina Maier
Siemens

Evelina Kurgonaite

Martina Maier was appointed Chief Compliance Officer of Siemens AG and head of the global Siemens Compliance Organisation in December 2018. Before this, Martina served as Chief Counsel Competition of Siemens. Prior to joining Siemens in September 2017, Martina was Unilever's General Counsel Competition. Before going in-house, Martina worked for 21 years (15 years as Partner) in international law firms in Paris and Brussels. She studied law at the Free University of Berlin/Germany and Public Administration at the Ecole d'Administration Public (ENA) in France.

Evelina Kurgonaite is the founder and chair of "Women At" (W@) – a platform that connects and promotes women professionals around the world. She also leads W@Competition – a W@ branch dedicated to women in antitrust. Evelina is the Secretary General at the Fair Standards Alliance. She previously served as Head of Policy Strategy and Legal Counsel at Samsung Electronics in Brussels. Evelina has 15+ years of experience in EU & competition law and public affairs. Having spent seven years in private practice – including at Sidley Austin and Morrison Foerster – she established and managed the European arm of global news service PaRR, part of the Financial Times group at the time.

You joined Siemens in September 2017 as Chief Counsel Competition, having previously been a partner in private competition law practice and building on 20+ years of professional experience in the field, including a stint at Unilever as a General Counsel Competition. Which aspects of your prior experience proved most relevant and useful for your role at Siemens?

My 20+ years of experience as a competition lawyer in private practice have been extremely helpful for my role in-house. First, I already knew the antitrust law and merger control law from several jurisdictions very well. I could therefore concentrate – since day one – on applying the law to the concrete situations that I was dealing with. Second, I was used to working on numerous different topics and with very different economic activities in parallel, and to quickly identifying and understanding the key characteristics of previously unknown topics and sectors. Third, for me it is easy to cooperate and work with external lawyers since I know their ways of working. As a result, I found the work, as such, easy to manage and could concentrate on learning how to operate as an in-house (in contrast to external) lawyer.

Within less than one year of starting at Siemens, you were promoted to Chief Compliance Officer of the company. Why did you accept this position?

I left private practice looking for new challenges outside of competition law. For me, competition law was only the known door into a new professional world. Seen from today, it was the right decision to start with leading competition teams. But since starting at Unilever, I took training on non-legal topics, such as finance, leadership and media, to widen my experience and skills.

Compliance was not really what I had in mind as my next career step. But now it feels right. I love what I do. Compliance is an area that gets more and more important for companies – and it gets more and more complex, in particular in fields such as export control and human rights.

In a company like Siemens, it is a key function with intense interaction with senior management, the business and other functions such as audit, finance and HR.

What key challenges have you faced in your prior and current roles, respectively?

In both roles, I saw my key role as helping companies with global activities to develop the business in full compliance with applicable laws and internal policies. Advising a company with global reach encounters numerous challenges, in particular with respect to dealing with evolving applicable laws, jurisprudence and societal expectations – which are sometimes contradictory and difficult to understand and to explain. In any case, communication is certainly a key challenge, since communication is needed within the company and externally: towards regulators, judges, journalists, NGOs and others.

One of the most debated European Commission decisions of the decade – namely not to clear the Siemens/Alstom transaction – was made last year. What is the key take-away that you would be able to share in relation to this major project?

I'm not in charge of merger control anymore and do not miss this field of activity.

With respect to the *Siemens/Alstom* transaction, I'm convinced that this prohibition reflects a missed opportunity for Europe to create a strong European company for international competition.

The deal could have been cleared by the European Commission with reasonable remedies. But the Commission's requests for remedies were such that the companies could not accept those requests without effectively compromising the deal.

The fundamental problem for the deal was the way that the European Commission is assessing mergers, namely with a backward-looking and data-based approach which does not match economic realities. One major problem we were facing in this deal was that the Commission takes only open markets into account when assessing market shares. In consequence, the Commission defined the "world market" as the world minus China, Japan and Korea since western companies cannot sell their products in those countries. This meant that Siemens and Alstom were seen as world market leaders – despite the fact that Chinese, Japanese and Korean competitors can operate and are operating around the world. Taking the sales in those countries into account, Chinese competitors are by far the world market leaders. And they can and will leverage their market power (combined with public financing and political support, e.g. through the Belt and Road Initiative) into other countries around the world. In this context, the decision of the European Commission to disregard those realities makes no sense from a business point of view.

Over the course of your career to date, what have been the biggest changes you have observed in competition law enforcement generally and merger control in particular?

When I started in law in the 1990s, competition law was a rather exotic field. EU merger control law was just introduced and only a small number of EU countries had national merger control laws. Today, competition is a mature field of law and nearly all countries around the world have their own national competition laws, including merger control. This also makes things very complex and often frustrating for companies operating internationally. While I very much welcomed the use of economic theory in competition cases, economics now has too big a place in this field. From my point of view, contemporary procedures and decisions, and merger control in particular, did not become better, but simply more complex and burdensome.

If you could go back to the early 1990s, when you had just completed your legal training at the European Commission's DG COMP, the Higher Regional Court of Berlin and the German Bundeskartellamt, what three key pieces of advice would you give yourself?

I would once again study macroeconomics and politics, in addition to law. I would also once again focus on languages and international experience. But in order to work in private practice, I should have qualified also in microeconomics or industrial economics, since competition economists are in more demand than competition lawyers.

If your daughter considered becoming a competition lawyer, what key considerations would you tell her to keep in mind before making up her mind whether that is a professional path for her?

I would recommend her to be open-minded and to see competition law as one option among others. Competition law today is rather mainstream. She should rather look for new areas with growth potential such as data protection, international trade, human rights and cybersecurity.

You have had a stellar career as a competition lawyer. How do you manage to stay at the top of your game for decades? What have been the main motivation factors that have kept you going at high speed for all these years?

Intellectual fun, interesting people that I meet through my job, family and good friends.

Sophia Real
Google

Carina Lange

Sophia Real works as competition counsel in Google's EMEA Competition Team and is based in Brussels. Before joining Google, Sophia spent more than 10 years working as a competition lawyer in private practice in London, Rome and Brussels, initially at Freshfields Bruckhaus Deringer and then at Baker McKenzie, where her practice focused on advising clients in relation to abuse of dominance and merger control proceedings. At Google, Sophia advises her clients on all aspects of competition law, with a particular focus on competition law issues in Germany.

Carina Lange is a freelance competition economist and strategic consultant. She works with competition lawyers and their clients on State aid cases as well as cartel damage claims, by providing the supporting economic and financial analysis required for these cases. Her special area of expertise is quantifying damages for indirect customers of cartels. Carina also works as interim or project manager, supporting private or public bodies with their strategic decision-making or by providing economic advice. Before starting her own business, AILI Consulting BV, Carina worked for PwC as economic and strategic adviser, as well as for economic consultancies in London.

Introduction

To kick off the interview, I would like to start with a personal question. You recently joined Google after more than 10 years of working in private practice. What was your main motivation behind your move from private to corporate, and to Google in particular?

The short answer is that I could not think of a more exciting role as a competition lawyer right now than to be working for Google. The slightly longer answer is that after 10 years of working as a competition lawyer in private practice in London, Brussels and Rome, I was looking for a new challenge, a role that would stretch me and where I could learn a lot. Thanks to a secondment as in-house competition counsel at a major pharmaceutical company I already had some idea of what life in-house involves, and that I liked the fast pace and direct exposure to the business you get as an in-house lawyer. So when the opportunity to join Google's in-house competition team came along it was impossible to say no – I get to work with some of our generation's smartest (legal) minds all while looking at competition law issues that go to the very heart of what competition law is about, something I find very rewarding.

Having spent some time getting acquainted with the new company and your new role, what are the main challenges and tasks that Google and other digital organisations are facing with respect to the future of competition law in the age of digitalisation?

The current debate about competition law and digital markets goes to the heart of what competition law is about and whether we need to adapt the existing legal framework to ensure it remains fit for purpose in the digital age (that some legal changes are coming our way seems inevitable). In fact, we are now starting to see the first proposals for competition law reform, e.g. in Germany.

With multiple jurisdictions taking a keen interest in all things digital, we are facing an increasing number of competition law investigations across the globe, including through sector inquiries and market investigations, often with overlapping scope. So there is a risk of fragmentation of decisions and approaches.

We could see different legal standards applied to digital players – with some countries potentially adopting far-reaching reform packages and others maybe adopting a more "wait and see" approach. At the same time, there is a potential for any legislative reforms to introduce considerable legal uncertainty – e.g. we may see the introduction of broad new legal rules based on novel theories of harm, as well as novel legal concepts.

On a more practical level, we are also seeing a trend towards increasingly lengthy and complex RFIs in the context of competition investigations. This is not surprising given the nature of our products and our business model. When it comes to issues like how to value and think about access to "data" for example, there is much work to be done (including by us) to build the right framework and evidentiary base for decision-making.

Those practical challenges aside, it is clear to us that rules need to adapt, and to be adaptable, to changes in society and technology. At Google, we think that constructive engagement is the best way to find solutions and dispel myths. Our experience has been that there are others in industry and government who feel the same way, which gives us reason to be optimistic about the future.

Abuse of Dominance (Article 102 TFEU)

In recent years, there have been many discussions about whether the traditional toolkit to control abusive practices, which is to (i) define markets, (ii) assess market power, (iii) analyse efficiencies and (iv) assess the overall effect of practices, remains fit for purpose when applied in the context of digital markets. What do you think are the main challenges faced by the classical framework to prevent abuse of dominance, when it comes to digital markets?

I think all of the elements of the traditional toolkit are challenging in the digital markets. For example, how do you define multi-sided markets and how do you assess market power in multi-sided markets? Similarly, how do you ensure effective competition enforcement in such a fast-paced sector, when competition investigations can often take several years from opening of proceedings to final decision (not even counting any appeal process in the courts)?

However, the size of the challenge should not be overstated. For example, I am not aware of a single case where the Bundeskartellamt was not able to proceed because it was unable to establish dominance. Even the criticism by the Düsseldorf Higher Regional Court of the *Facebook* case was not about the Bundeskartellamt's approach to market definition or its approach to the question of whether Facebook is dominant. Moreover, the *Facebook* case, which took three years, is a good example that swift enforcement action is possible using the existing toolkit.

The real challenge lies in striking the right balance between (i) strict enforcement of any conduct by digital players that hinders their competitors' ability to innovate and (ii) making it clear that digital players introducing innovative new products and services or new business models will not later be recast as anticompetitive. And that is a challenging task. It may not always be easy to tell when competition on the merits leads to the market exit of less efficient rivals or when such exits are due to anticompetitive foreclosure.

We should not be too quick to abandon the existing toolkit, since it provides an important framework for the legal analysis in competition cases. The first step seems to me to have a clear problem statement for how that toolkit has been shown to be deficient, and to work from that position on improvements in process and analytical tools.

In your position at Google, you also focus on German jurisdiction. Germany recently published the draft ministerial bill on the 10th Amendment of the German Act Against Restraints of Competition, also referred to as the "digital antitrust law". What are the main amendments for controlling abusive practices in digital markets? Do you think these amendments will be effective in bridging the enforcement gap of the previous system?

The draft proposals include a number of significant amendments that will allow the Bundeskartellamt to control allegedly abusive practices by digital players. This includes (i) a broadening of the concept of relative market power beyond SMEs, and (ii) the lowering of the standard of causation for abuse of dominance cases from "strict causality" to "normative causality". More importantly, the reform proposals also introduce a new legal concept of superior cross-market power.

Whether the proposed amendments will bridge the enforcement gap under the previous system is an interesting question, in that it presupposes that there is an enforcement gap under the current system. However, there does not yet appear to be any consensus on this among academics, lawyers or economists on this point. If there is an enforcement gap, it is not clear to me that this cannot be closed using existing tools. Take, for example, the proposed provisions on undertakings with superior cross-market power – we are not aware of any cases where the Bundeskartellamt could not intervene because it was unable to establish a dominant position. In fact, in its report the German Kommission Wettbewerbsrecht 4.0 (Commission of experts on Competition Law 4.0) recommended further economic analysis in relation to cross-market foreclosure, instead of immediate legislative changes.

What is clear is that the proposed changes, if implemented, will allow the Bundeskartellamt to intervene more frequently, and an earlier point in time than under the current rules. So there is a potential risk of catching potentially procompetitive conduct – which would appear to run counter to the lawmaker's objective of creating favourable conditions for the digital economy in Germany and Europe. However, much will depend on how the Bundeskartellamt applies the new provisions in its decisional practice, and what checks and balances the German courts will put in place.

I think that it's important that discussion of these kinds of difficult questions involves debate between industry, government and all affected stakeholders. My experience in Germany has been that all those involved are willing to engage in constructive and open dialogue, which I think is a good thing and reflects a desire by government to base their decisions on evidence.

Germany has become a pioneer in antitrust regulation in digital markets in recent years, especially when it comes to controlling abusive practices. What are the main differences between German and European legislation? What is your view on this fragmentation in the decision-making practice between different jurisdictions and authorities? How effective do you think it is?

While German competition law is in many regards similar to EU competition law, there are some subtle differences which can have a significant impact in practice. Taking the abuse rules as an example, Germany has a broader notion of market power and includes provisions sanctioning the unilateral behaviour of companies where they only have so-called "relative market power". Under EU rules, unilateral conduct can only be sanctioned where a company can be considered dominant. However, the German abuse rules can kick in below that level. The initial objective behind this was to protect SMEs.

So under existing rules there is already a risk of fragmentation in the decisional practice of the Bundeskartellamt and the European Commission. Germany is now looking to introduce some sweeping reforms to its competition rules. While competition law reform is a hotly debated topic in Brussels as well at the moment, there is an obvious risk of increased fragmentation depending on the specific changes to the existing sets of rules we will end up with in Germany and Brussels.

Fragmentation has a number of downsides. There is a clear risk of inconsistent decisions and increased costs with different jurisdictions potentially requiring different solutions to the same or similar problems, which then also potentially become more costly to design and implement. But even before we get there, fragmentation increases legal and business uncertainty, which not only makes compliance more challenging, but could potentially also lead to delays in product launches.

Based on my discussions in Germany and Brussels, I believe that these are issues that people are generally alive to.

Merger Control

Another anticompetitive concern when it comes to the digital economy is that dominant platforms might engage in strategic acquisitions, taking over relatively small start-ups in order to maintain their dominant position. As start-ups do not have large enough market shares yet, some of these acquisitions might escape the European Commission. In order to prevent this, Germany and Austria have introduced transaction value thresholds in merger control. What is your view on the effectiveness of such transaction value thresholds? Should similar rules be implemented at a European level?

Transaction value thresholds are meant to capture transactions that would typically not be notifiable to national competition regulators or even the

European Commission, either because the target company does not yet generate any turnover yet or because its turnover falls below existing merger filing thresholds.

When these rules were first introduced in Germany and Austria, it was clear that the purpose of these rules was to capture so-called "killer acquisitions". A concept originating in the pharmaceutical world, when applied to the digital sector it refers to large established digital players buying up nascent or smaller rivals with a view to integrating products and services which might otherwise have grown into direct competitors (by contrast, in the pharmaceutical sector, the term killer acquisition typically refers to a larger player buying a smaller rival and *terminating* their R&D projects).

From a merger control enforcement perspective, this raises the question of whether the integrated products and services would have fared better had the target company not been bought by a larger rival. A recent study commissioned by the UK CMA was inconclusive on what would have happened had a number of digital mergers been blocked. At the same time, both national competition authorities and the European Commission have reviewed a number of established digital players' acquisitions of smaller rivals under the existing rules (e.g. Google's acquisitions of Motorola, DoubleClick and Waze).

The absence of clear empirical evidence of an enforcement gap does not mean competition authorities should not engage in rigorous merger review, in particular in concentrated markets. However, it does probably mean that the European Commission Special Advisers' Report was right to conclude that no changes to the EU merger filing thresholds are needed at this stage, and that a better understanding of these types of acquisitions is needed before making changes to the existing legal framework – the experience with the transaction value thresholds recently introduced in Germany and Austria will be informative in that regard.

Conclusion

In a speech on the future of competition law from September 2019, the president of the French Autorité de la Concurrence, Isabelle da Silva, concluded that, "if 2019 was the year of Reports, let's hope that 2020 will be the year of Action!". Having discussed the challenges the current competition law is facing with respect to the digital economy, what are your recommendations on the main actions competition authorities should take, going forward?

There is a fear that long-running competition investigations are rapidly outpaced by changing technologies. The seven-year long *Google Shopping* case is sometimes used as an example of the slow pace of enforcement action. To counter this issue, there are some suggestions (including in Germany) to simplify or speed up the overall length of proceedings, e.g. through reversing the burden of proof, making do without written statements of objection in certain cases and making it easier for competition authorities to impose interim measures.

And yet, not all cases in digital markets have been this slow – e.g. the Bundeskartellamt's *Facebook* case, which, although involving complex digital technologies and a novel theory of harm, managed to go from case opening to reaching its conclusion in just under three years.

So I would say that swift enforcement is possible under existing rules. Attempts to speed up the length of investigation, including through an increased use of interim measures, should be carefully weighed against the need for thorough and evidence-based competition investigations, even in fast-moving technology markets, and the need to avoid sanctioning conduct that has an overall positive or neutral impact on competition.

As I mentioned previously, I do believe that it's natural and appropriate to reflect on how rules should evolve in changing markets, not just digital markets – issues relating to, say "data", cut across many of the industries that we think of as more traditional. No rules sit in a vacuum. Whether they are fit for purpose has to be a function of what society expects from technology at a particular moment in time.

These are tough questions to grapple with. I would encourage competition authorities investigating issues in digital markets to involve us early on in the process. We have had great experience with NCAs doing that, including in France. Such a collaborative approach, e.g. through more frequent calls, meetings (including workshops led by technical experts rather than lawyers) has considerable benefits for both sides. It allows competition authorities to better understand our sector, the business models of digital players and their products and services, which then allows them to focus on what they consider to be the key issues and to use targeted RFIs to gather further information. For digital players, this reduces the strain on the business and gives them a better insight into the authority's thinking and possible concerns, and how they could be addressed.

Emily Smith-Reid
HSBC

Sandra Potlog

Emily Smith-Reid is Deputy General Counsel at HSBC. She splits her time between two roles: general counsel support to the Global Retail Banking business; and being Global Head of Competition Law. She also sits on the Group Legal Risk Executive Committee, which oversees legal risk management across the whole organisation. Prior to HSBC, Emily was at British Telecom where she led teams handling major competition investigations, litigation and merger control. While at BT she also spent three years working outside of legal, in business roles in new product development and corporate strategy. Emily originally trained and qualified into the Antitrust, Competition & Trade team at Freshfields, working in their London, Washington, DC and Singapore offices.

Sandra Potlog is Legal Counsel at Telefónica UK, Sandra's practice focuses on EU and UK competition law, advising on a wide range of antitrust and regulatory matters. Previously, Sandra was Managing Associate at DLA Piper, where she focused on regulated sectors, particularly telecom and life sciences, and Legal Counsel at Samsung Europe. Having obtained degrees in law from universities of Bucharest and Sorbonne, Sandra also holds an LLM in Competition Law from Queen Mary, University of London.

You are the Global Head of Competition Law in a major financial institution, leading global teams across a wide range of jurisdictions, where you encounter unique challenges within the framework of very specific competition law regimes. What are the main challenges to implementing a seamless competition risk mitigation programme across such a diverse legal landscape?

My current organisation is present in over 65 countries – and we are a universal bank with a highly diversified set of businesses and products – so yes, there are a fair number of challenges.

In this context, I approached the challenge of creating a global competition risk mitigation programme with a strong focus on identifying the biggest risk drivers (the ones most likely to cause major financial, reputational or customer damage if you get it wrong), looking for common principles of global application and keeping the level of cost/complexity to a reasonable level so that the whole thing is operationally sustainable.

At a principles level, I think there is a high degree of commonality between competition law regimes globally. I also believe that if you are aiming to upskill a very large global workforce on how to do the right thing, it is most effective to focus on the key principles – and to help them understand what those principles mean in their world. So I have actually found it more important to tailor the risk mitigation programme to reflect each of the business areas my team supports, rather than for different legal jurisdictions.

In terms of operational sustainability, it is no good building a programme that perfectly controls every nuance of law or risk in every country, if the complexity or cost of that is simply unmanageable or unreasonable. So whenever you are thinking about adding a new rule or a new control to a risk mitigation programme, it's helpful to check whether the operational cost of doing that – and the additional complexity you might be introducing to an already complex risk framework – is justified by a corresponding benefit.

As a female top competition law practitioner and a champion of diversity, what is your advice for young female practitioners beginning their career? How does your experience reflect on how you have built your team, for example on how you choose your team members and what features are you looking for in a competition lawyer?

I think it's hard to generalise about that because it really depends what the women in question want from their career. The best general advice I can give is: get an excellent technical legal grounding; try to get early experience of working directly with commercial clients (not just other lawyers); seek out diversity of experience – don't be afraid to experiment a bit; and focus on doing a great job whatever role you're currently in, but let people know sooner rather than later when you feel ready for the next challenge. Also, seek out mentors and/or sponsors from an early stage – many of the most successful people attribute part of that success to those who guided them or championed them along the way. Lastly, try to be yourself. If I think back, I spent earlier parts of my career trying to project a brand or an image that wasn't wholly me. Over the years I've become more confident to just be myself and I've realised that works a lot better: I am more effective and my relationships with people around me are better as a result.

These days when I am recruiting, I am looking for people who are interested in business and markets and what makes those things tick, and who are excellent communicators. Breadth of experience and intellectual curiosity and openness are also important qualities. Given the proven importance of diversity of thought to successful organisations, I am also consciously focused on how to build diverse teams of people who will gel together but also complement each other without being too similar. So if I'm looking to bring a new person on to a team, I'll be thinking about what new life experience, perspective or character traits they can add to the existing team.

Having started your career in private practice, what, in your view, is the biggest challenge for lawyers crossing over to the industry side? What advice would you give to a private practice lawyer aspiring to move in-house and become a trusted partner for the business?

I've guided a number of younger lawyers through their first transition from private practice to in-house, so I can offer a perspective on this beyond my own experience of making that transition. There are many challenging aspects, but I'll just pick out a few.

The first is what I would term immediacy and actionability. In-house, there is little or no buffer between you and the person (typically not a lawyer) who wants your advice. One minute you are sitting there working on something else, the next minute someone is on the phone or literally standing by your desk wanting your immediate advice on an urgent issue. So you're really thinking on your feet a lot, but also judging when you have to say you need more time to consider the issue.

Secondly there is no one in between you and the client translating the legal advice you are giving into what that means for them in their world, on their project. It's you who now has to make sure not only that you get the law right, but that you give your colleague advice they can actually do something with, like decide whether or not to go ahead with a proposed course of action, or what adjustments to make to mitigate any risks in a proportionate way.

That brings me to another key challenge, which is commerciality: seeing the bigger business or external market context in which you are advising, understanding the potential commercial/customer benefits of a given proposal and making a balanced evaluation of risk vs benefit and what the options are to optimise that equation. Good private practice lawyers do this well. But successful in-house lawyers need to do it even better.

Lastly, I think all really good in-house lawyers should ask not only is it legal, but is it right. So it's about building the credibility, trust and confidence within your organisation to do more than simply deliver legal advice and instead to partner with colleagues in helping to create sustainable and ethical growth.

At an earlier stage in your career you spent time in purely commercial roles, including product development and corporate strategy. How do you use the experience of these roles in your day-to-day work as Global Head of Competition Law? What has your commercial experience changed in the way you partner with the business and deliver the legal guidance they need?

That experience was pivotal for me. It gave me a much more hands-on understanding of how a business works (from R&D, to business-case development, strategy, finance, marketing, running pilots, P&L account management etc.) and of the types of pressure that people working in a range of roles in business routinely come under. When colleagues now come to me as a lawyer for advice, I'm much better able to understand the commercial context, the challenges they are facing and what it will take to really help them. I also ask better questions.

Crucially, the experience also put me on the receiving end of legal advice, as a client myself. It wasn't a great experience! I was frustrated that the lawyers were explaining the rules to me, but not in a way that helped me understand whether I could actually do what I was proposing to do: the advice wasn't actionable or practical. I learned a lot from that.

The Financial Conduct Authority (FCA) has recently applied its first ever fine as a competition law enforcer, analysing illegal information exchanges between competitors as a result of a leniency application. The FCA's Executive Director of Strategy and Competition noted that the FCA will act when markets that play a vital role in helping companies raise capital in the UK's financial markets are put at risk, and also touched on potential regulatory action against individuals. How do you see the FCA's role as competition law enforcer in the coming years and the level of its intervention?

There is no doubt that the FCA becoming a concurrent competition law enforcement agency greatly increased the likelihood that breaches of competition law in the financial sector would be detected and penalised. It is particularly well placed to spot breaches thanks to the self-reporting obligations for regulated firms, the market review work it undertakes and the intelligence that is available from its broader supervisory and financial regulatory enforcement functions.

Overall I have no doubt the FCA will remain highly focused on addressing anticompetitive behaviour as well as intervening in markets that it considers are not delivering effective competitive outcomes for consumers.

But the FCA has a broad toolkit and will often have a choice between using competition enforcement powers or other powers (e.g. under FSMA – the Financial Services and Markets Act 2000) which are arguably procedurally more attractive for it to use. Trying to run cases under both sets of powers in parallel is complex – so it will be interesting to see what choices it makes going forward about which parts of the toolkit to use.

PSD2 (the Revised Directive on Payment Services) is a recent piece of legislation with a major impact on the well-established financial institutions. Some have argued that it will end up opening the existing bank infrastructure to competition from fintech start-ups capable of providing financial services that are relatively cheap, easy and fast, thanks to smart innovations in areas such as artificial intelligence, machine learning, mobile payment and blockchain. The Competition and Markets Authority (CMA) in the UK has also been championing a more transparent and competitive banking environment. Against this industry-wide effervescence, how do you think established institutions should respond in order to stay on the right side of competition law?

Whenever the external market or regulatory environment changes, it is always important to reassess what impact that has on your business's legal risk drivers and whether you need to do anything differently to safeguard compliance going forward. In connection with the fintech and open banking developments you're asking about, one obvious thing to do is to think about what impact this is having on the types of third party your colleagues are talking to, partnering with or buying from – and whether that raises new compliance questions or challenges. Beyond that, it's not my place to provide a route map for financial institutions in general – they can (and will) consult their own lawyers!

We should keep in mind that competition law risk is just one relatively small piece of the much bigger risk picture for established financial institutions in this context. They are grappling with fundamental questions like what a successful business model will look like in future, how best to focus their own investment in innovation and how to remain cost competitive.

My next question is related to the previous one – a big part of PSD2 links into big data, which seems to be on the agenda of more and more competition authorities across the world. How do you expect the competitive landscape in the financial services sector might change as a result of the increased access mandated by PSD2? Are there any lessons for other industries where data might be seen as a barrier to entry or at least as a key factor of competition?

I think it's very likely that when we look back 10 years or so from now, the introduction of PSD2 and other "open banking – style" initiatives in various countries will be seen as a key inflection point in the development of competition, choice and innovation in the financial services sector. I don't think that necessarily means we will see big established players being marginalised, but it is driving a lot of change. I also think this is one area where the EU has been fairly world-leading. The timing of these regulatory changes is key: it's at a time when the development of enabling technologies like cloud computing and artificial intelligence make possible new propositions and business models that can take advantage of the regulatory landscape.

Given that we haven't yet really seen how PSD2 will impact on the competitive landscape in financial services in practice, I think it's a bit early to be talking about lessons for other industries to follow. One thing you can certainly say is that the cost and complexity to regulators of designing the European PSD2/open banking regime – and then to industry of implementing it – has been huge. Governments or regulators thinking about mandating more open access to privately held data pools in other industries should consider very carefully things like: what problem are they trying to fix, or what policy aim are they pursuing; what will be the (intended or unintended) potential impacts on incentives to compete (including to acquire data); are there risks and trade-offs to take account of in areas like privacy and security; and overall what is the strength of evidence that the benefits of intervention will outweigh the costs.

Financial sector regulators across the world appear to increasingly warm to the notion of "regulatory sandboxes" as valuable opportunities for allowing small-scale, live-testing of innovations in a controlled environment (for example, under a special exemption or a limited time-bound exception). Some would argue this has encouraged dialogue between regulators and service providers and has supported innovation for the benefit of consumers. How, in your view, has this changed the competitive landscape in the industry? Is this an aspirational model for other industries in the following period?

I tend to agree this has been a healthy development. Where sandboxes are created, I think it's important that they are available not only to new entrants and smaller firms but also to more established firms that want to test innovative new products or services (as is the case in the UK).

Competition law has always had "consumer benefits" close to its heart, but over recent years this seems to have developed into a clearer point of focus for competition law enforcers, suggesting that competition is gradually becoming more and more consumer protection – oriented. Would you agree this is also the case for the financial services industry? And, if so, what do you see as the main challenges of an in-house competition lawyer in this industry when dealing with fairness in customers' treatment, as highlighted in recent papers from the FCA and the CMA?

At the outset, we should distinguish competition law enforcement in the sense of *ex post* actions for breach of the laws against anticompetitive practices or abuses of dominance, from the types of intervention that are aimed at fixing perceived problems with the competitive process in a given market. Both can be influenced by consumer protection agendas, but the latter more so than the former.

I think authorities – certainly in the UK but also in a range of other countries and regions – are becoming more focused on the *outcomes* that markets are producing for consumers and not just on whether there appears to be anything wrong with the *process* of competition in the more traditional sense. This seems to stem at least partly from much wider concerns in society and among politicians/governments about unequal distribution of wealth and benefits among the general population – the sense that there are large sections of society that have not shared fully in the benefits that market-driven competition in the economy can bring.

There are then wider underlying policy questions like: whether you think competition law should focus on consumer welfare or total welfare; whether the litmus test of an effectively competitive market is that benefits (e.g. access to low prices and innovation) are distributed evenly across the population; or whether it is sufficient that those benefits are accessible to all or most consumers (even if they are not in fact accessed by some of them). On the latter question, you might accept that a degree of uneven distribution (e.g. in the form of price or service-quality differentials that are not cost related) is not problematic provided that the differential is not too great, or if those who are deemed to be "missing out" are not in that position because they have particular vulnerabilities that are being exploited. I think we are at a really interesting point in the cycle where a number of authorities around the world – including the FCA and CMA in the UK – are actively engaging with these kinds of policy questions.

We often focus on the points of tension between competition policy and consumer protection, but there can also be positive reinforcing effects. I think Rod Simms of the Australian Competition and Consumer Commission explains that well when he points out that when consumer protection interventions are aimed at ensuring consumers are well informed and not misled, they become an essential part of the process of healthy competition because they help ensure the demand side can engage effectively in making choices that keep the supply side on its toes. But when intervention motivated by consumer protection objectives reduces choice or scope for innovation, it is important to evaluate very carefully and honestly the trade-offs involved and the potential adverse consequences for dynamic competition.

Turning more specifically to the financial services sector, since the financial crisis – and even before – there has been a strong regulatory focus on consumer protection. So it isn't surprising that competition policy in the hands of a financial regulatory authority like the FCA would be influenced by that agenda.

In terms of fairness, I think this is at the same time a hard principle to argue with and a hard principle to apply in practice. The main difficulty is that it is inherently subjective. So it is challenging to translate what principles like fair competition or fair pricing actually mean a firm can or can't (or should or shouldn't) do in practice. This isn't a wholly new challenge for the financial services industry in the UK, given we have been working with the regulatory principle of "treating customers fairly" for some time now and can draw on experience of how fairness is interpreted in that context.

Looking at the future of the in-house legal environment, between budget constraints, innovations in process automation, and an increasing workload which can easily divert attention from the bigger picture, how can the legal function in a company work strategically to add value and support business objectives?

It's obviously critical for lawyers to understand the commercial strategy and goals of the organisation they support and to partner with colleagues in the rest of the organisation to achieve them (both the short-term annual operating plan or quarterly results reporting-driven goals and the more medium to long-term strategic goals). A lawyer is most likely to be viewed as credible and trusted – and therefore involved at an early stage – if they are perceived as understanding the wider commercial context, goals and challenges, and as part of the team who can help colleagues find solutions.

Adaptability is also increasingly key: for example when supporting teams building new digital channel propositions, lawyers are likely to need to adjust to very different ways of working than they are used to, to fit in with the "agile" development methods those teams use.

You can often add significant value by finding time to step back and focus on emerging risk identification and on giving proactive, practical guidance on how the organisation can get ahead of those emerging/horizon risks. This is particularly important in industry sectors that are undergoing, or are under threat of, significant disruption and change – whether driven by technology, regulation or other factors.

Where possible, the legal function can also play a wider role that takes it beyond giving legal advice and mitigating legal risks. Where an organisation aspires to uphold high ethical standards, a culture of good conduct and to build revenue/profit streams that are sustainable, lawyers can be well placed to help in constructively challenging and guiding not only on "is it legal?" but also on "is it right?".

Auraellia Wang
Google
Wendy Thian

Auraellia Wang is Senior Competition Counsel for APAC at Google. She has been in practice for almost two decades, first in private practice and more recently, in tech. She advises on all aspects of competition law arising in the region for Google. Auraellia is an advocate for mindfulness in business. In her work she implements more compassionate ways of working in a real and tangible way, thereby increasing welfare as well as productivity. In her spare time, she teaches meditation, enjoys time with her children on the beach and plays the violin and piano.

Wendy Thian is part of Baker McKenzie's Global Antitrust & Competition practice. As knowledge lawyer for Asia Pacific, she oversees the group's knowledge strategy and initiatives for the region. Wendy is an experienced competition lawyer and has practiced in Australia and Hong Kong. She previously led the competition practice at another large law firm in Hong Kong and was part of the management team that established the Hong Kong Competition Commission. Wendy has a broad practice with a focus on TMT, financial services, supermarkets and airline industries, and has assisted clients on cartel investigations and in securing merger clearance and exemptions from competition authorities. She also managed investigations in a wide range of sectors as a former senior enforcer within the Australian Competition and Consumer Commission's mergers branch.

You look after all of Google's APAC competition law matters, having joined the company after 10 years in private practice, and you have also worked in London and Washington DC. Tech firms today are some of the highest valued companies in the world, and the global business and regulatory landscape is much changed since you began your legal career. Competition enforcement and scrutiny of tech firms have also become increasingly complex over this time. How has this evolution shaped your role at Google?

I count my blessings every day that I am in this job. My role entails overseeing Google's Asia Pacific (APAC) competition law matters, encompassing not only tasks traditionally associated with the role of a lawyer but also beyond that. Suffice to say, there's never a dull day!

I should mention at the outset that all views expressed here are my own and not that of Google.

Since day one at Google, over six and a half years ago, I have witnessed the steady increase in the number and complexity of the matters we handle. As the size of the company grew and its range of products expanded, so have the complexity and quantity of the regulatory hurdles. And all of these developments aren't taking place in vacuum – we are really witnessing a greater seismic shift in the landscape of competition – where we see governments querying the validity of their policy objectives and the sufficiency of competition laws, general changes in societal attitude towards so-called "big tech" and increased concerns beyond traditional competition factors.

These changes have required me to develop an entirely new set of skills that I would not have needed in a comparable role 10 years ago. Far gone are the days when one simply advises on how competition law principles apply to factual scenarios. Instead, as an in-house competition lawyer interested in doing the best job one can, one must now be well equipped to read the trends and implications of the latest developments in competition law, policy, politics, and the extent of media influence in that country and beyond. And to do this well, one needs to cultivate a deeply open mindset in order to compute a vast range of input, and in turn, to make the best strategic determinations.

This multifaceted way of looking at competition issues really adds to the excitement of my work. On the other hand it also means that there are more factors to weigh up and perspectives to consider. At the company we have tremendously talented people who are subject-matter experts in Asia Pacific and beyond. To me, doing a good job requires me to communicate well so they know what I need, and to have good skills to elicit the relevant information and insight. It goes without saying that with a diverse group of individuals there are bound to be differences in views – this is healthy. In such situations I always adhere to the guiding question: what is the optimal way forward for the company? This has enabled me to unite internal stakeholders – we can always arrive not only at what I believe to be the optimal outcome, but also experience the process in as positive and collaborative a manner as possible.

The past decade has seen unprecedented developments in APAC, with the majority of jurisdictions now having sector-wide competition laws in force. The region has also become a hotspot for the digital economy. Established enforcers including Australia, China, Japan, Singapore, South Korea and Taiwan have expressed clear intentions to actively examine issues relating to digital and data-driven markets, though have yet to follow related major decisional practices in Europe. What is your general take on these developments and how have they influenced your interactions with agencies over recent years, including those that are in the capacity-building phase?

Having been in Asia for over 15 years now I see how much competition law regimes across the region have evolved in unique ways. I see the shift

– a healthy one – where more and more Asian regulators are starting to step forth and speak with pride and conviction of their laws and cases, and share their thoughts on policy.

This shift means a few things. One cannot simply transpose arguments that were prepared for the European or US agencies and expect that they will satisfy APAC agencies. Increasingly APAC agencies are building their own understanding and developing case law specific to their laws and policy concerns. If one does not take these developments into account, one does risk missing opportunities for advocacy – or more seriously – calibrating risk incorrectly.

Amidst all of these changes I have found it of critical importance to communicate effectively. Specifically, for us to be in a position to successfully communicate our position to regulators, it is pivotal that internal stakeholders understand this new landscape/risk calibration in order that they can contribute and allocate resources accordingly.

This has been a steep learning curve for me – particularly as APAC regulators became active unexpectedly in some cases. For example, the ACCC's wide-ranging digital platforms inquiry was one of the first of its kind in Asia – and in my view, showed that the scope and nature of the ACCC's agenda has expanded. I needed to not only come to grips with that change in regulatory stance, but also to learn to communicate it to my internal stakeholders effectively, in order to get the resources and support I need.

For agencies in capacity-building phase – I think they are worth watching closely to know what their latest thinking is, and what they are inspired and influenced by. The plethora of academic conferences and publications, and increasing participation in supranational organisations such as the ICN and OECD, and cross-national education efforts by leading competition enforcers, mean that these agencies are also quickly climbing the learning curve, and should not be underestimated.

In a region with such local divergences in laws, market conditions, degree of regulatory transparency and policy objectives, what do you see as critical to building trust and constructive engagement with competition authorities that are increasingly collaborating and learning from each other?

Trust is critical when engaging with regulators. In fact, trust is the foundation for all communication.

This starts with critical self-assessment on the part of companies, asking the questions: how are we understood in the world? How much goodwill do we have? For this to be a useful exercise the company needs to adopt a culture of true open speak, and to speak without fear. I have seen many companies over the course of my career suffer from the cultural error of fear – fear of speaking out, fear of standing up. Much is lost by this collective fear of speaking up or being unpopular. If a company does not have full information about its weaknesses because of a culture of fear, that will ultimately be reflected in interactions with regulators.

Having conducted a truthful and as correct as possible assessment as to how much trust the regulator is likely to have in the company, the next question is, how do we build trust?

There are many ways of building trust. A good place to start is by putting yourself in the shoes of the other person. This is not just lip service. I've observed this in practice where, for example, a regulator asks certain questions that may be seen as an overreach of jurisdictional powers, and companies and advisers react negatively to not only the questions themselves, but to the regulator. It is in this common human emotional reaction that we lose the opportunity to truly understand what the regulator is seeking to do and understand. Granted, there are times a case officer may be driven and ambitious, but there is always a good reason; when one examines the questions deeply and without the interference of irritation, one will always glean insight into the regulator's mindset, and be better prepared to respond.

I see trust-building as a series of interactions, and each interaction is cumulative. By interaction I don't just mean in-person meetings, but every single touchpoint between the regulator and the company or its advisers. Every request for information is a touchpoint, as are dawn raids (as unwelcome as they might be) and chats at conferences.

As I sit in Hong Kong and cover APAC, I cannot be at all meetings or calls that take place. I have to delegate heavily (and I'm still learning!) to my teams and outside counsel. I place a great, great deal of importance on cultivating my internal and external teams, as they are an extension of the company. I think it's critically important that those who represent you are on the same wavelength as you in terms of how you approach an issue and how you present the company. By wavelength I don't just mean legal acumen and expertise – that is already a given – but compatibility of your advisers. To give an obvious example – if you hire an adviser who is known as a hard-nosed negotiator and you are dealing with a market study where such skills are not perhaps required, you have to ask yourself whether you have hired the right person for the job. Even if you believe your adviser is on the same wavelength as you, and you can trust them to present the company and the issues in the way that you believe to be optimal for the company, one must never get complacent that they will automatically continue to do that.

With my internal teams I take great care in communicating my views and reasoning with them, even though it takes time and energy. I feel it to be mutually beneficial – they get the opportunity to understand where I'm coming from and to share their views, and we can always converge to a satisfactory point. This is a very resource-intensive, but also a deeply meaningful and joyous part of my role. This is how I grow as a mentor and manager, and how my team members expand their ability and confidence.

Related to the previous question, given the number of highly active and diverse jurisdictions in your remit, how do you manage Google's engagement on the same or related issues and the risk of different and potentially conflicting outcomes? What are your day-to-day challenges?

It's indeed challenging to recognise the commonalities in what is motivating certain lines of inquiry from regulators, and also to be carefully focused on the country-level considerations that are likely most important for a regulator.

It can be difficult to gather the knowledge from engagements all over the globe and to reflect them in our cases, especially since similar inquiries may unfold in parallel. This is logistically demanding but also requires constant reflection on what has been learned, even before the conclusion of a matter. To achieve the best outcomes for the company, where our obligations are as much aligned as possible globally, we need a constant information feedback loop.

To power this feedback loop effectively, communication skills are vitally important. They are needed to manage internal expectations as to timing and the bounds of what product changes are acceptable given regulatory developments. I train my team to be clear in communicating the feasibility of deliverables so that we are consistent and aligned in this message. Flexibility and generosity are also vitally important – understanding that everyone in the company is working across many different sets of goals and demands, of which competition hurdles are just one set. When we can effectively communicate to a team working in one jurisdiction the effect on their work of a decision or development in another jurisdiction, in a spirit of flexibility and helpfulness, we can mitigate some of the difficulties that come from having such a complex set of engagements.

There has been debate over how traditional competition law enforcement fares in the assessment of digital markets. Regulators and policymakers worldwide are increasingly looking across borders to explore how to adapt existing frameworks and improve cooperation to address interrelated concerns around competition, consumer protection, privacy and media/advertising. Is there opportunity for all stakeholders to participate more transparently in such discussions, including beyond the usual analytical framework?

Certainly many have said that we are in a totally different time now when it comes to how we think about competition law vis-à-vis digital platforms. And there seems to be some recalibration of the role of the State versus private and consumer interests. Competition law has had a lot of attention, but it's not the only area, a prime example of another area is privacy.

I think these are important issues and they need to be considered carefully. For many years, regimes around the world pursued deregulation and actively encouraged each other to deregulate. And now the trend seems to be to question the sufficiency of competition law when it comes to digital platforms and to move towards an *ex ante* model of enforcement, which to me is a dramatic shift in approach. I do think that any such shift should be preceded by a robust and principled debate in full public view, where all stakeholders – including companies and consumers – can participate and feed-back on policy shifts that will affect them dramatically.

Competition law is a relatively small and highly specialised field, particularly within the broader in-house community. Women also tend to be under-represented in the tech sector. Can you share how you have developed your support system, especially in an increasingly fast-paced and high-intensity business environment?

Support is absolutely vital in this profession – which is cut-throat and dynamic. I consider myself extremely fortunate to have so much support these days. It was not always like this – I did not have a mentor as such when I started out in London, nor when I moved to Asia.

How did I find so much support now, when none seemed forthcoming in the early days of my career? What shifted for me was my perspective – the way I saw myself and the world. This shift came from my training in what is now popularly known as "mindfulness" – or, more accurately, the science of consciousness. I began my study seriously over eight years ago, and it is paying dividends in all aspects of my life, including my work.

Through this training, I came to see that it was my perception of myself and everything in the world that determined the quality of my existence, including my satisfaction level at work. This might sound a little abstract, so let me explain more. Part of this training is to become mindful – or conscious – of one's unconscious patterns of thinking that block one's potential, including potential to develop in one's career. Through practice – which includes deep meditation and cultivating wisdom and awareness – I developed awareness of destructive inner-wiring that stopped me from getting what I need at work, be it opportunities for advancement or support.

This negative inner-wiring is not unfamiliar to human beings – in fact we have all gone through the gauntlet of conditioning and many of us suffer from these negative streaks, such as excessive self-criticism and self-doubt. As a profession, lawyers experience an extremely high level of negative wiring and, as such, lawyers have overtaken dentists with the highest rate of suicide of any profession in the US. This is sobering information.

With training, I have been able to chip away this negative wiring. I came to understand and see that when I operate from such an unkind place of over-criticism and self-doubt, I was actually feeding into fear – fear of not being good enough, not smart enough and so forth. And when I am in fear, I am actually not delivering my highest potential. Fear constricts and at times, paralyses. I also cultivated the understanding that letting go of fear doesn't mean that one becomes sloppy – instead, one learns to approach work from a place of love – which is this feeling of pure flow, enjoyment and excitement. When one approaches work from this place, one takes ownership in the work, tending to it with great care and excitement, and it is not only outcome-orientated, but also process-orientated. That is something I strive to be.

Once I'd let go of enough of these fear-based negative streaks and learned to embrace work with love, I found myself open to so much more. I became more open to receiving feedback – positive or negative. Letting go of negative streaks means you become more positive – and it makes it so much easier to build bridges when you are positive. I found that support came my way in all sorts of ways – people showing up at the right time, giving me honest feedback, guiding me to new routes and ideas. It is truly incredible.

And this goes both ways – nowadays I see it as a responsibility to ensure that I nurture all those who work alongside me and with me, to support them and to help them to evolve and not be run by these internal negative streaks. This virtuous feedback loop is what life is truly about.

What are some of the initiatives and projects you have found most rewarding over the course of your legal career so far?

I am an advocate of bringing much-needed change to the modern-day workplace. This is an initiative I started when I presented my paper "ChangeMakers" at the International Section of the American Bar Association in October 2017.

For too long, we have been too caught up in the always-on and over-achiever culture, not truly realising that it is costing us in terms of wellbeing, which then impacts efficiency and effectiveness, to the detriment of all concerned. This change is urgently needed and we need to evolve into a compassionate and sustainable way of working.

Much of the underpinning of this current unsustainable system of working stems from fear. This fear is common to all human beings and it comes from our conditioning. In the context of work, we are conditioned to believe that if we don't work hard, lead the pack and excel at all times then we are not okay – that somehow, we will have failed, and such failure is simply unthinkable. This fear is very much about preservation of the self, and does not take account of greater goals. In our brain chemistry, this fear-based conditioning has become so entrenched that we have come to mistakenly equate fear of failure with that of the caveman survival instinct.

This fear of failure can seemingly drive us, but in truth it actually costs us greatly as it is dysfunctional. As this fear is self-serving, it stops us from having clarity and integrity to see what needs to be done in order to advance the interest of the project and of the company. It also cripples us, preventing us from standing up for what is true and the rightful thing to do. It does not enable us to access our innate talents, for fear blocks and constricts – when we are in fear we are busy defending ourselves, covering up the fear with anger or frustration, our precious energies cannot be used to resolve the issue at hand. Fear also stops us from accessing our creativity, as fear puts a lens of constriction on us as we seek alternative solutions. And, of course, when we are in fear, we feel awful and stressed-out. Over time, it costs us mental, emotional and physical wellness. This is a cost companies are increasingly recognising to be undesirable.

In short, fear stifles us from excelling, and creates much havoc on our wellbeing. It is smart business to root out a fear-driven culture and replace it with a compassionate and sustainable culture.

In order for this shift to happen it requires change in different directions.

It calls for an inner shift for each of us, to remove the fear-based way of relating to the world, to a place of no (or at least less) fear. It also calls for us to care beyond our own survival and interests, and expand to care for others: our teams, colleagues in other teams, the company – and beyond. To make a fundamental shift, we need to embrace a new way of working – and that is to work with love, not fear. When one works from the place of love, one is filled with excitement and joy with the attitude of openness to feedback, to learning and to surprises! Operating from love at work also means being receptive to new ways of looking at an issue with no fear, and being open to the unknown and the unquantifiable. At the end of a long working day, one may feel physically tired but energised and enthused at the same time, as opposed to the fear-based way of working where one is not only physically tired, but deflated and despondent.

We also need strong leaders who endorse and uphold the importance of this inner shift at an individual level. Leaders need to also change the way they manage people – to move away from fear-based mentality to this love-based model. Managing people in this way requires the manager to gain deep insight into the individual, to help them move out of their fear-based constrictions and limitations and to flourish and grow.

This inner shift will gather momentum when more and more of us progress to this new way of being.

Is this new model of working possible? Absolutely. I practise and implement this compassionate work culture wherever I can. For example, in my meetings and calls I endorse and implement an open-speaking culture, and I discourage self-interested rivalry. I spend time cultivating this common understanding with the key stakeholders I work with – everyone I have spoken with has been incredibly receptive, and there is an amazing cascading effect. For big meetings where there are strong divergent forces and personality clashes, I might get the group to do breathing exercises at the outset and throughout meetings. These tools are so precious and they really do work!

The challenge lies in being able to be consistent – can one be consistent in the face of great difficulties and pressure? Can one persist when people do not behave in the highest way possible? And this is a moment of choice, do we choose the old fear-based way, which we know leads to a suboptimal outcome, or are we game enough to try the way of compassion? I choose love, I choose compassion, for it is the only sustainable way to proceed, and is benevolent.

You meditate. How does it contribute to your life and your work?

I've been a serious daily meditator for over eight years now, and the benefits are enormous – beyond what the human mind could have known.

Meditation is increasingly incorporated in the wellness and ad hoc welfare programmes of many corporations and law firms. Meditation has tremendous benefits that are widely reported – and include improvements to our physical health, stress levels, alertness, concentration and wellbeing. It is a smart, and business-orientated decision for companies to incorporate it into the workplace.

There are many types of meditation. For the fundamental inner shift, to move away from fear-based belief systems that hamper our performance, meditation needs to be deep, deliberate and focused. It also needs to be of sufficient regularity and duration to enable the rewiring of our brains. We must abandon the well-established neuron pathways of outdated fear-based patterns and beliefs, and build new pathways that lead to higher, life-affirming and benevolent thought patterns.

Take a moment and examine carefully whether these fear-based patterns and beliefs will actually help us: do they constrict us, keeping us in fear, or do they open and liberate us? Do they keep us small, or do they allow us to expand into the unknown? Do they give us room to blame others and not evolve, or do they allow us to be honest with ourselves and take responsibility? Recognising these outdated patterns and beliefs is only the beginning to shifting paradigms: we actually need to retrain so we no longer revert to these familiar thought patterns.

Meditation also enables you to attain mastery over your thoughts, emotions and physical responses. When one has a sufficient level of mastery it is possible to quiet the mind at will, and when the mind is quiet and not racing from one errant thought to another, one can become more intuitive and holistic in approach. I have found that my practice has moved so far from just applying black letter law to facts – I need to have such a deep understanding of so many factors: the nitty gritty of the issues at hand, the facts and their optics, the regulator's mindset, the brain space of the case team etc. There are no clear answers anymore. Instead, I have to exercise a high level of intuitive seeing in order to see the bigger picture, so I can drive the strategy effectively. I credit my meditation practice in being instrumental in helping me navigate very tricky situations.

Meditation can also be used to bring teams together, and to achieve certain goals. For example, I often get teams preparing for a big project or meeting to meditate and visualise positive outcomes. At all-day meetings I break up the day with regular short breathing exercises, to prevent the onset of mental and physical fatigue. These focused meditations do not need to be long – even when brief they are deeply energising and they also enable people to work together effectively.

Companies would do very well to introduce meditation programmes for their staff – it is smart business.

Working in the legal industry around the world, across multiple jurisdictions, have you seen a conscious shift towards pioneering and supporting women? In what way could this shift be further endorsed?

It's a great question, and a huge one to do justice to.

By and large, women are under-represented in the senior echelons of business, and the law/tech space is not an exception.

I see an imbalance in our current system. Other than the systemic fear that I spoke about earlier – we also measure success on patriarchal values. As a woman who joined the workforce in the early 2000s I accepted the system as it was, but have always found it incongruent with my being. It was not until later that I realised that women have so much to contribute to the world, to business.

The Dalai Lama has said that,

> According to our biological nature, we are animals that thrive in an environment of compassion, caring, affection, and warm-heartedness … The essence of compassion is the desire to alleviate others' suffering and promote their wellbeing. Women are somewhat better than us men when it comes to developing these inner values such as benevolence, patience, forgiveness, generosity and tolerance.

It is these attributes that can bring together divisive forces, win hearts, and nurture teams for the benefit of all. It is also these traits that can enable us to move into the new paradigm of work based on compassion and love.

We will not get more women into senior positions of influence through fighting with men or the system. We need to first accept the system for what it is without blame or seeing it as wrong. Specifically, we need to also take responsibility for clearing out any internal belief system that devalues or weakens women in some way. For example, do we – men and women alike – harbour any belief that a woman is only likeable if she appears to be apologetic for being strong or firm? When something goes wrong or not according to plan, is there a habit for women to self-blame unnecessarily rather than focus precious energy on resolving the issue? Is there an innate discomfort when a woman speaks highly of her accomplishments or her ambition?

I do see efforts at companies to support women. Unconscious bias is one such example. We still have a long way to go before this imbalance is addressed, but we are starting to wake up, and that is a good place to be.

Part III
Lawyers

Silvia D'Alberti
Gattai, Minoli, Agostinelli & Partners

Barbara Veronese

Silvia D'Alberti leads the antitrust team at Gattai, Minoli, Agostinelli & Partners. She has practiced Italian and EU competition law for more than 20 years. She has extensive experience of counselling and representing clients before the European Commission, the Italian Competition Authority (ICA), EU and Italian courts on complex merger cases, behavioural investigations on restrictive horizontal and vertical practices, cartels, abuses of dominance, consumer protection investigations and antitrust damages litigation. Silvia has been the partner leading the Italian antitrust group at Allen & Overy for 18 years and has also worked for five years at the ICA as an official and case handler. She holds an LLM from Yale Law School.

Barbara Veronese is a partner at Oxera. She has advised private and public sector clients on national and EU-wide matters (competition and mergers, damages litigation, and regulation), including, BT, ENI, EasyJet, Metro, Marionnaud, SEA Airports, Ofcom, Sky, Telecom Italia, Toyota, Vivendi, YOOX and multinationals in the chemical, pharmaceutical, logistics and consumer goods. Dr Veronese has in-depth expertise, drawing from cases in a number of EU states in broadcasting and communications, including auction matters and spectrum policy. As an experienced econometrician she has also advised extensively on the quantification of effects and damages. Recommended in the GCR competition experts from 2013, she graduated from the University of Venice and holds a PhD in Economics from the London School of Economics.

There is a huge debate nowadays on whether digitalisation, platform intermediation, collection of data and the ability to quickly process data will require major changes in competition law enforcement. There is no general agreement on this (yet?). Alongside competition, we seem to talk a lot about unfair competition and consumer protection. We can take a long-term perspective on all this thanks to your experience.

First of all, how does this period compare with the moment Italy adopted a national competition law? What were the expectations back then?

When Italy adopted the national Competition Act back in 1990, the debate focused on fairly different priorities: for decades, a collective culture based on elements other than competitiveness, individual risk and competition had prevailed in Italy. The mentalities of both companies and individuals were full of expectations placed more on the State than on the market. We were at the dawn of liberalisation in the energy, telecommunications and transport markets, and the newly established Italian Competition Authority (ICA) had the difficult task of educating both economic operators and consumers on the new competition rules.

The first interventions did not only concern former legal monopolies. Sectors that were less concentrated but characterised by a high propensity to collusion (concrete, freight forwarders, public businesses) have had to change – to their amazement – their deeply rooted habits.

Did we see "competition" as closer to "unfair competition" back then?

"Unfair competition" and "competition" at that time were two completely separate categories. On the former there was already an important track record of our civil court judgments and the aim was to keep the two areas completely separate, in light of the different underlying interests: protection of competitors in private unfair competition cases and protection of the public interest of competition in public enforcement proceedings.

Are we going to protect companies a bit more, and not just the competitive process?

We cannot exclude the development, in the years to come, of a trend aimed at protecting companies, not only the competitive process. This arises, for example, from the growing focus given in the debate on competition in Italy to topics that (going beyond strict enforcement by the ICA) aim at protecting companies from the distortions to which they may be subject in the context of competitive dynamics in a European and global context. I am thinking, for example, of the speech made by the President of the ICA, Mr Rustichelli, on the occasion of the ICA's Annual Report presentation in July 2019, which was largely devoted to the competitive consequences of the lack of harmonisation of tax regulation between Member States of the European Union. It was a programmatic speech, which expressed the desire not only to protect competition but also to promote it. These are, of course, powers that are alien to those of national competition authorities (NCAs), which can only use their own advocacy powers in this matter while awaiting further action at European level.

Do you believe we are about to change (or that we should change) our paradigms in the application of competition law, e.g. reversing burden of proof, stretching the concept of dominance into "strategic status/gateway" and so on? And/or do we mostly need to revisit regulation where competition enforcement has insufficient clout?

I do not think it is necessary to change the principles underpinning competition law or the paradigms of its application, neither at EU level nor national level. We are certainly witnessing rapid changes in the economic environment that European companies, especially in strategic sectors, are facing, such as the increasingly penetrating competition from large global players, as well as the transition from an industrial economy to an economy based on intangible assets.

However, even if the context evolves, the principles governing competition law are unchanged. Maybe the role of NCAs and the European Commission is becoming more complex from a technical standpoint.

With regard to requests for regulatory intervention, I believe that these should be limited to those cases in which antitrust proves to be an insufficient tool for dealing with critical issues and avoiding distortions of competition.

Do you believe there have been years/ways in which EU antitrust has been Americanised? Or else, is the US becoming more a European-type enforcer on some fronts?

Although EU and US have two broadly similar systems of competition law that share a commitment to maintaining competition in the marketplace and which employ similar concepts and legal language in making antitrust decisions, differences in social values, political institutions and legal precedent have inhibited close convergence.

As a result, in recent years, the US Supreme Court has been narrowing the antitrust rules that the US enforcement agencies and courts apply to dominant firms and monopolists, while the European Commission (as well as some European NCAs) has heavily fined dominant firms engaged in abusive behaviour. As to cartel enforcement, the situation changes completely. Neither the European Commission nor the majority of NCAs may apply criminal sanctions, while the US Department of Justice has sent many individual cartel participants to jail.

In general terms, then, and from a global perspective, a gap has recently arisen between European antitrust activism (just think of the fines imposed on Google) and a more permissive US antitrust position.

In early 2019 we had the Italian High Court pronouncement on the right of defence and lack of impartiality of the ICA. Do you sense that there is a plan going forward and/or could you tell us if there have been better practices in ensuring the right of defence that we could revisit now to address concerns (e.g. see Stefania Bariatti's position on this topic in this book).

From a formal point of view, the procedure before the ICA is covered by a number of guarantees offered to the parties to the procedure. I am thinking of the right of access to documents, the right to an oral hearing or, as regards the institutional structure of the ICA, the formal separation between the investigation units and the Panel. In fact, however, as the cited Italian Constitutional Court's judgment has pointed out, in their practical application the guarantees referred to above appear to be totally insufficient to represent an effective tool for the protection of the rights of the defence.

It would be desirable to reform the investigation procedure, aimed, among other things, at guaranteeing full access to the documents of the proceedings – or at least to those with a key role in the reconstruction of the prosecution charges – at any time and not, as often happens, only at the end of the investigation phase when the statement of objections is sent to the parties. Also hearings before the ICA Panel should have the object of "restructuring": million-euro sanctions, of a substantially criminal nature, higher and higher by virtue of frequent recourse to parental liability, require that a full and actual adversarial approach be established during the hearing phase, in which ICA investigation units, Panel members and the parties to the proceedings can speak in detail on the merits of the evidence gathered and not be confined, as it happens today, to a very brief presentation (not exceeding 15 minutes for the parties, frequently without the possibility of reply).

Finally, I believe that reform of the timing of the final phase of the investigation proceedings is particularly required. While the duration of the entire investigation is equal, on average, to two years, parties are given a short time limit for the exercise of their defence and the submission of the final pleading (usually 30 to 40 days) after the statement of objections is served. This is far too short a time limit to guarantee a truly level playing field.

Merger control is back into the spotlight. Do you think the rules should change again in Italy? Have you got views on whether, as some argue, we've been too lenient at DG COMP?

The issue of merger control has been made even more topical by the recovery after the crisis of the national and cross-border M&A process – globally, in Europe and in Italy – and by evolution in the assessment of the effects of this process in a profoundly changed market context, also due to the importance of the digital sector and its major operators. Especially in digital markets, particular attention is paid to the role of start-ups and the risk of their early exit from the market through acquisitions by established companies.

At European level, the debate to recalibrate European implementation practice and competition rules in the field of mergers has become particularly interesting and heated, following the position lastly expressed at the beginning of February 2020 by representatives of the French, German, Polish and Italian governments, who strongly requested that the EU Commission for Competition should define a precise and effective action plan to tackle potential abusive behaviour in the single market of economic operators outside the EU. The discussion is focused on interesting proposals like that to revive and strengthen the role of the Advisory Committee in merger control procedures, and the request for cooperation between DG COMP and industry specialists from other DGs for a comprehensive and complete approach to the relevant markets is very interesting and welcome.

As regards Italy, from 2013 onwards, we have witnessed to an extremely significant reduction in the number of mergers assessed, a problem that has not been fully resolved even with the reduction of the second turnover threshold (from €50 million to €30 million) set by the 2017 Italian annual market and competition act. It is therefore necessary to find solutions that will allow for a more extensive verification by the ICA. Making the obligation to notify dependent on when certain turnover thresholds are exceeded is not always the most appropriate solution. In this regard, the final report of the Italian Big Data Fact-Finding Survey also called for a reform at national and international level that would allow antitrust authorities to assess mergers capable, since their start, of restricting important forms of potential competition (such as acquisitions by large digital operators of particularly innovative start-ups, known as killer acquisitions), regardless of the turnover data of the companies involved.

Class actions take two. Italy has a new law. What is your assessment?

Certainly, we are currently witnessing a change. The approved reform shifts the discipline of class action from the Consumer Code to the Code of Civil Procedure and provides that class action is an instrument of protection available to anyone (business or consumer) who has a right to compensation for contract and tort liability damages relating to the violation of homogeneous individual rights.

The most significant innovations are (i) the claimant's right to join the action after the final judgment and (ii) the provision of reward payments to be paid by the losing party to the joint representative of the members and the lawyers who assisted the applicants. Such last provision, in my view, alters the merely compensatory function of damages and encourages litigation. This appears to be in contrast with the proposal for a directive on collective redress, now being discussed at European level, which requires that the system of remuneration for lawyers does not create incentives for litigation.

The main critical issues for defendant companies seem to be related to: (i) the extension of active standing and the magnitude of rights involved,

(ii) the rules facilitating access to evidence for those who have the right to damage claims and (iii) the extreme difficulty of assessing *ex ante* the risk of such litigation, especially considering the possibility of joining the action after the final judgment, which creates uncertainty for the defendants and jeopardises the very possibility of reaching settlement agreements.

Is private enforcement crowding out more public enforcement?

Private and public enforcement, in my opinion, go hand in hand. Private actions before national courts should remain complementary to the public enforcement of competition law.

The threat of private litigation acts as a strong deterrent and would lead to a higher level of compliance with competition rules. Moreover, increased numbers of private actions would further develop a culture of competition among market participants, including consumers. In addition, private litigants may take action against infringements which the Commission and NCAs would not pursue, or do not have sufficient resources to deal with. Lastly, if rights are properly protected in court, public enforcement can focus on priorities in the public interest, as it has also been recognised by the ECN+ Directive.

Where do we stand? Is the system "having it all" now or there are unwanted consequences?

Both at national and European level, we witnessed a general increase in litigation for damages.

Speaking of Italy, the binding nature of ICA decisions in civil proceedings and the presumption of damage in cartel cases are elements that will contribute to a further increase in follow-on actions. Likewise, the passing-on rules and relevant presumptions will facilitate actions, above all on the part of indirect purchasers. Conversely, there will probably be fewer follow-on actions in non-cartel cases closed by the ICA with commitment-based decisions.

With reference to the new rules on class actions, and as a result of the new provisions concerning disclosure and presumptive evidence in cartel infringements, we can expect to see an increase in collective actions on the part of consumers, small and medium-sized enterprises and public administrations.

Certain aspects characterising antitrust disputes – such as proving the damage and establishing the criteria applied in quantifying damage – and proving the causal nexus, will continue to be a source of complexity in antitrust litigation. Nevertheless, the Italian act that has implemented the Private Enforcement Directive has incorporated in national law a clearer and more developed legislative framework for private antitrust actions in terms of procedural rules, judge's expertise, speed and predictability. This, combined with the judicial costs (still lower in Italy than in most other major EU Member States), may play an important role in increasing the number of damages actions, thus contributing to the effectiveness of the second pillar of antitrust rules enforcement.

Women and careers, "*quote rosa*" (reserved seats in boards), Goldman Sachs moving against (no IPOs for) companies with male-only boards. "The Times They Are a-Changin'"?

It would be really desirable. I am part of a generation that has fought hard for equality and has always encountered a lot of resistance.

I am not a fan of quotas, but I must admit that quotas have helped to open access to boards. This is not enough, though. The problem is how boards get formed and how you fill vacancies. It might be unconscious bias. However, when there is an opening, usually men try to involve men who are part of their network rather than attracting women and socially diverse directors who may bring diversity of thought and ideas. This means that women have to engage men to reach equality – and not only at board level! Italy is still a country where women are left alone to take care of the family business and have very little support from the State and civil society at large. Men must play a role in this respect and help women to achieve their professional goals sharing the family business responsibility.

I worked hard to become a partner of a big law firm but I am sure I did it thanks to the daily help of my husband, who not only shared the loving care of our daughter with me, but has always pushed me to do more and to exceed my limits.

Stefania Bariatti

Chiomenti

Sabrina Borocci

Stefania Bariatti is currently full professor of Public International Law, Private International Law and International Insolvency Law at the School of Law of the University of Milan and of Counsel Former Partner at Chiomenti, where she practices primarily Italian and EU competition law, international insolvency law, and international litigation. Since December 2017 she is the chairperson of the Board of Directors of Banca Monte dei Paschi di Siena and since May 2019 she is the Vice-President of A2A. She has been the chairperson and the member of the board of other Italian listed companies, universities and non-profit entities. Since 2014 Stefania represents Italy in the Governing Council of UNIDROIT.

Sabrina Borocci leads the Italian Antitrust practice of Hogan Lovells and is a member of the firm's EU-Global Antitrust practice. She is also a professor at Bocconi University. Since the beginning of her career, she has been advising clients with a focus on Italian and European antitrust, competition, and merger control law. Sabrina focuses on cartel and abuse of dominance investigations in various industries and merger control filings.

Constitutional Court and ICA

The recent pronouncement of the Italian Constitutional Court (Corte costituzionale) concerning the Italian Competition Authority (ICA) has drawn a lot of attention in and out of academia. The ICA had argued that it carries, inherently, the role of a judge when it imposes fines, and in this function it is independent and impartial just as much as is a judge. The Constitutional Court had a different opinion: it ruled that ICA lacks impartiality, that it cannot be considered a judge and that it cannot therefore raise a challenge of unconstitutionality before the Court. Concerning the specific decision, was the outcome in line with your expectations?

Yes, it was indeed. Day-to-day experience shows that the ICA is not a judicial authority that applies the law impartially, but rather is an agency which – at the same time – (i) carries out investigations (through the DG Competition (DG COMP), *Direzione Generale per la concorrenza*, composed of officials and staff), (ii) authorises the Statement of Objections (prepared by the same DG), and (iii) adopts the final decision (by the Collegio, composed of the president and two commissioners).

The Corte costituzionale's approach is fully in line with that of the European Court of Human Rights in *Menarini*, where it was implicitly acknowledged that the ICA is not an independent and impartial court established by law.

And what about the specific reasons that were adduced to conclude that the ICA lacks impartiality?

The Corte costituzionale expressly stated that within the ICA there is no "clear separation" between its investigative and decision-making functions and bodies, due to the existence of a functional link between the Secretary General and the President.

Moreover, according to the Corte costituzionale, the ICA – in its entirety – pursues a specific public interest (the promotion of market competition) and, therefore, is not neutral vis-à-vis the addressees of its decisions.

The absence of a clear separation between the investigative and decision-making bodies of the ICA, as well as the lack of neutrality, is reflected in the structure of the ICA proceedings. Just to mention a concrete example: during the whole proceedings the Collegio is constantly informed by the investigative bodies on the status of each investigation and is required to verify that the Statement of Objections is not manifestly ill-founded, before authorising the Direzione Generale per la concorrenza to send it to the parties. In other words, the Collegio is aware of, and to a certain extent, controls, the activity of the investigative body. By contrast, the parties' statements of defence (which often amount to thousands of pages and are accompanied by elaborate economic analysis) are submitted only five days before the final hearing before the Collegio, which then adopts the final decision in the following few weeks or even few days. This timeframe seems frankly insufficient to allow the commissioners to carry out a deep analysis of the parties' arguments and to impartially balance the different interests at stake. If one considers that the administrative judge – to whom the ICA's decisions are challenged – usually takes more than one year to decide, it is clear that the swiftness of the analysis by the Collegio is mainly due to the fact that it already knows the position of the staff pretty well (and possibly it shares its findings, since it authorised the service of the Statement of Objections to the parties) and that the time dedicated to examining the positions of the parties is somewhat compressed.

What are consequences of this decision? Shall the structure of ICA be reshaped?

The message of the Constitutional Court is clear: the ICA lacks impartiality. Even if the consequences of the decision are difficult to predict, I hope that it will trigger a lively debate on the opportunity to reshape the proceedings at the ICA and the relationship between the Collegio and the staff, particularly in view of the probable increase of fines level which will follow the transposition of EU Directive No 2019/1.

Right of Defence and Proceeding in Front of the ICA

Broadening the scope of the question, there is a lively debate on the nature of the public antitrust proceedings and whether there is a full right of defence in public enforcement. For instance, in Italy, some argue that a few sore points include:

– delayed and partial access to the case file;
– a lack of debate on the set of proofs;
– insufficient depth at the hearings, taking into account also the tight calendar setting a few days between the submission.

What is your view on these specific issues and do you see real criticalities?

I definitely see real criticalities. Indeed, full access to the case file – particularly to leniency applications – is granted only upon service of the Statement of Objections, i.e. about one month before submission of the final brief. The latter, indeed, will be made on a set of evidence acquired by the other parties at a very late stage, with the risk that they might not be able to build a strong defence.

There is also a clear lack of debate on the set of proofs: also due to procedural timeframe constraints, economic analysis submitted by the parties is considered only superficially. Further, the accuracy and reliability of the leniency applications are often taken for granted, to the extent that the leniency applicant sometimes does not even submit a structured final brief to support its arguments.

Finally, during the final hearing there is no real debate, as the parties are granted a very limited time to present their defences to the Collegio (in the range of 10–15 minutes).

Again, all the above would not seem fully proper in proceedings which may lead to hundreds of millions of fines and may trigger multi-million actions for damages, jeopardising the company's reputation and sometimes its own existence.

Industries More Affected by Antitrust Enforcement

At times it seems some industries are more subject to public enforcement and that this goes in waves: construction and cement, telecom, pharmaceuticals. Would you subscribe to the view that there is some cyclicality of intervention in certain economic areas?

I agree, but I think that the ICA's intervention is mostly driven by the market itself and by other EU antitrust authorities' ongoing activities rather than by the ICA's own will. Just to mention an example, the current ICA's interest in digital markets and "big data" comes from both the disruptive changes that markets are facing and the ongoing investigations before the EU Commission and other European antitrust authorities. It is clear that the ICA follows European antitrust trends as it does not want to "miss the boat".

This being said, it is worth noting that, following the implementation of Directive No 2019/1, the ICA will be empowered to set its own intervention priorities.

Is banking and insurance one of the frontiers now? After 10 years of restructuring and state aid focus, is now this industry the eye of the storm with a blend of privacy, data issues, disruptive digital models?

At the moment the banking and insurance sectors appear to be appealing for the ICA only in terms of the repression of unfair commercial practices. However, as mentioned before, privacy, data issues and disruptive digital models are definitely at the frontiers of antitrust law, regardless of the specific industry in which they may emerge. Potentially, in fact, no industry today seems to be immune from these topics: data-driven technologies, indeed, can be present in any industry, from food to retail, from transport to banking and insurance. It remains to be seen where competition issues will emerge and how European and US antitrust authorities will deal with them.

Antitrust and Policymaking

Is antitrust enforcement a legitimate instrument in the toolbox of industrial policymaking? Some recent decisions seem to be more policy than antitrust oriented: is it in your view one of the roles of the competition authorities to deal with public policy?

I do not think that public policy should be included in the interests to be considered by antitrust authorities, especially in cartels and abuse of dominance cases. Public policy is indeed something blurred and debatable by definition, and making room for it in the ICA's toolbox would just bring more uncertainty and even more discretion to a proceeding that, as seen, is purely "vertical" (i.e. oriented by a specific public interest).

A different issue concerns whether antitrust enforcers should take into account other interests, i.e. the need to create EU and/or national champions in order to better compete internationally with undertakings that are subject to less stringent rules and requirements.

Antitrust and "*matière pénale*"

From the Menarini case onwards there is a need to reconsider the antitrust as a "matière pénale". Recent cases in front of the ICA have shown massive fines due to pure parent (objective) liability. This may encounter some important limit in the national law and principles. In Italy, for instance, criminal liability is "personal".

How do you see these frontiers to be adapted to the national legal systems?

Parental liability based on the mere shareholding, as applied in the very recent ICA decision, is indeed something new to our system. In previous cases, in fact, the ICA always backed the "100% control" approach with a supplementary analysis of the actual involvement of the parent company in the contested illicit activity of the subsidiary. In very recent cases, instead, the ICA simply relied on the "Akzo presumption" without making any further investigation on the effective responsibilities.

This approach is foreign to the Italian system, which, as mentioned, does not admit objective liability.

I am rather inclined to believe that the milestones of domestic law should not be compromised by the application of European case law principles which are highly questionable. This has been already made clear in other jurisdictions such as Germany and France.

Verticals and RPM

After a summer wave of DG COMP cases (on a rather diverse set of goods which hardly suggest they were related product markets), should we brace for the return of resale price maintenance (RPM) clauses?

The interplay between vertical agreements and new features of distribution systems (online platforms, use of algorithms) is attracting competition authorities. In fact, as shown in a recent case, the use of algorithms can allow manufacturers to track resale price-setting and to intervene swiftly in cases of price decreases. Similarly, DG COMP is also considering whether systems of online price-matching are spreading prices imposed to retailers across a market, where other retailers use algorithms and automatically copy that price.

Would you subscribe to the view that issues related to vertical competition aspects have been unduly neglected by enforcers?

Yes, I believe that enforcers have unduly neglected vertical competition issues. Suffice it to say that the DG COMP decision in the case just mentioned, issued in 2018, is based on rules on RPM that had not been enforced since 2003.

Some companies took clear advantage of the enforcers' negligence: for instance, a renowned sports brand engaged in licensing and distribution agreements in breach of competition law for around 13 years without being discovered.

Probably, therefore, thanks to the growing interest in digital markets, and in particular in the use of algorithms, some illicit practices such as RPM will be assessed more seriously by enforcers.

How are vertical cases going in Italy?

Vertical cases are quite rare in Italy, and most of them have been closed with the acceptance of commitments. A recent ICA decision – concerning booking companies for taxi drivers and the alleged existence of vertical restraints – has been annulled by the administrative judge, also due to the fact that the ICA did not prove the existence of a parallel web of agreements. Another signal, probably, of a lack of interest in the topic of vertical restraints

DG COMP Role and Policy

Current or former most-senior economists seem to be calling for more attention, without falling into hysteria, on antitrust, merely based on traditional economic thinking and empirics. They see many pointers to under-enforcement. Professor Valletti has called for more attention on digital, Professor Motta, reviewing many economic studies, structural industrial indicators and other evidence, has taken the position that if firms are large, it is appropriate to have a reverse burden of proof for horizontal mergers. What do you make of it?

I do not know whether reversing the burden of proof for large companies would be in line with the principle of equal treatment and/or would be acceptable from a procedural standpoint. Moreover, as recently highlighted by Johannes Laitenberger, the EU competition law system is "made of durable principles". Reversing the burden of the proof in merger control review would openly contradict such character.

Merger control review should not be based only (or mainly) on market share. Innovation should play a significant role in enforcers' assessment.

In relation to recent merger cases, how does competition policy create a dialogue with public policy?

As I said before, the discussion is now focused on whether antitrust enforcers should take into account other interests, i.e. the need to create EU and/or national champions in order to better compete internationally. I tend to believe that the analysis should take into consideration the fact that markets' structure has changed in many fields due to the access to global competition by some emerging economies. In this scenario, the competitiveness of European undertakings might be frustrated by obligations and requirements that are designed to serve the objective of safeguarding consumers. The decision-making process should then try to meet the new needs and support the activity and expansion of European undertakings.

These concerns can be addressed by independent authorities, like the European Commission and national competition authorities, but their activity should be somehow guided by policymakers – as in the Italian "golden share" rules in the context of foreign acquisition of 5G networks – in order to avoid uncertainty and to guarantee that all the interests at stake are taken into due consideration.

Career and Women

You are not only one of the most reputable lawyers in Italy, but also a full professor in one of the most important universities and President of the Board of Directors of one of the most important financial institutions in the country. Very few women in Italy are in such roles while in other countries (US above all) boards, law firms and universities have an impressive number of women in leadership roles. What is your view? What are cultural reasons? What can be done for the future generations?

Women are struggling to reach equality in many countries, not only in Italy. If one looks at graphs and statistics, improvements towards equality are very slow almost everywhere. And when I say equality I mean a 50–50 situation. Quotas have helped to open access to boards, but it is just a starting point. Quotas at 30–40% make people think that equality is there, and that once that percentage is reached, it suffices. It does not. We must work and cooperate with men in order to reach equality through equal opportunities at all levels in any organisation.

Reasons for gaps vary from one country to another. In Italy women are often stuck between the care of children and care of parents, and have little or very limited support from the state in this regard. A new organisation of work that takes into account family needs would also make the difference.

What I see from my observatory as a professor of law is that girls are very motivated and often are better students than boys, let alone the fact that there are more female than male students. Female lawyers are still very motivated when they enter the law firm and they pursue their career with the same enthusiasm as male lawyers, but at a certain point they slow down and reduce their expectations. It may happen when they have children, but also earlier, when they marry or start a relationship. Women tend to believe that it is appropriate to dedicate more time to their sentimental and family life than to their professional growth. A balance has to be found, but the impression is that only women make a choice in favour of the former, rather than trying to balance the interest of all their "stakeholders".

What can we do for future generations?

1. Cooperate with men in order to share responsibilities at home and to get more support for pursuing our career, if we wish to have one.

2. Educate our sons to equality and equal opportunities, teach them to respect women. Their future partners will live an easier life (see point 1).

3. Educate our daughters to equality and equal opportunities and convince them that they are first-class citizens. Educate them in self-respect and self-esteem, the magic words to equality.

Sometimes, when I discuss these issues with men who are fathers of daughters, I also find it useful to ask them how they would react if their daughters, who have studied, graduated and entered the work arena, one evening come home saying that they have been discriminated because they are women, maybe in the same way as these men are discriminating against their female staff. These fathers are usually stunned, they never thought before in terms of the situation of their beloved daughters.

In your view, in which of these three areas is career development more complicated for a woman?

I have started my career as full-time academic and I have worked hard in order to become full professor. Children did not stop my career, but in academia it may be easier to reconcile everybody's needs. When I entered private practice in a big law firm I did not have to start from scratch, my competence and skills were recognised and I became partner quickly. However, I see that usually female lawyers have a longer path, and in order to advance they have to prove that not only they have the same skills as their male colleagues, but that they are better. If you look at statistics, the percentage of female partners in law firms in Italy and the UK is low and almost the same.

I do not believe that being the chairperson of a listed company is part of a career in the company, it is mostly the effect of the law on quotas, even if I have served in the boards of universities and other entities before the entry into force of the law. It is sad to say so, but it is true. If I look at the companies I have worked with as a lawyer or that I have come to know as a board member, women are left behind, but things are changing rather rapidly, mainly in big companies. The approval of sustainability goals, in particular goal no 5, is helping a lot in creating a virtuous circle.

Do you have the feeling some European countries have a long way to "real" equality?

I know the Italian situation, and I know that there is lot to do, I do not know enough of other EU countries.

Fiona Carlin
Baker McKenzie

Ethel Fonseca

Fiona Carlin is a Partner and Chief Executive of Baker McKenzie's EMEA+ Region. She is the former Chair of the Firm's Global Competition and Antitrust Practice comprising more than 320 lawyers in over 40 countries. Fiona has been listed in "The International Who's Who of Competition Lawyers" since 2009, and is among Global Competition Review's Top 100 Women in Antitrust. Fiona chairs the European Advisory Board of Catalyst, a non-profit organisation dedicated to expanding opportunities for women in business. She was a founding member of Baker McKenzie's Global Diversity & Inclusion Committee.

Ethel Fonseca is a partner at RBB Economics. She is described in Who's Who Legal as "an excellent economist" who is "very easy to work with". Ethel has extensive experience in merger assessment, having worked on many Phase II investigations raising horizontal, vertical and conglomerate concerns. Having specialised in applied microeconomics and econometrics during her PhD studies, Ethel has particular expertise in the application of quantitative techniques to the assessment of competition policy issues. Ethel has run training seminars in competition economics and taught at the Postgraduate Diploma/Masters in Economics for Competition Law at Kings College, London. Ethel is a member of the W@Competition Board.

The European Commission is currently seeking feedback to reform its Vertical Block Exemption Regulation and accompanying Guidelines. What would you expect to be the key issues for review? And would you expect any major controversies coming up from this review, in particular considering the approaches of national competition authorities with, for example, the Dutch Authority for Consumers and Markets having recently announced stricter enforcement of vertical restraints and officials from the Bundeskartellamt having made public statements about tighter rules on online sales bans?

I do not see any need for a radical overhaul of the Vertical Block Exemption Regulation (VBER) as such. As a framework, the VBER has worked quite well: it provides a 30% market share safe harbour for all vertical agreements, subject to a limited list of hard-core, prohibited restrictions. The VBER was designed to provide legal certainty and, by and large, it has.

However, there are issues that need to be addressed.

First of all, legal certainty in certain key areas (such as e-commerce restrictions, selective distribution and pricing/price recommendations) has been eroded by divergent enforcement on the part of certain national competition authorities (NCAs) and national courts. This is a matter of real concern. The Commission is aware of this and committed in the final report on the e-commerce sector inquiry to ensuring a more consistent application of the VBER through a strengthened dialogue with the NCAs in the European Competition Network. The Commission should go further and intervene proactively in national cases where the correct and uniform interpretation of the VBER is at stake. It can do that, for instance, by submitting amicus curiae briefs before national courts, reviewing NCA approaches well before the formulation of final decisions, and removing the competence of NCAs to apply Article 101 TFEU in specific cases where appropriate).

Secondly, there is the philosophical question of how detailed the accompanying guidelines should be, bearing in mind (1) that absent significant market power vertical restraints are ordinarily benign, and (2) the fast-paced change in market dynamics with the growth of e-commerce and the advent of further transformational technological change. Any revised set of rules must allow brand owners and retailers the flexibility to adapt to future changes, and to provide consumers with the seamless omni-channel experience they expect.

Finally, the importance of access to data, including sales and pricing data, and the need for brand owners and retailers to have informed discussions about that data should also be reflected. I would submit that the current approach to discussions about resale prices and resale price recommendations is unnecessarily strict, especially in the franchising context.

While competition authorities have historically pursued very few cases against excessive pricing, in the last couple of years a number of such investigations were opened by antitrust watchdogs around the world, especially in the pharmaceutical sector. What explains this trend? Has competition policy suddenly become the most appropriate means of dealing with excessive pricing concerns? And could there be risks associated with over-enforcement?

There has been a recent resurgence of excessive pricing investigations in the pharmaceutical sector with decisions in the UK, Italy and Denmark, and the pending *Aspen* case at EU level. These cases all concerned old off-patent medicines and I think they are outliers that do not presage any attack on the pricing of innovative medicines. Each EU Member State has a plethora of regulatory checks and balances designed to control the prices of new medicines. I think that authorities clearly understand that competition law intervention would have detrimental knock-on effects on innovation incentives.

In practice, the authorities can face significant hurdles in determining when a price is excessive or unfair. For example, in June 2018, the UK Competition Appeals Tribunal (CAT) set aside the Competition and Markets Authority (CMA) Decision regarding the alleged excessive pricing of phenytoin sodium by Pfizer and Flynn. While the CAT supported the CMA's findings in relation to market definition and dominance, it was critical of the CMA's assessment of the alleged abusive conduct. Specifically, it found that the CMA "did not correctly apply the legal test for finding that prices were unfair; it did not appropriately consider what was the right economic value for the product at issue; and it did not take sufficient account of the situation of other, comparable, products, in particular of the phenytoin sodium tablet". Could this complexity reduce the appetite of competition authorities around the world to engage in such investigations? We are awaiting the views of the UK Court of Appeal on these questions, which will be of interest even post-Brexit!

The European Commission faced intense political pressure during its investigation of the *Siemens/Alstom* merger, with the run-up to the prohibition decision catalysing the debate about the creation of "European champions". Indeed, a number of EU governments have proposed updating the EU's antitrust rules in order to facilitate the emergence of European industrial giants able to face fierce competition from, for example, the US and China. Are there any risks of reforming the EU Merger Regulation, in particular regarding the delineation of the wider public policy considerations?

The European Commission showed its independence by prohibiting the *Siemens/Alstom* transaction in the face of considerable political pressure to allow the emergence of European champions.

France, Germany and Poland subsequently published a joint manifesto calling for greater political input into merger control decisions, to counter threats from China and the US.

I worry that altering the balance in favour of "European champions" could have dangerous consequences in terms of the predictability of a rules-based system. I agree with the statement made by the heads of five Nordic competition authorities last summer that competition, not politics, should determine EU merger policy. Effective and transparent competition policy enforcement creates a level playing field in which more efficient and innovative industries can emerge and thrive.

I also agree with Commissioner Vestager that legitimate third country threats should better be dealt with through legal instruments other than the competition rules. Under the new Commission, I expect we will see increased recourse to trade defence mechanisms (such as anti-dumping measures and an expansion of foreign direct investment controls), to enable EU companies to better compete with third country rivals.

It is of course sensible to ensure that the merger control rules remain "fit for purpose", especially as markets and technology rapidly evolve. But most companies value the fairness and relative predictability of the current EU system. There is no sense that wholesale reform is needed, not least since other regimes look to the EU system as a model and we don't need more barriers and legal uncertainty in the transactional space.

With more than 100 countries now having obligatory premerger filing requirements, different substantive and procedural regimes can make a multi-jurisdictional transaction a complex and time-consuming process. What are the key challenges faced by companies and their external legal advisers when embarking on M&A deals which have a multi-jurisdictional element? To what extent do investigations by "experienced" authorities have knock-on effects on investigations by "younger" authorities, if at all?

Merger control law is indeed a global phenomenon. The level of active enforcement has multiplied around the world. We routinely file transactions in as many as 20 or 30 jurisdictions. Agencies are also increasingly imposing fines for failure to file and for implementing transactions in breach of their laws.

Navigating a global merger through this multi-jurisdictional mine-field raises a number of strategic and practical considerations. Similar challenges arise in managing foreign investment review regimes. The critical task is to front-load as much preparation as possible. Here are some of the key aspects to bear in mind:

- *the "timing challenge"*: merger control filings are typically the gating item to large cross-border transactions, particularly in Brazil, China, India and other jurisdictions with lengthy regulatory processes. It is essential to develop a merger review timeline in any cases likely to give rise to concerns, so that agencies are looking at the substantive issues (and potential remedies) at an appropriate time. Ultimately, you want to ensure that you have a clear road map so that the client's expectations are managed effectively.

- *the challenge of "divergent outcomes"*: having a core competition narrative for the issues in a case is fundamental. The substantive analysis can be advanced quickly across all jurisdictions if it is developed and understood centrally and then modulated specifically on a local/regional basis as needed. This also avoids potentially contradictory approaches being taken before different, but potentially cooperating, agencies.

- *the "value leakage challenge"*: where an agency has substantiated concerns, a remedy will typically be required. Having a well-thought-out global strategy before going in to the agencies can significantly reduce the risk of having to make too many concessions when negotiating remedies under time pressure, once the clock is ticking.

– *the "document burden challenge"*: agencies are increasingly relying on internal documents to assess the incentives of parties and the potential effects of mergers. In its review of *Bayer/Monsanto*, the European Commission reportedly required 2.7 million documents to be disclosed to it. Other authorities, such as the UK CMA, are increasingly demanding in their requests for internal documents, and are actively fining companies for failing to properly comply. Ensuring that document disclosures are complete, correct and understood before submission is critical.

– *the "gun-jumping risk"*: once companies sign a deal they typically want to get on with integration planning. Mandatory and suspensory merger laws require parties to "stand still" until the deal is approved by the applicable agencies. Careful compliance is required to ensure that the parties do not "jump the gun" – an infringement that has attracted fines of over US$300 million across 30 jurisdictions in recent years. This is likely to be a continuing trend. Allowing the parties to do as much preparation as possible without stepping over the line requires care and attention.

While, broadly speaking, competition authorities, and the European Commission in particular, have a strong preference for structural remedies, is it fair to argue that the bar is lower for non-horizontal effects mergers, where behavioural remedies have been accepted?

Non-horizontal mergers can give rise to considerable benefits (e.g. the elimination of the double margin) but occasionally concerns arise (such as foreclosure). It is true that the Commission has been willing to accept behavioural commitments in some sectors such as energy, media, technology and telecommunications.

We saw this in 2018 when it approved Qualcomm's purchase of NXP. Qualcomm made a number of behavioural commitments over an-eight-year period on licensing and interoperability. In the 2017 *Broadcom/ Brocade* decision, the Commission required commitments from Broadcom to protect third-party confidential information and to cooperate with other suppliers to guarantee interoperability between competing switch devices.

More recent public comments by senior Commission officials indicate that the wind may have changed. Behavioural commitments are difficult to monitor and agencies do not want to become sectoral regulators. The ICN Mergers Working Group recently analysed how NCAs assess vertical mergers and is looking at conglomerate issues, and the US has just issued Draft Vertical Merger Guidelines. So vertical mergers are back in the spotlight and the bar may be rising. In short, merging parties are well advised to plan proactively to identify structural remedies if contractual solutions fail to win clearance.

DG COMP's former Chief Economist, Tommaso Valletti, said at a conference in late 2018 that the European Commission should conduct more retrospective studies to determine whether it made the right decision on merger cases. How much insight can be extracted from a retrospective review? More generally though, could this signal an interest by antitrust watchdogs in *ex post* merger control regimes, allowing them to review potentially anticompetitive deals after they have closed?

Retrospective reviews should be welcomed. It is essentially a self-policing exercise: while such reviews can raise uncomfortable questions and may involve work for companies to respond to questionnaires, the process can provide valuable insights on how to improve the remedy design and negotiation process.

The European Commission undertook a retrospective merger review in 2005 that was broadly positive, but it did identify some areas for improvement in the design and implementation of remedy packages. It would be timely for it to repeat the exercise. The US FTC published its second retrospective study in 2017 (the first was undertaken in 1999).[1] The study examined 89 merger orders issued by the US FTC between 2006 and 2012, including those requiring divestitures, as well as non-structural relief. The report demonstrated that in the vast majority of cases the FTC's remedies practice did protect and restore competition. It also confirmed that structural divestments are particularly successful.

In 2019, the UK CMA commissioned the Lear Report which investigated the potential competition theories of harm to be assessed when evaluating mergers in digital sectors; whether the assessment in four digital merger clearance decisions was reasonable based on the evidence available at the time (*Facebook/Instagram*, *Priceline/Kayak*, *Amazon/The Book Depository* and *Google/Waze*); and whether the outcome of the decisions was detrimental to consumers based on the market evolution following the mergers.

The Lear Report made a number of recommendations: that the CMA improve the information available to it in order to analyse and define the counterfactual; look at a timeframe longer than two years when assessing digital mergers; use transaction value to identify those mergers which may warrant a more in-depth analysis; and better understand online advertising. When the Report was released, the CMA's CEO stressed that there should be "evolution not revolution" of merger tools in the digital space, but the CMA has since stated in its draft Annual Plan for 2020/21 that it is actively considering whether there is a need for changes. In my view, any such changes need to be approached with caution. *Ex post* reviews (a feature of some voluntary merger regimes, including the UK's) should be avoided as much as possible in the interests of legal certainty.

---

1   FTC, *The FTC's Merger Remedies 2006–2012* (January 2017) <https://www.ftc.gov/system/files/documents/reports/ftcs-merger-remedies-2006-2012-report-bureaus-competition-economics/p143100_ftc_merger_remedies_2006-2012.pdf>.

If 2017 was the year of innovation theories of harm and 2018 and 2019 were the years of concerns associated with "big tech" firms and digital markets, what should we expect from 2020?

I fear that 2020, much like 2019, will continue to be the year of political pressure for more intervention and rising populism. Big tech/big data, acquisitions of nascent competitors, high drug prices and the threat of China will continue to be popular themes. We are likely to see agencies beginning to take concrete steps to address these issues. The challenge will be to ensure that any new measures do not chill innovation and investment. It will be important for regulators to continue to take evidence-based decisions in a global political climate of increasing protectionism.

Sustainability and environmental issues are also, rightly, at the top of the agenda. Most sectors of the economy will be profoundly affected in ways that are not yet fully appreciated. Obviously, transformative initiatives are more likely to be effective when taken by a large part of the market. Greater guidance will be needed from competition authorities on the extent to which companies can legitimately cooperate to achieve broad societal goals without infringing competition law. This is likely to be addressed in the ongoing review of the rules on horizontal cooperation.

On a more personal note, having chaired Baker McKenzie's Global Antitrust Law Practice, you are now Chief Executive of the firm's EMEA+ Region and you also continue with your practice. Can you share any highlights of your stellar career, any work you are particularly proud of?

I'm proud of the work we did together, Ethel, for FedEx in the *UPS/TNT* transaction. I'm also privileged to work for many clients in the life sciences sector. It's a fascinating sector that faces many regulatory and political challenges and where the pace of innovation and the resultant benefits to patients is simply inspiring. Perhaps, most of all, I'm proud of the work I've been able to do in the Diversity & Inclusion space, within Baker McKenzie but also with organisations like Catalyst and

W@Competition. I've had many amazing opportunities to share stories and touch on the lives of a great many promising women and supportive men. The journey from promoting gender equality to a broader agenda of inclusion and belonging at an organisational level has been truly transformative for me personally.

Cani Fernández
Cuatrecasas

María Pilar Canedo

Cani Fernández is a Senior Competition and European Law Partner at Cuatrecasas. She is also, Council member of the IBA and non-governemental advisor of the European Commission and Spanish CNMC before the ICN. She was previously case handler at the European Court of Justice and Officer of the International Task Force Antitrust Section at the ABA. She teaches competition law at BGSE and TSE and European law at Universidad Carlos III, Madrid. She is consistently recognized as top practitioner in several directories in Competition and EU Law and ranked "Star Individual" in Chambers Europe and has distinguished her with the "Outstanding Contribution to the Legal Profession Award".

María Pilar Canedo is Member of the Board of the Spanish National Commission on Markets and Competition since July 2017. Before this, she was the president of the Basque Competition Authority for 7 years. She is a Professor of Private International Law at the School of Law of the University of Deusto (Bilbao, Spain) and has devoted her research career to European competition law. She has been visiting professor at several Universities all over the world; was the Director of an Erasmus Mundus Master and PhD on European Trade Law and holds a Jean Monnet Chair in Transnational Law.

You are partner of the competition division of Cuatrecasas, you have for many years coordinated the EU and Competition Division, and you have "done everything" in the field. How did you decide to devote your life to competition and become a competition lawyer?

I first became acquainted with competition law in 1982, at a summer seminar organised by then Professor Gil Carlos Rodríguez Iglesias at Granada University. I was in my first year at university (in Zaragoza), and I got a fellowship for this summer seminar in wonderful Granada. My boyfriend got the same fellowship, and we thought this would be a nice holiday week. But then I listened to Professor Michel Waelbroeck, from the Université Libre de Bruxelles, explaining some of the cases in the competition field that he had pleaded before the ECJ … Four years later, he was my professor at the Institut des Études Européenes (IEE) in Brussels. While I was completing my Licence Spéciale at the IEE, I was working at the Brussels office of six Spanish law firms that had decided to set up a Brussels branch following Spain's accession to the EEC (as it then was). I was dealing with anything related to community law, but vividly remember a case related to Spanish legislation on the obligation to respect minimum distances between pharmacies: I was preparing my complaint and discussed it with a Spanish civil servant who had recently arrived to the Commission – his name was Cecilio Madero.

I then went back to Spain. I wanted to practice competition law, or community law in general. But this was Spain in 1988, and whenever I tried to convince clients of the firm to stop talking prices with competitors, they looked at me with a dismissive air and replied: "Listen little lady: almost up to yesterday, the Ministry was calling us, meeting with us all together and instructing us to agree on prices to control inflation. What on earth are you telling us now? You do not have a clue on how the market works."

However, I did not despair: I really wanted to practice competition law. So, while working as an M&A associate (quite hard, by the way, because Spain was "on sale": investors relied on the new legal and economic framework adopted following our accession to the EEC), I worked in parallel to help Enric Picanyol produce the Spanish version of Bellamy & Child's *Common Market Law of Competition.*

I was (even obsessively) seeing the competition angle in almost every transaction around, and doing a lot of "business development" to convince clients of the firm to engage us in competition cases. For example, I remember having drafted, in 1989 or 1990, a note ("Futbol.not") with Carolina Fernandez (then my junior associate) when we saw in the media that Real Madrid and Juventus had signed an exclusivity agreement for the mutual exchange of players. We wanted to "sell" the case to FC Barcelona. But the law was too new, we were too young, and the clients saw "a pair of girls".

Our next big case was 3C Communications against Telefónica. This was 1990, at the start of the process of liberalisation of telecoms in Spain. 3C came to Spain in view of the 1992 International Exhibition and the Olympics, with the purpose of installing telephone terminals with a credit card payment functionality. 3C needed the supply of lines by Telefónica, who was playing dilatory games while negotiating agreements with credit card companies. I had to convince the client to file a complaint (they were reluctant because at any rate they would depend on Telefónica, then holding a monopoly in the line supply). But even worse, I also had to convince some partners in the firm (I was just an associate at the time) that a Community regulation prevailed over a Spanish "organic law" (a kind of law that has almost constitutional rank in the Spanish legal system). I remember this case very well, because I tried for over a year to convince the client to file a complaint before the Spanish Servicio de Defensa de la Competencia or the European Commission, and the client finally agreed to do so five days after the birth of my first child.

The partner responsible for our team at the firm did not know what to do, whether to inform me or not, because he wanted me to have some time off with my baby (there was no maternity leave for lawyers at the time). My colleagues told him that I would probably kill him if he did not tell me after my one year trying to convince the client to file the complaint. Luckily he did, and my team and I prepared the complaint at home, while changing diapers and rocking the cradle.

One year later, for personal reasons (I became a widow with a one-year-old child and needed some fresh air and more reasonable timetables), I left the firm to became a référendaire at the Court of First Instance of the EEC (today General Court of the EU). It was a true privilege to have quality time to go in depth into the analysis of competition legal issues and precedents while drafting judgment projects, which helped me comprehend and consolidate my knowledge. In addition, the view from the Court complemented my practitioner approach.

You have participated in several relevant cases and advised several companies in the digital sector. This inspires several (some shorter) questions:

What is your assessment of the current discussion on competition law developments in the digital world? Do you think that we need to change our rules in order for them to give efficient answers in the new situations or do you think they are useful as such for protecting markets and consumers?

There is an aspect of the digital world that is clearly not well addressed by competition law, in my view, which is privacy. The Bundeskartellamt decision on Facebook is based on a particular element of German competition law and judicial precedents related to a wide concept of "exploitation". Still, this falls short of solving the problems we are facing in the area of privacy.

Do you think that artificial intelligence will make it possible for robots to collude without human intervention, or do you think that humans can (and should) design algorithms that avoid collusion?

Everything designed by humans involves human liability. We work knowing the rules; we should design whatever it is that we design knowing them as well.

Should we consider data as an essential facility? Under what circumstances?

As with any other input, the question is whether it is essential and not replicable.

The EU is rethinking its vertical restraints approach due to the use of new technologies. Thinking of Coty, Guess ... do you think that we are protecting general interest when accepting some of the traditional vertical restraints?

In my view, *Coty* and *Guess* are two very different situations. In *Coty*, the main question is whether a business model in which a consumer physical experience or advice is part of the product could lawfully request and justify the obligation of providing such an experience (as a necessary complement to the mere online sale). In *Guess*, the issue is geo-blocking, which in itself involves the idea of jeopardising the achievement of the single market (a threat to the same idea of European integration). If the existence of different business models, which provide more choice (and more products) to consumers (so, consumer welfare), justifies the imposition of restrictions, I am fine with it. When there is no justification from a consumer welfare perspective, those restrictions do not seem to have such a justification and therefore I believe they should be banned.

The situation we have experienced with the recent EU Commission relating to certain mergers has aroused contradictory reactions coming from different governments, companies and even competition agencies. This makes me ask you several questions:

Do you think that innovation and consumer welfare would be more protected by competition between companies or by the creation of European champions?

The answer for me is obvious: competition is the best way to procure consumer welfare.

Lina Khan's "Amazon's Antitrust Paradox" questioned the traditional approach to dominance in relation to digital giants. How do you assess her view on the matter and the impact it has had in approaches that are more traditional?

Before Lina Khan, I was an admirer of Louis D Brandeis, and before him, of Ida Tarbell (my first antitrust hero, a courageous woman, who in my view is the real mother of antitrust). Both Tarbell and Brandeis wrote against the accumulation of power, and they are closer to the thesis of Lina Khan than those considered to have a "more traditional approach to dominance". Therefore, there is nothing new under the sun, in my view, but there is always a benefit in reminding us of the evil of unconstrained market power, irrespective of how it arises.

Do you think that we would need to rethink our merger control regulations in order to achieve its objectives in a more efficient way?

Given the absence of "turnover" in many situations in the digital area, we may want to reconsider "turnover" as a criteria and use "valuation" instead (or other meaningful criteria).

We are experiencing a quite convulsive political situation in the world. There is a rise of protectionism and populism in different countries and a different equilibrium between political forces. Do you think that this could (or should) affect the development of competition law (including, for example, labour standards, environment issues or consumer protection as such, as relevant parameters in the decision-making)?

I can see the benefits of, for example, introducing some obligations on merging firms to provide training to reintegrate merging layoffs into the market, in particular after the last crisis we experienced. The problem is that "industrial policy" does not mean the same thing in different countries, so I rather prefer sticking to the "consumer welfare standard" as the purpose of competition. Consumer welfare is not in my view limited to lower prices; choice, innovation, and other benefits for consumers are also part of this standard.

We do not know what will it happen with Brexit, but we know that UK has a more robust competition culture than some other European countries. Do you think that European competition law will change when the UK finally leaves the European Union?

I do not think EU competition law will change in a Brexit scenario. However, I do think the more liberal view of the UK regarding markets and their approach to less regulation will probably be missed once they leave, and we may face a more regulated internal market.

You have devoted attention to training of younger generations in antitrust professionally, and, more generally, in very prestigious academic institutions. What made you devote time and energy to this activity? Apart from a social concern that could lead you to share your experience with younger people (and therefore with society), do you consider that participating in those programmes gives any benefit to your professional approach and career?

I have learned a lot from my students. A candid "why?" does more in the process of self-understanding than any kind of personal study. Preparing for a lecture is one of the most rewarding experiences, because you need to be able to transmit in a clear and cogent way what you believe you know. In the process, you cement your knowledge, and sometimes you realise you did not truly understand the concepts until you have to explain them.

Finally, let me ask for some advice that we could share and use. Academically: how would you encourage a young law or economics student to devote their life to competition, and what advice would you give them? And, being a member of the board of a competition authority, I ask what do you think we could underline in order for our work to be more efficient?

When we are young, we tend to be passionate about ideals. We study law and believe we are there for the defence of human rights, to do something good for humanity. Or we study economics and want to fight against poverty. And the truth is that competition policy may serve both these purposes. Because when we procure consumer welfare, we contribute to a better distribution of wealth, a more efficient, and thus fair, allocation of resources. That would be my way of encouraging students to devote their life to competition. And that would be as well my message to competition authorities: devote your resources to what really matters in terms of consumer welfare.

Renata Hesse
Sullivan & Cromwell
Louise Åberg

Renata Hesse is co-head of Sullivan & Cromwell's Antitrust Group. Her practice focuses on representing some of the world's biggest companies on a range of high-stakes antitrust matters, including antitrust counselling, cartels and merger clearance. Ms Hesse is frequently recognised as a leading and influential antitrust lawyer, with a particular emphasis on the intersection of antitrust and intellectual property matters in high-tech industries. She joined S&C in 2017 following a distinguished career in government, including leading the Antitrust Division at the Department of Justice twice as Acting Assistant Attorney General and serving that division for more than 15 years.

Louise Åberg is an associate in the antitrust law practice group of McDermott Will & Emery. She has worked in both the Paris and Washington, DC offices and has experience advising clients on complex cross-border matters and investigations. She focuses her practice on US, EU and French antitrust law, including merger control, cartels, and abuse of dominance. She has counselled clients of all shapes and sizes in a broad range of industries, including the automotive, consumer products, life sciences, and telecommunications industries.

You worked on the *WholeFoods/Amazon* transaction which the Federal Trade Commission (FTC) decided not to challenge. Were you surprised by this?

This was a very fun and interesting matter on which to work, and I was excited to be able to work on a transaction like this shortly after coming out of the government. I think it was most interesting to me personally because it happened at the same time that a larger public policy discussion about how the American economy has changed and is continuing to change was developing. Which isn't really an antitrust discussion at all, but is an interesting topic nevertheless. And that's one of the things that I love about antitrust – and what I loved about working in government. You get to think about interesting issues at the core of how our economy works and sometimes you are lucky enough to be in a position to push the discussion in new directions. Amazon had a great team working on the transaction and they are a great client to work with.

Do you think current antitrust rules are adequate to deal with the challenges of the digital economy, including big data, multi-sided markets and network effects? Or do we need to rethink our current framework of analysis?

To me, the question is much less about what the statutes say, and much more about what you do with those statutes. I started out as an IP litigator and I worked a lot in the area of software copyrights early in my career. People used to ask the same question about the Copyright Act. And I always believed that the beauty of these old statutes is that they were flexible enough to handle change – as long as you are flexible enough to recognise change when it is happening and to adjust with it. I am personally not convinced that we need to do a fundamental rethink of the framework that undergirds our antitrust regime. That isn't to say that we shouldn't ask the question of whether our enforcers are getting it right or that the enforcers shouldn't ask that of themselves. It is very important to keep pushing ourselves and both the law and the economics forward, so that we have the capability to ensure that our markets – all of them, not just the ones that are in vogue right now – remain competitive.

This, I think, requires both the agencies and private practitioners to think less about how matters fit into particular analytical "boxes" and more about what is actually happening in the marketplace, whether that is good or bad for consumers and, if bad, what is causing the harm? The answer to that last question is the most important one from an enforcer's perspective, because it will prevent you from missing problems that do stem from a loss of competition just because the harm doesn't fit neatly into a particular box. It's also important from a private practitioner's perspective because it will help you advise your clients better. If we cling too tightly to the way things "have always been done" we run the risk of missing things on both sides.

What's your take on the attacks on the consumer welfare standard?

It probably won't surprise you that I have a middle-of-the-road answer to this question. The most compelling case that I have heard for needing to think more expansively about harm has been in the context of labour markets. The interesting thing about that discussion – and I credit Jon Jacobson for distilling this argument down during a panel discussion we had at the FTC hearings – is that I think that it fundamentally challenges conventional thinking about efficiencies. We have to recognise that and then decide whether upending how the merger guidelines address efficiencies – and how companies think about them in the context of transactions – is what we really should be doing. I think that the agencies have generally shown themselves to be quite capable of recognising actual harm from a loss of competition when they see it, as opposed to concerns that people sometimes raise that, while not illegitimate in the broader landscape, don't really implicate the antitrust laws.

You had a 15-year career in government, during which you served twice as acting Assistant Attorney General in charge of the Justice Department's Antitrust Division (DOJ). Did your years in government have an impact on who you are as a private practice lawyer?

Absolutely. Having had the opportunity to work both in government and in private practice has helped me be a more well-rounded lawyer. I am able to provide better, more nuanced, advice to our clients because I have a good understanding of what is likely happening on the government side. It allows me to help clients understand when what the government is saying or doing is indicative of an actual issue that one needs to potentially be concerned about, as opposed to when it is simply the process working its way out. I think my government experience also helps me communicate with and, when needed, negotiate with the regulatory authorities more effectively.

You had oversight of the criminal programme when you were Principal Deputy Assistant Attorney General at DOJ. What do you think of the DOJ's new policy to incentivise antitrust compliance? Do you think it is appropriate for the DOJ to give credit to companies that have pre-existing compliance programmes at the charging stage?

I think the Division's recent announcement and guidance regarding the possibility of giving credit for compliance at the charging stage, and not just at the sentencing stage, is an important development and addresses a long-standing criticism of the private bar that the Division's position on compliance programmes has been, up to this point, too inflexible. I think it's going to be very interesting to see the circumstances under which credit at the charging phase is given. I really hope that the Division provides some commentary when that happens so that we are able to understand better how the Division is actually going to apply the guidance.

More and more countries around the world are making it easier for private litigants to bring damages actions against cartelists. Do you think that the cost of seeking leniency has become too high for companies? Do you often recommend to your clients to apply for leniency?

I think the benefits of leniency are so significant that it is still worth it for companies to be the leniency applicant if they have that opportunity. If a client uncovers that it has a criminal antitrust problem, I would still recommend going in for leniency. That is not to say that developments around the world aren't having an impact, of course, but I think leniency remains very valuable to a company with a criminal antitrust problem.

How do you think antitrust agencies can strike a balance between protecting intellectual property rights and innovation and the principles of antitrust law?

I think that the agencies have been doing this, and doing it well, for a very, very long time. I really believe that this idea that intellectual property rights and antitrust law are inherently in conflict is just wrong. They both work to achieve the same thing – more innovation. Granted, they get at that from different angles, but it is not new to apply antitrust laws to intellectual-property-related conduct and to limit the behaviour of intellectual property holders in certain contexts. So setting the discussion up as if it is an either/or situation is not the right way to think about it. The two disciplines should work together and historically have worked well together.

I recommend that people look at all of the reports and studies that both the FTC and the Division (sometimes jointly!) have put out over the years. I think you will find a very coherent and appropriate articulation of a balanced approach to these issues in those writings.

What do you think of the framework established by the European Court of Justice in *Huawei v ZTE* (Case C-170/13)?

I am not a European-licensed practitioner, but I admire the European Commission's attempt to provide people with a framework that they can use to guide their negotiations in this area.

You brought W@Competition, a platform for women competition professionals founded in Europe, to the Americas. Why do you think it is important for women in antitrust to support each other?

So the interesting thing about W@Competition, and one of the reasons that I support it and agreed to bring it to the Americas, is that it is actually about getting women out there into the public eye and not about "supporting" each other. Women are often overlooked, whether you are thinking about hiring outside counsel or a consulting economist, providing an opportunity to work on an interesting case, looking for someone to fill an in-house legal position or looking for someone to fill a speaking role at a conference. The idea behind W@Competition is to make it easier for everyone – not just women – to find these fantastic female lawyers and economists and give them opportunities. Another very important distinguishing feature of W@Competition is that its events are not just for women – we really want men to come to the events and participate too.

The fact that W@Competition focuses on developing the profiles of up-and-coming women – using the networks and resources of the more senior women on the Americas Board – makes it a unique and, I think, particularly meaningful group. The slogan of the organisation is "Be found. Be seen. Be heard." That says it all to me and I am very proud to have brought the initiative to the Americas and to be working with such an amazing group of women. On our board for the Americas group, we have me, Melanie Aitken, Alejandra Palacios, Jamillia Ferris, Suzanne

Wachsstock, Terrell McSweeny and Liz Bailey. Our team consists of Louise Åberg, Elisa Hauch, Samantha Hynes, and Marianela López-Galdos.

As an example of the kinds of things that W@Competition Americas does, we have an incredible initiative going on in the US right now called the B3 Initiative, where we have up-and-coming women working together in teams to put on programmes. And the programmes feature not just the senior women that everyone already knows, but the up-and-coming women themselves. We had the first one of these on 3 October 2019, and it was really great. I saw women lawyers and economists who I had never seen in action before conducting a mock trial-style programme. It was inspirational not just to watch them at work, but also to feel the energy and enjoyment in the room.

What advice can you give to young women in antitrust?

I could go on for quite some time on this question, so let me just try to focus on a couple of key issues. First, there is no "right" way to do anything and the most important thing that you can do is to get to know yourself and your own style. Watch the people you admire, and even those who you don't, and develop whatever combination of skills and practices you see that fits best with your personality and your goals. This advice holds for both your professional life and, in my view, your personal one. Women agonise about the work/life balance, when or whether to have children and, if you have children, whether to stay at home with them. And my advice there is that you should unapologetically do what feels right to you – no one can tell you what that is and don't let anyone make you feel bad for making choices or compromises that work for you.

Second, try to be open to change. Many of the most amazing things that have happened to me in my career happened because I said "yes" when someone called and the opportunity sounded interesting. To be sure,

I was lucky to get some of the calls that I got, and I did make sure that I felt like the changes would be interesting and challenging ones. But just being willing to say yes, for example, to moving across the country and transforming from an IP litigator to an antitrust lawyer changed my life. Sometime I think women talk themselves out of taking opportunities because they think they are not qualified enough or it might not work out. Try not to do that – have faith in yourself and your ability to take on challenges and try new things and don't take yourself out of the running before the race starts. Just because you apply for a job doesn't mean you have to take it, for example.

Finally, try to learn to take pleasure and pride in the small successes of life. I once was speaking on a panel where a group of women were asked to share their biggest successes. As we went down the line, people started talking about winning big cases or getting a big client and such. When it came to me, I said that I sometimes felt really successful when I managed to get out of my house in the morning (a) on time, (b) with coffee and (c) without having had to drag my kids out of bed for school. I was trying to be humorous, but my comment was also a serious one. Doing well in your job, whatever it is, is obviously important. But success is defined by what makes you feel like you've accomplished something, and it is not measured only by the points you put on the board in your job. Many, many other things matter a lot and it is very easy to lose sight of that.

Heather Irvine
Bowmans

Nicola Ilgner

Heather Irvine is a partner in Bowmans' Johannesburg Competition Practice. Heather specializes in complex mergers, competition law complaints and pricing disputes in various African jurisdictions. Heather has BA and Honours degrees (both cum laude) and an LLB (magna cum laude), from the University of Cape Town. She was a researcher for Justice Albie Sachs at the Constitutional Court in 2000, and currently serves as an external examiner in the undergraduate and master's competition law courses for the University of the Witwatersrand.

Nicola Ilgner is Senior Associate at Nortons Inc. Her principal area of practice is competition law, including prohibited practices, corporate leniency applications, dawn raids, market inquiries, merger control, merger interventions, compliance training, competition audits, legal research and general competition/antitrust litigation before the South African Competition Authorities, as well as other African competition authorities (such as Namibia, Botswana, Tanzania, Zambia and Zimbabwe). She has also been involved in commercial litigation and arbitration proceedings.

Let's start with some background on your journey into competition law in South Africa and Africa, having since been recognised by Global Competition Review as among the world's top 40 under 40 competition lawyers, as well as one of the 100 most successful women in the field of competition law. In addition, you were recently acknowledged in the W@ Competition "40 in their 40s" Notable Women Competition Professionals: Private Practice – congratulations! How did competition law evolve into an area of expertise for you, after having worked as a researcher for Justice Albie Sachs at the South African Constitutional Court – as (I suppose) this was before competition law matters were determined by the Constitutional Court.

Thank you!

I joined a boutique corporate law practice in Johannesburg shortly after the South African competition legislation came into effect. We assisted clients with merger notifications as part of our M&A practice, and my boss at that time, Paul Coetser, was engaged by the monopoly fixed telephony provider, Telkom, in relation to a complaint in terms of the Competition Act by internet service providers – one of the first major complaints about alleged exclusionary conduct by a dominant supplier in South Africa. I was fascinated by the intersection of law and economics, and had the opportunity to read up on lots of foreign case law, since there was very little precedent to guide us in South Africa. This was something I had learned to do while working at the Constitutional Court, so it was a logical progression for me. This experience sparked my interest in competition law issues in the communications and online space. This is still a significant focus area in my practice.

What can be done to attract more women to this particular field of law?

I think South Africa has done quite well compared with some other jurisdictions, when it comes to attracting women – a number of the top competition law teams in South Africa are led by women, or have a number of very senior female partners. It is important for aspiring female lawyers to see other women achieving success in the field. We are also lucky to have some highly qualified women in leadership positions in both the Competition Commission and the Competition Tribunal.

Who is a woman in history that you admire and why?

I really admire Marie Curie – she pursued a scientific career at a time when it was almost unheard of for women, and continued her pioneering work even though the radioactive isotopes she was experimenting with made her ill. Her work is still in use today, in treating various cancers. As a cancer survivor myself, I really admire her courage.

What have been your greatest professional achievements?

Being chosen by Judge Albie Sachs to work as his researcher at the Constitutional Court in 2000, and being appointed to lead the Deneys Reitz (later Norton Rose) competition law team in 2008.

You acted in several of the seminal competition law complaint cases in South Africa, including the applications to the South African Constitutional Court involving Omnia and Loungefoam, which tested the boundaries of the Competition Commission's powers to initiate and refer complaints to the Competition Tribunal. What are your views on how the approach has since evolved?

These cases established that although the work of the South African competition authorities is important, companies accused of contravening the Competition Act are protected by the right to just administrative action in the South African Constitution. These successful challenges to the exercise of public power by the Commission have created a more conducive environment for test cases, and more willingness on the part of respondents in complaints to challenge the Commission. We are seeing more successful exceptions to the Commission's complaint documents, more cases going to trial and more acquittals. Companies no longer feel they have no option but to settle if they receive a complaint – there are procedural as well as substantive grounds for a defence.

The most significant recent development in competition law in South Africa is the Competition Amendment Act which was recently signed into law, although it has not fully come into effect yet. You acted for the South African Minister of Economic Development in the *Walmart/Massmart* merger almost a decade ago, and this matter formed the basis for the development of public interest reviews in South Africa and a number of African jurisdictions. Now that the public interest provisions under the Competition Act of 1998 have been amended by the Competition Amendment Act to clarify their importance in the merger assessment process, and to highlight the objectives of transformation and de-concentration, what impact do you anticipate these amendments having on the South African competition law regime?

The *Walmart/Massmart* merger firmly established the basis for intervention on these grounds in merger reviews, particularly by the Minister but, at least initially, these factors only took centre-stage in a relatively small number of high-profile mergers, usually featuring foreign buyers. Now, however, we see these concerns – especially in relation to job losses and the impact on South African supply chains – playing out more frequently, in smaller or less newsworthy transactions, particularly when third parties, like trade unions or customers and competitors, have concerns about a transaction. I expect that there will be considerable litigation over what the new public interest factors in the Amendment Act mean – and what kind of evidence is required to establish an impact on these factors. Unfortunately, this may lead to longer merger reviews. Dealmakers hate delays, and there is a risk this reduces foreign investment. We all have to work very hard to strike an appropriate balance.

I understand that you have had a considerable amount of experience in Africa, how have the public interest considerations evolved in other African jurisdictions in comparison with South Africa?

South Africa led the way, but public interest issues have slowly become a priority for competition authorities in East and Southern Africa. Kenya and Zambia now regularly impose employment-related conditions on merging parties in order to mitigate job losses. However, since the amendments to the legislation in South Africa, the range of public interest factors in our jurisdiction is much broader. It remains to be seen whether other jurisdictions in Africa – including in regional blocs like COMESA – will follow our lead once again.

Although Africa is sometimes seen as the last frontier of competition law given that African competition regimes are still relatively young, have you seen other stakeholders in jurisdictions on other continents give more consideration to public interest issues?

I think that very similar concerns – about inequality, the impact on workers, national champions, tariff protection – are being raised around the world. Sometimes these concerns are dealt with by competition authorities, in terms of antitrust laws, or sometimes they are dealt with separately, for example, by a government department. But I think that the days when mergers were permitted as long as they didn't harm competition, and the evaluation of complaints against dominant firms took no account of historical privilege, are behind us. Competition law enforcement – like all law – is connected to the political and social context, and will evolve.

As the African Regional Forum Liaison Officer for the Antitrust Committee of the International Bar Association (IBA), what has been your experience with "reciprocal learning" from and by African competition practitioners?

I have worked extensively with lawyers from all over the continent, particularly on merger-related work, and have always been impressed by the expertise of our fellow practitioners and their generosity when it comes to sharing their expertise. However, there are still relatively few opportunities to gather and swap research and insights, like conferences and publications. The IBA has created some of these opportunities in the past, through the African Regional Forum, and will play a key role going forward. Given how many new competition law regimes there are in Africa, this is a big area of focus for the IBA Antitrust Committee. It is a very exciting time to be here.

The Competition Amendment Act also makes provision for the constitution of a government committee, which could block the acquisition of a South African business by a foreign acquiring firm if the merger is likely to have an adverse effect on South African national security interests. Are you concerned that this could potentially concern foreign investors, thereby possibly affecting the levels of (foreign) investment in South Africa in order to stimulate job creation and grow the South African economy?

Yes, I am concerned, particularly given the high levels of corruption in South Africa we have seen over the past few years. It is not yet clear who will sit on this committee, or how it will function. However, we know that foreign investors insist on predictable and efficient decision-making. If South Africa is serious about increasing foreign investment, it is crucial that this additional review mechanism is transparent, fair and completely free of corruption.

Although a cliché, competition law is a merger between law and economics, and therefore both competition law attorneys and economists play a prominent role in merger assessments and competition litigation.

Lawyers and economists really have to work together in this area of enforcement, because although the law sets out the rules, the evidence required to establish that a merger is anticompetitive – or that a particular business practice has harmed competition – is economic in nature. Lawyers have to at least "learn the lingo".

"Competition in the digital age" – the digital agenda seems to be a key theme in the global competition law enforcement agenda and, in particular, although this could become a long debate, there is a certain perceived tension between competition policy and privacy and consumer welfare. Do you foresee this becoming a priority within the South African context soon?

I think we are a bit behind the global curve on these issues, although the president is concerned about the impact on South Africa of the Fourth Industrial Revolution, and, in that context, there has been an increased focus on the digital agenda. I think we can expect South African consumers to become increasingly concerned about the use of their data by "free" online service providers, and we may see the competition authorities being asked to step in where there is ineffective regulation by the Independent Communications Authority of South Africa or other regulatory bodies.

Concurrences
Competition Laws Review

Concurrences Review

Concurrences is a print and online quarterly peer reviewed journal dedicated to EU and national competitions laws. It has been launched in 2004 as the flagship of the Institute of Competition Law in order to provide a forum for academics, practitioners and enforcers. Concurrences' influence and expertise has garnered interviews with such figures as Christine Lagarde, Bill Kovacic, Emmanuel Macron and Margarethe Vestager.

CONTENTS

More than 12,000 articles, print and/or online. Quarterly issues provide current coverage with contributions from the EU or national or foreign countries thanks to more than 1,500 authors in Europe and abroad. Approximately 35 % of the contributions are published in English, 65 % in French, as the official language of the General Court of justice of the EU; all contributions have English abstracts.

FORMAT

In order to balance academic contributions with opinions or legal practice notes, Concurrences provides its insight and analysis in a number of formats:
- Forewords: Opinions by leading academics or enforcers
- Interviews: Interviews of antitrust experts
- On-Topics: 4 to 6 short papers on hot issues
- Law & Economics: Short papers written by economists for a legal audience
- Articles: Long academic papers
- Case Summaries: Case commentary on EU and French case law
- Legal Practice: Short papers for in-house counsels
- International: Medium size papers on international policies
- Books Review: Summaries of recent antitrust books
- Articles Review: Summaries of leading articles published in 45 antitrust journals

BOARDS

The Scientific Committee is headed by Laurence Idot, Professor at Panthéon Assas University. The International Committee is headed by Frederic Jenny, OECD Competition Comitteee Chairman. Boards members include Bruno Lasserre, Mario Monti, Howard Shelanski, Richard Whish, Wouter Wils, etc.

ONLINE VERSION

Concurrences website provides all articles published since its inception, in addition to selected articles published online only in the electronic supplement.

WRITE FOR CONCURRENCES

Concurrences welcome spontaneous contributions. Except in rare circumstances, the journal accepts only unpublished articles, whatever the form and nature of the contribution. The Editorial Board checks the form of the proposals, and then submits these to the Scientific Committee. Selection of the papers is conditional to a peer review by at least two members of the Committee. Within a month, the Committee assesses whether the draft article can be published and notifies the author.

e-Competitions Bulletin

CASE LAW DATABASE

e-Competitions is the only online resource that provides consistent coverage of antitrust cases from 55 jurisdictions, organized into a searchable database structure. e-Competitions concentrates on cases summaries taking into account that in the context of a continuing growing number of sources there is a need for factual information, i.e., case law.

- 15,000 case summaries
- 3,000 authors
- 85 countries covered
- 30,000 subscribers

SOPHISTICATED EDITORIAL AND IT ENRICHMENT

e-Competitions is structured as a database. The editors make a sophisticated technical and legal work on all articles by tagging these with key words, drafting abstracts and writing html code to increase Google ranking. There is a team of antitrust lawyers – PhD and judges clerks - and a team of IT experts. e-Competitions makes comparative law possible. Thanks to this expert editorial work, it is possible to search and compare cases by jurisdiction, legal topics or business sectors.

PRESTIGIOUS BOARDS

e-Competitions draws upon highly distinguished editors, all leading experts in national or international antitrust. Advisory Board Members include: Sir Christopher Bellamy, Ioanis Lianos (UCL), Eleanor Fox (NYU), Damien Géradin (Tilburg University), Fred Jenny (OECD), Jacqueline Riffault-Silk (Cour de cassation), Wouter Wils (DG COMP / King's College London), etc.

LEADING PARTNERS

- Association of European Competition Law Judges: The AECLJ is a forum for judges of national Courts specializing in antitrust case law. Members timely feed e-Competitions with just released cases.

- Academics partners: Antitrust research centres from leading universities write regularly in e-Competitions: University College London, King's College London, Queen Mary University, etc.

- Law firms: Global law firms and antitrust niche firms write detailed cases summaries specifically for e-Competitions: Allen & Overy, Baker McKenzie, Cleary Gottlieb Steen & Hamilton, Jones Day, Norton Rose Fulbright, Skadden, White & Case, etc.

The Institute of Competition Law

The Institute of Competition Law is a publishing company, founded in 2004 by Dr. Nicolas Charbit, based in Paris, London and New York. The Institute cultivates scholarship and discussion about antitrust issues though publications and conferences. Each publication and event is supervised by editorial boards and scientific or steering committees to ensure independence, objectivity, and academic rigor. Thanks to this management, the Institute has become one of the few think tanks in Europe to have significant influence on antitrust policies.

AIM

The Institute focuses government, business and academic attention on a broad range of subjects which concern competition laws, regulations and related economics.

BOARDS

To maintain its unique focus, the Institute relies upon highly distinguished editors, all leading experts in national or international antitrust: Bill Kovacic, Mario Monti, Eleanor Fox, Laurence Idot, Fred Jenny, Ioannis Lianos, Richard Whish, etc.

AUTHORS

3,800 authors, from 55 jurisdictions.

PARTNERS

- Universities: University College London, King's College London, Queen Mary University, Paris Sorbonne Panthéon-Assas, etc.

- Law firms: Allen & Overy, Cleary Gottlieb Steen & Hamilton, Baker McKenzie, Hogan Lovells, Jones Day, Norton Rose Fulbright, Skadden Arps, White & Case, etc.

EVENTS

More than 350 events since 2004 in Brussels, London, New York, Paris, Singapore and Washington, DC.

ONLINE VERSION

Concurrences website provides all articles published since its inception.

PUBLICATIONS

The Institute publishes Concurrences Review, a print and online quarterly peer-reviewed journal dedicated to EU and national competitions laws. e-Competitions is a bi-monthly antitrust news bulletin covering 85 countries. The e-Competitions database contains over 15,000 case summaries from 3,000 authors.

15 years of archives
27,000 articles

4 DATABASES

Concurrences Review
Access to latest issue and archives
- 12,000 articles from 2004 to the present
- European and national doctrine and case law

e-Competitions Bulletin
Access to latest issue and archives
- 15,000 case summaries from 1911 to the present
- Case law of 85 jurisdictions

Conferences
**Access to the documentation
of all Concurrences events**
- 350 conferences (Brussels, Hong Kong, London, New York, Paris, Washington DC)
- 250 PowerPoint presentations, proceedings and syntheses
- 450 videos
- Verbatim reports

e-Books
Access to all Concurrences books
- 34 e-Books available
- PDF version

NEW

New search engine
Optimized results to save time
- Search results sorted by date, jurisdiction, keyword, economic sector, author, etc.

New modes of access
IP address recognition
- No need to enter codes: immediate access
- No need to change codes when your team changes: offers increased security and saves time

Mobility
- Responsive design: site optimized for tablets and smartphones

www.ingramcontent.com/pod-product-compliance
Lightning Source LLC
Chambersburg PA
CBHW042313210326
41599CB00038B/7118